The Circuit of Apollo

EARLY MODERN FEMINISMS

Series Editor
Robin Runia, Xavier University of Louisiana

Editorial Advisory Board
Jennifer Airey, University of Tulsa; Susan Carlile, California State University; Karen Gevirtz, Seton Hall University; Mona Narain, Texas Christian University; Carmen Nocentelli, University of New Mexico; Jodi Wyett, Xavier University; Paula Backscheider, Auburn University

Showcasing distinctly feminist ideological commitments and/or methodological approaches, and tracing literary and cultural expressions of feminist thought, Early Modern Feminisms seeks to publish innovative readings of women's lives and work, as well as of gendered experience, from the years 1500–1800. In addition to highlighting examinations of women's literature and history, this series aims to provide scholars an opportunity to emphasize new approaches to the study of gender and sexuality with respect to material culture, science, and art, as well as politics and race. Thus, monographs and edited collections that are interdisciplinary and/or transnational in nature are particularly welcome.

The Circuit of Apollo

EIGHTEENTH-CENTURY WOMEN'S
TRIBUTES TO WOMEN

Edited by
LAURA L. RUNGE AND
JESSICA COOK

University of Delaware Press
NEWARK
Distributed by the University of Virginia Press

University of Delaware Press
© 2019 by Laura L. Runge and Jessica Cook
All rights reserved
Printed in the United States of America on acid-free paper

First published 2019

ISBN 978-1-64453-003-0 (cloth)
ISBN 978-1-64453-004-7 (paper)
ISBN 978-1-64453-005-4 (e-book)

1 3 5 7 9 8 6 4 2

Library of Congress Cataloging-in-Publication Data is available for this title.

Cover art: Portrait of Elizabeth Brownlow, Lady Exeter, by Godfrey Kneller, c. 1699. (Burghley House Collection)

Contents

Acknowledgments vii

Introduction 1

Tracing "The Circuit of Appollo": Poetic Forms and Identities
in Anne Finch's Tributes to Women Poets 21
CLAUDIA THOMAS KAIROFF

"Those Stately Palaces": Tribute and Estates in the
Work of Anne Finch and Jane Barker 36
NICOLLE JORDAN

Martha Fowke's Tributes to
Mary, Lady Chudleigh, 1711 and 1726 54
CHRISTINE GERRARD

Eliza Haywood, Fame, and the Art of Self-Homage 68
KATHRYN R. KING

"Who Praises Women Does the Muses Praise":
Mary Barber, Laetitia Pilkington, and
Constantia Grierson's Poetic Tributes 87
CATHERINE INGRASSIA

"Friendship, Better than a Muse, Inspires": Anna Letitia Barbauld
Claims the Sister Arts for Female Friendship 104
LAURA TALLON

Painting in Bright Characters: Helen Maria Williams's Poetic Tributes to
Anna Seward, Elizabeth Montagu, and Marie-Jeanne Roland 123
NATASHA DUQUETTE

Sapphic Circuitry: Anna Seward's Equivocal Tribute
to "Llangollen's Vanished Pair" 142
SUSAN S. LANSER

"I Delight in the Success of Your Literary Labours":
Friendship as Platform for Reinvention 155
KATHARINE KITTREDGE

Lyric Sociability: Object Lessons in Female Friendship
in Amelia Opie's Occasional Verses 176
SHELLEY KING

Afterword: Researching, Writing, and Teaching
Women's Tributes to Women 194
BETTY A. SCHELLENBERG

Bibliography 205
Notes on Contributors 219
Index 223

Acknowledgments

This collection of essays began as a Women's Caucus luncheon discussion at the ASECS meeting in Williamsburg, Virginia March 2014. The enthusiasm for the subject of celebrating women celebrating other women spread to the room, and our topic was voted to be one of the panels for 2015 in Los Angeles. The response to the call for presentations was equally enthusiastic and we were able to put together two full roundtables for short presentations by twelve scholars. In addition to the contributors in this volume, we heard papers by Julie Candler Hayes, Julie Murray, Deborah Weiss, Jessica Fripp, and Jocelyn Harris. We also convened a luncheon where plans for this book emerged. We agreed to invite others who had expressed interest to participate, and to make the revision process shared so that we could benefit from reading the other essays in the volume. Throughout, this has been a collaborative endeavor.

As such, the process of working together to edit this volume has mirrored many of the experiences we have documented for the eighteenth-century women in this book: women working together through correspondence (email) and meetings, sharing support, challenging each other's ideas, celebrating our successes. Our book illustrates the importance of networks for eighteenth-century women, but it also results from important networks among women scholars today. More so than ever, it seems important in 2018 to recognize and value women's relationships with other women. As Betty Schellenberg clarifies in the afterword, making these networks visible is only one step. Valuing the networks and sharing them with the next generation of scholars is crucial for the preservation of the story of women's contributions.

As editors we thank the ASECS Women's Caucus and its membership for creating the institutional space where these networks happen. We thank the contributors to this volume for their continued support and enthusiasm for the project. We also wish to acknowledge Ed Larkin at University of Delaware Press for his initial support for our proposal, Julia Oestreich for her work on the editing process, and the editorial board. We would also like to extend gratitude to Susan Staves, our external reader, whose work on women's writing and their networks in the long eighteenth century has inspired us both. Her detailed reading of the manuscript has made it stronger and better in many ways. We are grateful to Frederick Mackenzie, Bridgeman Images, and The Burghley House Collection for permission to publish their images.

We would also like to extend our thanks to our institution, the University of South Florida, the English department staff, especially Marissa Klippenstein, and Laura Runge's research assistant Lesley Brooks. Their care and kindness help in more ways than they know.

The Circuit of Apollo

Introduction

> The men think us incapable of real friendship you know, and I am determined to shew them the difference.
> —Jane Austen, *Northanger Abbey*

The Circuit of Apollo is a book about early modern women's networks traced through affirmations of respect, admiration, love, and sometimes competition. It emerges out of the desire to highlight what relationships among women in the long eighteenth century tell us about the emotional lives and the creative work of women. In the last twenty-five years, we have benefited from an abundance of serious scholarly work on early modern women authors, artists, and patrons, including biographies, bibliographies, scholarly editions, and archival work in correspondence, all of which has served to let women stand in their own light, not in the shadow of best-known men.[1] This cumulative attention to women makes visible important historical realities that counter damaging gender narratives, such as the idea that friendship was a virtue particularly suited to men, that women were excluded from artistic networks, and that women relegated to the home and outside of London were bitterly immured in domestic privacy. The essays collected here attest to the vital practice of commemorating women's artistic and personal relationships and in doing so illuminate the complexity of female friendships and honor as well the robust creativity and intellectual work contributed by women to early modern culture. The subjects of these essays cover nearly two hundred years of women's lives from the late seventeenth to the middle nineteenth centuries. The geographical diversity of people represented and the span of time covered underscore the consistency of the practice of women's tributes to other women, even when it took the form of critical engagement.

Our title is taken from a tribute poem by Anne Finch that celebrates the poetic legacy of women and the vibrant network of living female poets in Finch's local county. Based on the work in this volume, poetry appears to have been the vehicle of choice for women's celebrations of one another, but it is important to note that women's tributes to other women took many forms, from published letters of dedication to private circulation of gifts of friendship. The sociable and long-lived Mary Delany, who sent drawings along with verses and other mementoes with her letters, provides a helpful touchstone for our book's theme.[2] Delany was a treasured correspondent in a varied set of networks from Jonathan Swift to George III, but she is best remembered as the intimate of the Duchess of Portland's intellectual home at Bulstrode and a first-generation Bluestocking. Her correspondence, edited and published in six thick volumes by her descendant Augusta Hall in 1861–1862, reminds us how much personal friendships depended upon letter writing. When living in Ireland away from many friends and family, Delany received by packet a paper-cut landscape and an embossed floral frame from Lady Andover in 1752; she wrote about the gift to her sister: "it is the finest thing I ever saw of the kind,"[3] a fact underscored by the editor's note that the original remained uninjured 108 years later in the setting ordered by Delany. Elizabeth Eger has argued, "While historians have concentrated upon the role of female accomplishment in the marriage market as a means of advertising female charms to potential male suitors, few have acknowledged the profound importance of the circulation of objects, many of them self-crafted, between women."[4] Delany's letters record descriptions of the craftwork exchanged between women as emblems of friendship, from watercolors and oils, to shell work and needlepoint, to the cut paper collages that ultimately earned Delany fame. Thus, Delany also illustrates the simultaneous private *and* public nature of women's friendships and their tributes to one another.

Feminist scholars have long recognized the complexity of women's public relationships with other women, particularly famous women who preceded them.[5] In poetry by women, we trace women's acknowledgement of inspiration and guidance. Katharine Philips (1632–1664) and Aphra Behn (c. 1640–1689) offer important examples because both women were admired but for very different literary reasons.[6] Philips, popularly recognized by other writers as Orinda, achieved poetic fame with classical, intimate, chaste, or lesbian lyrics consistent with Christian virtue; her reputation as a literary model continued over time throughout the changing of gender and sexual mores. Behn, known as Astrea, adopted a libertine expression of female intimacy in her poetry and, notably, in her own commendations in dedicatory letters to Nell Gwynn and the Duchess of Mazarin.[7] At the turn of the eighteenth century, women were equally likely to invoke the image of both praiseworthy women who broke new ground as published authors. However, scholars such as Susan Staves have documented the change by mid-century, when Behn's literary model was discredited, and the public recognition of the woman artist came at the cost of erotic expression.⁸ As will be seen, this shift in attitudes toward public acknowledgement affected the ways women commemorate each other.

Safely in the twentieth century, Virginia Woolf remembers Behn in *A Room of One's Own* as "shady and amorous" but appropriately entombed in Westminster Abbey, the national site of commemoration.⁹ Closer to her era, Anne Finch obliquely said of Behn, "a little too loosely she writ." The line, taken from our eponymous poem, has become shorthand proof of Finch's early dismissal of Behn's erotic example, but the commemoration is more complicated than that. Finch's unsullied reputation puts her squarely in Philips's line and, accordingly, Orinda is praised in Finch's poem by Laura, a member of the Kentish circle. However, critics often overlook what Jane Spencer calls "an extraordinary tribute" to Behn.¹⁰ In the poem's narrative, Behn's death initiates Apollo's quest to find the best living poet in Kent. Whereas Orinda is praised in abstract, Apollo himself mourns the death of Behn:

> A summons sent out, was obey'd but by four,
> When Ph[o]beus, afflicted, to meet with no more,
> And standing, where sadly, he now might descry,
> From the banks of the Stowre the desolate Wye,
> He lamented for Behn, o're that place of her birth,
> And said amongst [females] was not on the earth,
> Her superior in fancy, in language, or witt,
> Yett own'd that a little too loosely she writ;
> Since the art of the Muse, is to stir up soft thoughts,
> Yett to make all hearts beat, without blushes or faults.¹¹

Finch's tribute to Behn gives lineal priority to her imagination, expression, and intelligence and raises her above all other women writers in the world. Spencer rightly notes that Finch's tribute articulates the dilemma of a female artist who recognizes the need "to make all hearts beat" while not compromising her personal virtue, a new artistic agenda that Finch proposes for herself.¹² Like other female writers who risked personal reputations, such as Mary Delarivier Manley, Mary Pix, Elizabeth Thomas, and Eliza Haywood, Behn enjoyed a period of adulation and gratitude from fellow women writers, and their commemorations illustrate complicated negotiations of fame, gender, and art. In *Aphra Behn's Afterlife*, Spencer argues that the history of Behn's reputation in the eighteenth century is not simply a trajectory of fame and regard transitioning to disrepute and disregard, but is rather more varied and differs across the multiple genres in which she excelled.[13]

The fate of Elizabeth Singer Rowe (1674–1737) makes for an interesting comparison to Behn and suggests that the cultural preoccupation with women's virtue exerted a negative impact on those perceived to be moral. Paula Backscheider's recent recovery of Rowe traces the overly simplified image of the "Pious Mrs. Rowe" in order to return her to the complexity of her historical context.[14] An extremely popular poet and prose writer, Rowe was memorialized repeatedly throughout her lifetime and long after her death in poetry, biographies, and engravings. Significantly, however, Backscheider argues that the one-dimensional character of pious retreat that comes down to us from the nineteenth century has done a disservice to the present-day literary reputation of Rowe, particularly with respect to her contributions in fiction. Backscheider says, "As text, [Rowe] was not a reified object but an active signifying practice, a cultural performer located in history, influencing the future, and negotiating personhood."[15] We find evidence of this in the poetic commemorations by women. For example, Elizabeth Carter (1717–1806) published her tribute "On the Death of Mrs. Rowe" in the *Gentleman's Magazine* on April 7, 1737, shortly after Rowe's death on February 20. When she calls Rowe "our sex's ornament and pride!" she claims Rowe's artistic achievements as a model worth emulating for women.[16] In particular, Carter singles out Rowe's sensibly applied "genius" that transformed prose fictions from wanton tales of romance "to virtue sacred and thy maker's praise."[17] Backscheider argues that Rowe provided the blueprint for religiously minded intellectuals that inspired the mid-century Bluestocking circle of Carter's friends, a legacy that "the most distinguished experts on the Bluestockings" fail to note.[18] Significantly, Backscheider's understanding of Rowe as a mobile abstraction used by others can be seen as a direct result of her continued commemoration. Rowe's example suggests that the convention of praising one's fellow female author activated a network of meaning extending far beyond personal contact. The construction of the commemorated female as an "active signifying practice" can be considered a core methodology throughout this volume.

In both of these instances, Finch on Behn and Carter on Rowe, the death of the respected author initiates reflection and public commemoration. Although many living women are celebrated in poetry, letters, and dedications, the ritual of mourning an author's death in poetry functions in a particularly public and communal way. The poetic voice, be it the speaker or a figure such as Apollo, expresses a collective set of values that includes sorrow over the loss of the female practitioner. In some ways, the woman's death makes her available for the "active signifying practice" of the community, shaping the figure into a model or a memory that honors the departed and soothes the living. As Catherine Ingrassia points out in her essay in this volume, the female author's reputation is a "valuable commodity whose memory invokes moments of potential success for the women" who commemorate her. Thus the terms of praise in these poems tell us about the shared values of the literary community of women, and they specify the unmet desires of the public in the wake of the female author's departure. Behn figures as an Olympian peer whose example is impossible to follow, whereas Rowe offers spiritual inspiration and rational artistic invention that gives Carter hope. Invoking the dead predecessor is a convention we see women employing repeatedly in the essays in this volume, but as active signifiers the memory of these women can be put to use in surprising ways. While a virtuous reputation might be used to shore up a patchy one, as Christine Gerrard suggests might be the case in Martha Fowke's praise for Mary Chudleigh, for others the effect of a woman's death might be imagined while she is very much alive, as Susan Lanser describes for the lesbian couple, Butler and Ponsonby. Eager to convert the iconoclastic couple into an active signifying practice, Anna Seward imagines the breach that Butler and Ponsonby cause when they exit—as we all will do—the mortal realm. Thus, eulogies provide a way of thinking about the legacy of women's artistic production, not just the legacy of the woman being commemorated, but also that of the woman writing the tribute, who establishes herself as the next link in a rich history of women's cultural contributions.

The focused attention to women's praise for other women in this volume illustrates a turn on female honor to which the patriarchal conception of female honor as sexual chastity stands in stark relief. Notions of honor and the related concept of friendship were under revision in the Enlightenment for both men and women. Social and political historians have long seen the eighteenth century as a time when vertical ties of kinship were challenged by the horizontal political ties of party and commerce.[19] For men, friendship became a particularly vexed arena of relations where honor was deeply implicated,[20] a transition highlighted by the rise of the gentleman's duel.[21] The eighteenth-century duel is particularly illustrative of gendered codes of honor because it lays bare the terms for which a man defended his honor. According to Markuu Peltonen, a gentleman's honor was understood as honesty, bravery, and inner goodness; it was reflexive and established among his peers. Any challenge to his honor needed to be met with an attack in order to publicly restore that honor or keep it intact.[22] In contrast, Ute Frevert explains, "The honour of women, who were primarily sexual beings, was not on the [Enlightenment] agenda since their distinguishing feature, in other words, 'chasteness', had been established for all time and did not require any further delineation. Male honour, on the other hand, was embroiled in a web of complex relationships."[23] The term "honor," then, had distinctly gendered meanings, as the Earl of Rochester's song, entitled "Womans Honour," makes clear:

> Consider reall Honour then,
> You'll find hers cannot be the same.
> Tis noble confidence in men,
> In Women mean mistrustfull shame.[24]

"Real" honor is masculine, public, and displayed through a physical bearing of confidence, whereas female honor relates solely to sexual behavior, which in Rochesterian irony translates chastity into shame. Women's honor belongs only, if at all, to the male who is publicly accountable for her sexual reputation, a decidedly truncated network of power and identity.

The counter narrative exposed in the tributes of women to each other challenges this limited view by crafting a public-private discourse of women's artistry through horizontal relations. Whether in letters or manuscript or publications for the market, women write other women into history in a much wider range of roles including intellectuals, authors, musicians, historians, patrons, arbiters of taste and morals, and more. In their letters, women reveal extensive networks of exchange and value with their intellect and creativity at the core. Moreover, women in this discourse do not suffer their honor to be dictated by men; they are agents of their own honor. Aphra Behn, who memorably wrote, "I value Fame as much as if I had been born a hero," is not the only woman artist to have cared deeply about her legacy.[25] As Kathryn R. King eloquently demonstrates with regard to Eliza Haywood in this volume, women writers have celebrated the fact that female authorship revolutionized culture. The tribute poem became a form of gifting between one woman and another that served a communal function "binding people in a network of obligations" that reinforced feminocentric values.[26]

Like honor, friendship in the eighteenth century was understood in gendered terms that privileged the male. Also as with honor, male friendship was conceived as fundamentally public and civic in the classical sense. Such definitions simply excluded women from the category of friend by virtue of their status as inferior or contingent to male relations. Susan Lanser notes that "discourses from Aristotle to Montaigne had defined friendship as a male affair and rendered friendships between women epistemically invisible."[27] Female friendships were allowed during adolescent years, but marriage was generally perceived to be a threat if not an end to female friendship. Lanser argues, however, that privileged women such as the queen consort Henrietta Maria of England (1609–1669), the philosopher and author Mary Astell (1666–1731), and Katharine Philips in various ways promoted female friendship and purposely sought to appropriate the discourse of friendship "to promote female excellence, to create social liaisons, and to justify material autonomy."[28] She identifies an "unprecedented publicity for female friendship that surfaced in seventeenth-century Europe and became institutionalized in eighteenth-century painting, poetry, fiction, and letters by women and men."[29] Yet the epigraph from Jane Austen indicates a suspicion of non-familial female bonding lingering into the nineteenth century. In the mouth of Isabella Thorpe, a false friend of the protagonist from *Northanger Abbey*, the defiant challenge to enduring prejudice also functions as ironic testimony to the patriarchal roadblocks to female friendship.

Moreover, the efflorescence of art on female friendship did not mean that cultural authorities in the eighteenth century endorsed unlicensed female intimacy. Scholars like Emma Donoghue demonstrate that, during the same period, a virulent anti-tribadic literature recast female-female relations safely within heterosexual norms.[30] Lanser claims "that by at least the 1740s, female friendship has ceased to be the property primarily of female pens and that keeping female bonds under control had become a hegemonic interest."[31] The physicality of women's relationships expressed in the early friendship poems of Philips virtually disappears in public tributes by midcentury. Shelley King's evocative account in this volume of the poems that Amelia Opie wrote on gift-objects to her lifelong friend Elizabeth Lemaistre demonstrates a shift to the emotional mediation of material things by mid-nineteenth century. According to Lanser, however, bodily representation continued in the private correspondence between women. As Amanda Vickery has shown, the letters of women record a world of female relations that might otherwise have gone unnoticed by history.[32]

To take the example of Mary Delany once again, her letters to her sister chronicle the deeply emotional ties of lifelong female friendship and bear witness to the centrality of its physical expression. "Upon my honour," she wrote to Ann Granville in 1733, "my heart is so full of wishing you and my mother multiplicity of happiness, that it is ready to burst, and I have been miserable in keeping of it in so long."³³ Mary's letters sparkle with physical details of materiality despite the fact that, as Janice Thaddeus recorded, the mores of her Victorian editor led to expurgations of many bodily references.³⁴ On a day in 1736 that Mary titles "Melancholy Monday," Anne Granville departed from Mary's London home, leaving her with palpable grief. She begins the letter tracing that day: "I heard you, my dearest sister, when you rose, but found my heart failed me, and judged it would be best for both of us if I lay quietly till you were gone. It was unnecessary for us to see one another's tears; we are both too well convinced of each others affection to want any heightenings of that kind."³⁵ She proposes to record how she spent that "dismal day," beginning with breakfast: "But alas! Your picture stared me in the face all the time; I was angry with it for not speaking." Her servant presents her with a bouquet: "I said little to her, but kissed the little nosegay made up of rosebuds, daisies, seringos, and heartsease—the lovely emblems of your friendship, which blooms and blesses me every year." After a disappointingly crowded visit to pay their courtesy to the Prince and Princess of Wales, she is treated with kindness by mutual friends who "like you too well not to feel for me to-day."³⁶ Despite their compassion, Mary runs away from them: "I could not live longer without speaking to you, my dearest sister!"³⁷ Here, life itself seems to depend on expressing her love through writing; as in the earlier example, Mary experiences a physical pain that is eased by writing to her sister. So while poetic tributes lose the vitality of the body in friendships between women, letters can sometimes express unfettered physical-emotional bonding.

This mid-century shift in the discourse on female friendship coincides with a change in female friendship poems as noted by Paula Backscheider. In her study *Eighteenth-Century Women Poets and Their Poetry: Inventing Agency, Inventing Genre,* Backscheider devotes an entire chapter to women's friendship poems, the only genre that "women inherited from women."³⁸ Some of our essays demonstrate that women's encomiums to other women are modulated through traditional artistic and cultural conventions. For example, Finch adopts the male oriented "sessions" poem and, according to Claudia Kairoff in her analysis in our first essay, turns it into a female tribute. The friendship poem, however, was a unique form in which women created a "safer, woman-centered place."³⁹ The genre descends directly from Katharine Philips's legacy of seventy-one friendship poems: "[Philips'] poems lay a firm foundation for the work of eighteenth-century women poets" in all of their varieties.⁴⁰ Philips's presence as a poetic precursor blends the friendship poem and the tribute poem, since many women looked to Philips (like

Behn) as a poetic icon they used to recognize the excellence of their peers. Mary Delarivier Manley's tribute to Catharine Trotter Cockburn, for example, envisions the author of *Agnes de Castro* as filling "the Vacant Throne" now with "Orinda, and the Fair Astrea gone."[41] Characteristically for this earlier period, Manley strikes a combative stance of female alliance against "Aspiring Man": "For thus Encourag'd, and thus led by you, / Methinks we might more Crowns than theirs Subdue."[42]

Lanser notes a decided increase in male-authored directives on female friendship by the 1740s, and so too Backscheider sees a change in the nature of the friendship poem at that time: "By midcentury, women poets were largely joining their sister novelists in retreating from the assertiveness of obvious participation in public controversies about the nature and capacities of women. Rather than insisting upon women's equality or even superiority in friendship, for instance, they portrayed for one another their separate sphere."[43] Laura Tallon in this volume examines Anna Letitia Barbauld's line from "To Mrs. P[riestly]," which encapsulates the strategy "Friendship, better than a Muse, inspires." By positing the female bond as the source of artistic creativity, Barbauld elevates the female-female relationship without threatening masculine aesthetic expertise. The trend Backscheider identifies for the friendship poem is evident in most of the essays in our collection, with the notable exception of Natasha Duquette's essay on Helen Maria Williams. Williams's public tributes to Elizabeth Montagu, Anna Seward, and Marie-Jeanne Roland in the late eighteenth century continue the pronounced endorsement of special female capacities in an explicitly public and political context.

The human networks traced in these essays have human subjects and limitations, and as such we find that tributes of friendship also serve naturally as vehicles for self-promotion and literary ambition. In crafting their praise of other women, the authors in these networks simultaneously demonstrate their own creative abilities, cultural knowledge, and literary connections. In taking seriously the work of other women, they model how their own work should be similarly received, and either implicitly or explicitly acknowledge their own desire for fame. In Finch's "The Circuit of Appollo," the Session of the Poets is a competition for the laurel crown, an indication that female tributes are not all fawning praise but can feature competition and critique. Just as Finch's praise of Behn includes some censure, the friendliness of her Kentish coterie still allows for rivalry; when one woman writes well, it challenges others to do better. The female collaborations featured in this collection range from the amicable, as with Finch's circle, to the occasionally combative, as Ingrassia demonstrates in Mary Barber's and Laetitia Pilkington's references to Constantia Grierson. In the latter case, a mutual animosity emerges from competing ambitions but also from differences in class, education, and social reputation.

Female collaborations can go awry, as the well-known example of the middle-class Bluestocking Hannah More and laboring-class poet Anne Yearsley illustrates. Yearsley, the wife of a yeoman farmer and mother of seven children, garnered More's philanthropic attention for both her poetic talent and her family's financial struggles. Yearsley initially paid tribute to More in "Night. To Stella" in her *Poems upon Several Occasions* (1785), but she fiercely criticized her benefactor in a second volume after the two bitterly quarreled over More's editorial and financial interferences.[44] What Yearsley saw as More's condescending dismissal of the laboring-class woman's autonomy, More took as Yearsley's gross ingratitude. Their example illustrates not only how a tribute in 1785 might devolve into hostility, but importantly also how factors other than gender can disrupt female allegiances.

Other examples suggest that critical engagement and friendship can coexist in female collaborations, as in the case of another laboring-class poet, Mary Leapor (1722–1746). Throughout her poetry, Leapor pays tribute to both her former employer Susanna Jennens and her friend and patron Bridget Freemantle, the daughter of a local vicar, as the greatest supporters of her writing. In her verse epistles to Freemantle, Leapor extends invitations to her home for tea and conversation, and asks to borrow Freemantle's skills as reader and editor of her work. In other writing, she refers to her poems as children she sends to "school"—to Jennens and Freemantle—for correction and improvement.[45] When Leapor died at the age of twenty-four, in the midst of preparing her poetry for publication by subscription, Freemantle took over the project, ensuring the collection was still published. Freemantle's introduction to Leapor's poetry serves as a remarkable tribute of its own to a laboring-class phenomenon.[46] In contrast to Yearsley and More, Leapor and Freemantle demonstrate how supportive interclass friendships could be for women personally, and also how instrumental they were to developing talent and disseminating literary work.

Leapor also illustrates the opportunities afforded by women's artistic networks based on geographical location. Though she lived in her native Northamptonshire for her entire life, her poetry proves her cannily aware of the London publishing world: she details sending her manuscript play to Colley Cibber, and—though far from the denizens of London—feared she would be classed with the Grub Street hacks.[47] Leapor's poetry also indicates that she saw herself at the center of her hometown of Brackley's literary life, even as something of a celebrity. In her poems, other characters constantly recognize (and mock) Leapor's poetic persona Mira as the "scribbling" kitchen maid.[48] Far from being shut out of the metropolitan literary scene, Leapor records herself as making a daring entry into that culture, even from rural Northamptonshire. In this sense, she bears a resemblance to the women of Finch's provincial coterie who compete for the laurel crown as the god Apollo makes his circuit ride through Kent, implying there is a literary culture worth seeing there.

Traditionally connected with the home, women spent comparatively less time in travel than their male counterparts did. It is perhaps not surprising, then, that women associated other women with places they inhabit. Women's commemorations of other women have frequently served as a material trace of their social and literary networks located within a specific geographical space. Nicolle Jordan, for example, emphasizes place in her analysis of women's relationships to their estates in Finch's poem to Lady Worsley and Jane Barker's dedication to the Countess of Exeter. Notably, this volume features a range of women living and writing outside of London, including in Kent, Lancashire, Ireland, Wales, and France. It is another indication of the advancement of the scholarship on women that our essayists have been able to analyze the provincial networks of women. Tracing non-aristocratic women in early modern history has been notoriously difficult. Susan Frye and Karen Robertson argue that women's relations "have proved not only less visible but also more difficult to reconstruct, often because women did not formally record their activities or seek memorialization in material structures."[49] The tributes analyzed in this volume are just such material structures, and they are emerging from the archive. As place markers, women's tributes make visible feminocentric networks of artistic, social, and material exchange in specific geographic contexts. Sarah Prescott argues that studies of eighteenth-century literary culture tend to overlook the provinces and women's participation in provincial literary culture, in particular.[50] However, as Prescott demonstrates, "provincial culture was not only vibrant and productive but also enabling for many women writers."[51] Evidence of similar forms of mentorship appears throughout this volume; for instance, as Katharine Kittredge discusses in her essay, Mary Leadbeater and Melesina Trench used their transcultural correspondence to encourage each other to write and offer, at times, pointed criticism of each other's writing.

The Circuit of Apollo: Eighteenth-Century Women's Tributes to Women fills the need for the "thick contextualization" of women's writing, a need that

Laura Mandell reminds us is renewed in the face of the digital turn in literary studies.⁵² The recovery of women writers is never a complete and stable history, and Mandell demonstrates that most of the initial large-scale databases and websites devoted to literary figures have been predictably dedicated to canonical male authors. In order to capitalize on the newfound depth in scholarly infrastructure for women, we need to maintain our focus on women's networks and look for connections in the archives. We can expand our attention to the lives of women in ways that resist the tendency of historical erasure and counter the notion that women's works are ephemeral, once-printed, and unworthy. When, for example, we study Sarah Scott's fiction *Millenium Hall*—a published novel by a woman at risk for erasure—we find that female artists have often embedded their encomiums to other women in the narratives of fiction themselves. Mary Delany makes a final appearance to exemplify our theme in Scott's novel in the figure of Mrs. Morgan: "Mrs. Morgan, the lady who was drawing, appears to be upwards of fifty, tall, rather plump, and extremely majestic, an air of dignity distinguishes her person, and every virtue is engraven in indelible characters on her countenance. There is a benignity in every look, which renders the decline of life, if possible, more amiable than the bloom of youth. One would almost think nature had formed her for a common parent, such universal and tender benevolence beams from every glance she casts around her."⁵³ Delany, who would have been sixty-two years of age when *Millenium Hall* was published, was known for, among other artistic endeavors, her drawing. Scott puts the character of Delany at the center of a utopian female network by having Mrs. Morgan found Millenium Hall with her best friend Miss Mancel. Scott pays further tribute by recounting a version of Delany's own loveless first marriage arranged by her family in the backstory of Miss Melvyn. Thus, Scott turns her friend Delany into an active, signifying print agent without naming her and exposing her to the immodesty of fame. Delany's identity, known only to those in Scott's immediate network, signals the representation of the Bluestocking circle, and indeed Scott's sister Elizabeth Montagu is thought to be represented somewhat less complimentarily in the figure of Mrs. Brumpton.⁵⁴

Scott's fictional character sketch repeats verbal cues from an earlier description of Delany, "Aspasia's Picture, drawn by Philomel, in the year 1742." Probably written by Anne Donnellan by the request of Margaret Cavendish, the Duchess of Portland, the sketch functions as another form of commemoration practiced among friends: "I am at a loss what terms to find strong enough to express her general benevolence or her particular tenderness to

INTRODUCTION

her friends; her benevolence is so strong it should seem as if she looked upon the whole world as her friends, and her tenderness to every particular friend so great as to fill up the measure of the whole heart."[55] Aspasia, Mary Delany's coterie name, is captured in this verbal portrait as a memento in time: "it is above twenty years since she was married," and yet she enjoys her bloom "the modest sprightliness of her eyes, the shining delicacy of her hair, the sweetness of her smile."[56] Calling to mind the physical being, the character sketch is a material tribute not unlike the miniature portraits of four friends that the Duchess commissioned for a luxurious multi-paneled snuff box of gold that she later gifted to Lady Andover.[57] The Duchess presented "Aspasia's Picture" to Delany's sister Anne when she left Bulstrode. By constructing and distributing multiple images of Mary Delany, the Duchess circulated her friend and created material traces of the precious and mortal human bonds of female friendship. These traces, with their rich implications of cultural value and historical meaning, command a place in our scholarly discussions.

The Circuit of Apollo: Eighteenth-Century Women's Tributes to Women is organized chronologically by author and can be divided roughly into two sections of the long eighteenth century. Claudia Kairoff's essay on "The Circuit of Appollo" appropriately leads the collection. In this poem, Anne Finch (1661–1720) reworks the misogynistic "Session of the Poets" form into a tribute to her female coterie's friendship, intellectual creativity, and artistic ambition. Kairoff explores the personal relationships behind the pseudonyms used in the poem, providing keys to both the women's real-life identities and the dating of Finch's manuscripts. She also argues that the poem is a significant material record of the importance of women's provincial networks for both friendship and literary support. Nicolle Jordan further explores how women benefited from such provincial feminocentric networks in her essay, "'Those Stately Palaces': Tribute and Estates in the Work of Anne Finch and Jane Barker." Jordan considers how both writers confront the masculinist literary conventions associated with writing about landed property in their tributes to female friends and patrons. While Finch's country house poem follows a restricting model due such poems' emphasis on male ownership, Jordan argues that the more flexible generic boundaries of the book dedication offer Barker (1652–1732) greater opportunity to subvert gendered literary conventions.

In "Martha Fowke's Tributes to Mary, Lady Chudleigh, 1711 and 1727," Christine Gerrard explores Fowke's (1689–1736) formal epitaphs in praise of her mentor and role model, Chudleigh (1656–1710). Gerrard compares the two poems, written at the beginning and end of Fowke's literary career, arguing that Fowke laments the loss of both Chudleigh's friendship and her brand of witty yet pious feminism, a persona that may have seemed difficult to imitate for the scandal-plagued younger author. In the essay that follows, Kathryn R. King also focuses on a writer whose scandalous reputation has limited our perceptions of her literary fame: Eliza Haywood (1693–1756). King recuperates both Haywood's image and the Enlightenment definition of fame as civic virtue and literary excellence. In her discussion of other women's tributes to Haywood—and the author's own homage to herself—King argues for the important role women's tributes can play in rewriting literary history. The first half of the volume concludes with Catherine Ingrassia's essay on the Dublin-based writers Mary Barber (1690–1757), Constantia Grierson (1706–1732), and Laetitia Pilkington (1709–1750). Ingrassia considers how friendship and competition intersect in the three women's poetic tributes to one another, most notably in Barber's and Pilkington's memorials to the deceased Grierson. Ingrassia argues that both women attempt to control Grierson's memory, and by extension, their own poetic legacies, revealing the way that tributes to other women can function as a covert method for acknowledging one's own literary ambitions.

The second half of our volume begins in the late eighteenth century with Laura Tallon's "'Friendship, better than a Muse, inspires': Anna Letitia Barbauld Claims the Sister Arts for Female Friendship." As Tallon demonstrates, women continued to revise masculinist literary forms in the late eighteenth century. In a poetic tribute to her friend Mary Priestley, Barbauld (1743–1825) announces her own participation in the historically masculine contest of the "Sister Arts" of painting and poetry. Tallon argues that, in this poem, Barbauld positions herself as artist and female friendship as her muse, thus challenging the gendered dynamics of artistic production in which men are agents of creativity and women mere objects of representation. Natasha Duquette explores a more public form of female friendship in her discussion of Helen Maria Williams's (1761–1827) poetic tributes to Anna Seward (1742–1809), Elizabeth Montagu (1718–1800), and Marie-Jeanne Roland (1754–1793) during the revolutionary 1780s and 1790s. Duquette argues that these tributes blend the political and the philosophical, the social and the spiritual, as Williams illustrates the transformative power of female friendship on both an individual and national level. Susan S. Lanser addresses the problematic side of public tributes to private friendship in her essay, "Sapphic Circuitry: Anna Seward's Equivocal Tribute to 'Llangollen's

Vanished Pair.'" Lanser argues that Seward's tribute to her friends, the celebrated lesbian couple Lady Eleanor Butler (1739–1829) and Sarah Ponsonby (1755–1831), concludes with the physical erasure of the women themselves. The tribute becomes an elegy to the memory of their love—despite the fact that neither woman was actually dead. Lanser highlights the inherent difficulties in writing a public tribute when the objects of praise disrupt normative gender and social expectations, as in the case of the same-sex couple.

In her essay, "I delight in the success of your literary labours: Friendship as Platform for Reinvention," Katharine Kittredge examines the correspondence of Mary Leadbeater (1758–1826) and Melesina Trench (1768–1827), demonstrating that, in spite of differences in age, class, and location, the two women not only offered each other friendship and domestic commiseration, but also encouraged their mutual interests in writing and social action. Kittredge argues that Leadbeater and Trench challenged each other personally and professionally, forcing both women to acknowledge their ambitions and redefine their notions of success. Finally, Shelley King concludes the collection with "Lyric Sociability: Object Lessons in Female Friendship in Amelia Opie's Occasional Verses," an examination of Opie's (1769–1853) tributes to her friends Frances Kemble Twiss (1759–1822) and Elizabeth Vassall Lemaistre (1771–1857). King argues that the sets of poems—one a public recognition of a famous friend's portrait, the second a series of gift poems sent as private tributes of friendship—suggest that female friendship serves not only as a source of poetic inspiration, but also as a foundational aspect of self-identity. Opie's annual birthday poems for Lemaistre, in particular, offer an example of sustained poetic tribute over a lifetime of friendship.

The women analyzed in this book clearly do not stand in the shadow of best-known men; the history of women looks different from the perspective of female tributes to women. Yet to students new to the era, the overt misogyny of the age makes an indelible impression, and many of our students imagine the lives of women only in the context of patriarchal oppression and dangerous childbirth. The persistence of Virginia Woolf's description of fifteenth-century daughters "locked up, beaten and flung about the room" may have something to do with it.[58] As one contributor mentioned early in the editorial process, our students need to see alternative stories of female-female experience in the early modern period. When we replace the fictional example of Judith Shakespeare with the actual case of Anne Finch, we discover a rich and persistent tradition of female encomiums to other women in which women's artistic production is taken seriously. Regarding the poems, like Barbauld's "To Mrs. P[riestley]," written to inspire a female friend to artistic production, Backscheider writes, "It is hard to find a woman poet who did *not* leave poems like these, *and they are an unbroken chain.*"[59] When we see the woman writer through the misogynist anecdote, we envision a lone, odd, violated woman—not someone to admire or recuperate. When we see the woman writer through the lens of female tributes, we not only see the vibrant competitive culture of women's writing, but we also see that behind the isolated female figure of the anecdote lie scores of other female artists sharing, reading, critiquing, inspiring, supporting, and teaching each other. Like the portraits and craftwork that survive from the eighteenth century, the writings explored here persist as tangible artefacts of human relations that—once read—activate a new network of potential meaning for audiences today.

Notes

1. Biographies abound, but recent work not mentioned elsewhere in this introduction include: Teresa Barnard's *Anna Seward: A Constructed Life* (Burlington, VT: Ashgate, 2009); William McCarthy's *Anna Letitia Barbauld: Voice of the Enlightenment* (Baltimore: Johns Hopkins, 2008); and Kathryn R. King's *A Political History of Eliza Haywood* (London: Pickering and Chatto, 2012). Relevant collected works and textual editions include: *The Works of Aphra Behn*, ed. Janet Todd, 7 vols. (Columbus: Ohio State University Press, 1992–1996); *The Poems and Prose of Mary, Lady Chudleigh*, ed. Margaret J.M. Ezell (Oxford: Oxford University Press, 1993); *The Galesia Trilogy and Selected Manuscript Poems of Jane Barker*, ed. Carol Shiner Wilson (Oxford: Oxford University Press, 1997); *Clio: The Autobiography of Martha Fowke Sansom (1689–1736)*, ed. Phyllis J. Guskin (Newark: University of Delaware Press, 1997); *Memoirs of Laetita Pilkington*, ed. A.C. Elias, Jr. (Athens: University of Georgia Press, 1997); *The Poems of Anna Letitia Barbauld*, eds. Elizabeth Kraft and William McCarthy (Athens: University of Georgia Press, 1994); *Selected Works of Eliza Haywood*, ed. Alexander Pettit, 6 vols. (London: Pickering and Chatto, 2001–2002); *The Collected Poems of Amelia Anderson Opie*, ed. Shelley King (Oxford: Oxford University Press, 2009); and *The Cambridge Edition of the Works of Anne Finch, Countess of Winchilsea*, eds. Jennifer Keith and Claudia Thomas Kairoff (Cambridge: Cambridge University Press, forthcoming). Bibliographies include: Mary Ann O'Donnell, *Aphra Behn: An Annotated Bibliography of Primary and Secondary Sources*, 2nd ed. (Burlington, VT: Ashgate, 2004), and Patrick Spedding, *A Bibliography of Eliza Haywood* (London: Pickering and Chatto, 2004). Archival work in letters includes *Elizabeth Montagu and the Bluestocking Circle*, http://www.elizabethmontaguletters.co.uk/the-project, and *The Correspondence of Amelia Alderson Opie: An Online Archive of Networks and Letters*, ed. Roxanne Eberle, https://ctlsites.uga.edu/eberle/ameliaopieletters/.

2. See the recent biography of Mary Delany by Molly Peacock, *The Paper Garden: An Artist Begins Her Life's Work at 72* (New York: Bloomsbury, 2010); also, the catalogue and essay collection accompanying the exhibit at the Yale Center for British Art and

INTRODUCTION

Sir John Soane's Museum, *Mrs. Delany and Her Circle*, ed. Mark Laird and Alicia Weisberg-Roberts (New Haven, CT: Yale University Press, 2009).

3. *Autobiography and Correspondence of Mary Granville, Mrs. Delany*, ed. Augusta Hall (Lady Llanover), 6 vols. (1861, 1862; Cambridge: Cambridge University Press, 2011), III.176.

4. Elizabeth Eger, "Paper Trails and Eloquent Objects: Bluestocking Friendship and Material Culture," *Parergon: Journal of the Australian and New Zealand Association for Medieval and Early Modern Studies* 26, no. 2 (2009): 120.

5. Janet Todd, *The Sign of Angelica: Women, Writing, Fiction 1660–1800* (New York: Columbia University Press, 1989).

6. See Jeslyn Medoff, "The Daughters of Behn and the Problem of Reputation" in *Women, Writing, History 1640–1740*, eds. Isobel Grundy and Susan Wiseman (Athens: University of Georgia Press, 1992), 33–54; Ros Ballaster, *Seductive Forms: Women's Amatory Fiction, 1684–1740* (Oxford: Clarendon Press, 1992); Jacqueline Pearson, *The Prostituted Muse: Images of Women and Women Dramatists 1642–1737* (London: Harvester Wheatsheaf, 1988).

7. Aphra Behn, "The Feign'd Curtizans, or, A Nights Intrigue," in *The Works of Aphra Behn*, ed. Janet Todd (Columbus: Ohio State University Press, 1996), 6:86–87; Aphra Behn, "The History of the Nun: or, the Fair Vow-Breaker," in *The Works of Aphra Behn*, ed. Janet Todd (Columbus: Ohio State University Press, 1995), 3:208–9.

8. See Susan Staves, *A Literary History of Women's Writing in Britain, 1660–1789* (Cambridge: Cambridge University Press, 2006).

9. Virginia Woolf, *A Room of One's Own* (San Diego: Harcourt, 1981), 66.

10. Jane Spencer, *Aphra Behn's Afterlife* (Oxford: Oxford University Press, 2000), 159.

11. Quoted in ibid., 159; Myra Reynolds, *The Poems of Anne Countess of Winchilsea: From the Original Edition of 1713 and From Unpublished Manuscripts* (Chicago: Chicago University Press, 1903), 92.

12. Spencer, *Aphra Behn's Afterlife*, 160.

13. Ibid., 12–13.

14. Paula Backscheider, *Elizabeth Singer Rowe and the Development of the English Novel* (Baltimore: Johns Hopkins University Press, 2013).

15. Ibid., 4.

16. Elizabeth Carter, "On the Death of Mrs. [Elizabeth] Rowe" in *Eighteenth-Century Women Poets*, ed. Roger Lonsdale (Oxford: Oxford University Press, 1989), 167, line 8.

17. Ibid., lines 9 and 20.

18. Backscheider, *Elizabeth Singer Rowe*, 44.

19. E.g., Lawrence Stone, *The Family, Sex and Marriage in England, 1500–1800* (New York: Harper & Row, 1977); J. G. A. Pocock, *Virtue, Commerce, and History: Essay on Political Thought and History, Chiefly in the Eighteenth Century* (Cambridge: Cambridge University Press, 1985).

20. See Peter Fenves, "Politics of Friendship, Once Again," *Eighteenth-Century Studies* 32, no. 2 (Winter 1998–1999): 133–55.

21. Both dueling and conflicts of friendship play conspicuous roles in the novels and drama of the period. To name just two, see Richard Steele's *Conscious Lovers* (1722)

and Samuel Richardson's *Clarissa* (1747–48). See also *The Encyclopedia of British Literature 1660–1789*, comp. Laura L. Runge (Chichester, UK: Blackwell, 2015), s.v. "Dueling."

22. Markku Peltonen, *The Duel in Early Modern England: Civility, Politeness and Honour* (Cambridge: Cambridge University Press, 2003).

23. Ute Frevert, *Men of Honour: A Social and Cultural History of the Duel*, trans. Anthony Williams (1991; repr., Cambridge: Polity Press, 1995), 26.

24. John Wilmot, Earl of Rochester, *The Poems and Lucina's Rape*, eds. Keith Walker and Nicholas Fisher (Chichester, UK: Wiley-Blackwell, 2013), 35–36.

25. Aphra Behn, preface to *The Luckey Chance; or, An Alderman's Bargain, A Comedy*, in *The Rover and Other Plays*, ed. Jane Spencer (Oxford: Oxford University Press, 1995), 191.

26. Robert Von Hallberg, *Lyric Powers* (Chicago: University of Chicago Press, 2008), as quoted by Kathryn R. King in this volume.

27. Susan Lanser, "Befriending the Body," *Eighteenth-Century Studies* 32, no. 2 (Winter 1998–1999): 180.

28. Ibid., 182.

29. Ibid., 180.

30. See Emma Donoghue, *Passions Between Women: British Lesbian Culture 1668–1801* (London: Scarlet Press, 1993); Lisa Moore, *Dangerous Intimacies: Toward a Sapphic History of the British Novel* (Durham, NC: Duke University Press, 1997); Jodi Wyett, "'No Place Where Women Are of Such Importance': Female Friendship, Empire, and Utopia," *The History of Emily Montague*, *Eighteenth-Century Fiction* 16, no. 1 (2003): 33–57; Elizabeth Susan Wahl, *Invisible Relations: Representations of Female Intimacy in the Age of Enlightenment* (Stanford, CA: Stanford University Press, 1999); and particularly Susan S. Lanser, *The Sexuality of History: Modernity and the Sapphic, 1565–1830* (Chicago: University of Chicago Press, 2014).

31. Lanser, "Befriending the Body," 187.

32. Amanda Vickery, *The Gentleman's Daughter: Women's Lives in Georgian England* (New Haven, CT: Yale University Press, 1998), especially the introduction.

33. *Autobiography and Correspondence of Mary Granville*, I.390.

34. Janice Farrar Thaddeus, "Mary Delany, Model to the Age," in *History, Gender & Eighteenth-Century Literature*, ed. Beth Fowkes Tobin (Athens: University of Georgia Press, 1994), 113.

35. *Autobiography and Correspondence of Mary Granville*, 1.555

36. Ibid., 1.556.

37. Ibid., 1.557.

38. Paula Backscheider, *Eighteenth-Century Women Poets and Their Poetry: Inventing Agency, Inventing Genre* (Baltimore: Johns Hopkins University Press, 2005), 175.

39. Ibid., 176.

40. Ibid., 180.

41. Delarivier Manley, "To the Author of *Agnes de Castro*," in *British Women Poets of the Long Eighteenth Century: An Anthology*, eds. Paula Backscheider and Catherine Ingrassia (Baltimore: Johns Hopkins University Press, 2009), 715, lines 1–2.

42. Ibid., 3, lines 13–14.

43. Backscheider, *Eighteenth-Century Women Poets*, 194.

44. Staves, *A Literary History of Women's Writing*, 438–39.

45. See, for example, her poem "The Muses Embassy" and her letter to Freemantle on "Mopsus; or, The Castle Builder," both in *The Works of Mary Leapor*, eds. Richard Greene and Ann Messenger (Oxford: Oxford University Press, 2003), 215–17, 303.

46. For Leapor's poetry and Freemantle's dedication, see *The Works of Mary Leapor*. For more on Leapor's and Freemantle's tributes to one another, see Jessica Cook, "Mary Leapor and the Poem as Meeting Place," *Eighteenth-Century Theory and Interpretation* 57, no. 3 (2016): 365–83.

47. See Leapor's "An Epistle to Artemisa" and "The Proposal" in *Works*, 175–80, 96–97.

48. See Freemantle's Introduction in ibid., xxxvii.

49. Susan Frye and Karen Robertson, eds., *Maids and Mistresses, Cousins and Queens: Women's Alliances in Early Modern England* (Oxford: Oxford University Press, 1999), 3, quoted in Carolyn Williams, Angela Escott, and Louise Duckling, eds. *Woman to Woman: Female Negotiations During the Long Eighteenth Century* (Newark: University of Delaware Press, 2010), fn 2, 42.

50. Sarah Prescott, *Women, Authorship, and Literary Culture, 1690–1740* (Houndsmill, UK: Palgrave, 2003), 1.

51. Ibid., 2.

52. Laura Mandell, "Gendering Digital Literary History: What Counts for Digital Humanities," in *A New Companion to Digital Humanities*, eds. Susan Schreibman, Ray Siemens, and John Unsworth (Malden, MA: John Wiley & Sons, Ltd., 2016), 511–23.

53. Sarah Scott, *A description of Millennium Hall, and the country adjacent: together with the character of the inhabitants, and such historical anecdotes and reflections, as may excite in the reader proper sentiments of humanity, and lead the mind to the love of virtue* (London: J. Newbery, 1762), 10.

54. Staves, *A Literary History of Women's Writing*, 353.

55. *Autobiography and Correspondence of Mary Granville*, II.177.

56. Ibid., II.176.

57. See Alicia Weisberg-Roberts, "Introduction (1): Mrs. Delany from Source to Subject," in *Mrs. Delany and her Circle*, eds. Mark Laird and Alicia Weisberg-Roberts (New Haven, CT: Yale University Press, 2009), 4–5.

58. Virginia Woolf, *A Room of One's Own*, 42.

59. Emphasis added. Backscheider, *Eighteenth-Century Women Poets*, 205.

Tracing "The Circuit of Appollo"
Poetic Forms and Identities in Anne Finch's Tributes to Women Poets

CLAUDIA THOMAS KAIROFF

Seventeenth- and eighteenth-century women's tributes to women include a spectrum of relationships, from protégées acknowledging mentors as Christine Gerrard, Natasha Duquette, and Nicolle Jordan explore in this volume to, as Susan Lanser elaborates in this collection, admiring poets grappling with the challenge of addressing a same-sex couple. Anne Finch's "The Circuit of Appollo," which gives this volume its title, acknowledges a competitive relationship between four women vying for recognition as the best Kentish poet. While these women are described as rivals by Finch, her tone is admiring rather than invidious, as in the case of the competing tribute poems discussed by Catherine Ingrassia in her essay. Finch's tribute to her sister poets illuminates several of her other manuscript poems, a poem by one of her fellow poets, and the verse forms favored by members of her circle. The tribute also exemplifies some basic obstacles facing readers of most early women writers. Women writers' tributes to other women writers, even the forms of these tributes, present gender-related difficulties with regard to form and style, and even the identities of the subjects praised. This essay will open discussion of these challenges by first addressing the form of Finch's poem before considering what we might learn by identifying—in some cases, tentatively—the women concealed by pen names in the poem.

Male poets' commendations of women required extensive alteration by women poets because they usually regarded women's physical or spiritual attributes as equal to, or instead of, their intellectual accomplishments. As Laura Tallon discusses elsewhere in this volume, women were often addressed as muses, inspiring the male poet through an erotic bond. In addition, women writers were constantly exposed to counter-examples of sermons, poems, plays, and other texts satirizing presumptuous female intellectuals. Women's tributes must therefore be understood in context, recognizing the challenges that had to be negotiated in expressing literary praise.

"The Circuit of Appollo" commends several fellow writers by refashioning a kind of poem recently associated with harsh and, when women were included, misogynistic satire, transforming the "Sessions of the Poets," fictitious competitions for the laureateship, into a celebration of sister poets. In "The Circuit of Appollo," Finch avoids the pitfalls of adapting a male-dominated genre, as described by Nicolle Jordan in her essay, partly by shifting the location as well as the tone and diction of her "session."

The tradition behind "The Circuit of Appollo," Finch's imaginary contest for the title of best Kentish poet, takes poets seriously despite an informal style. "Sessions of the Poets" were occasionally written throughout the seventeenth century after the example of Sir John Suckling's "The Wits" (c. 1637), retitled "A Sessions of the Poets" when printed posthumously in 1646. In Suckling's poem, Apollo, like the Justice of the Peace at a court sitting, summons writers to defend their claim to the laurel crown. Suckling's 118-line poem featured anapestic stanzas of four, mostly four-stress, lines linked by single words ("The Laurel that had been so long reserv'd, / Was now to be given to him best deserv'd. / And / Therefore the wits of the Town came thither," 3–5), creating a droll effect.[1] The venerable Ben Jonson is first denied the bays, because "merit . . . and not presumption / Must carry it" (26–27). In the course of the poem, Suckling interrogates and dismisses numerous competitors, including friends such as Thomas Carew and William Davenant. Davenant, for example, is denied the laurels because he has lost his nose to venereal disease (48). Suckling indicts himself as failing to appear in court because "He loved not the Muses so well as his sport" (76), preferring flirting or bowling to writing (77–78), for which Apollo declares he should be fined (80). Apollo ultimately outrages the poets by crowning an Alderman, because "the best signe / Of good store of wit [is] to have good store of coyn" (107–8).

Suckling's poem may have appealed to Finch for several reasons. Like Suckling, she was a Stuart supporter and had been a courtier. Suckling was among the original Cavalier poets, but died in France after attempting to aid Charles I at the onset of the Civil Wars.[2] His poem remained in manuscript during his life, although it became widely known after it was sung to Charles I during a hunting expedition.[3] Finch, likewise, intended her poem for manuscript circulation, and would have appreciated Suckling's implied preference for fellow manuscript poets like Thomas Carew, instead of professional writers like Ben Jonson. Suckling's facetious coronation of an alderman on the grounds that "the best signe / Of good store of wit [is] to have good store of coyn" would also have resonated with Finch when she wrote her poem in the 1690s, as she joined other conservatives deriding England's embrace of mercantile capitalism.

But while Suckling's political affiliation and his evocation of courtly writing circles would have attracted Finch, other aspects of his poem were problematic. Suckling ignored women writers, while Finch features only women and avoids harsh criticism. Suckling's style, as if to illustrate his literary carelessness deplored by Apollo, was replete with rhythmic irregularities and run-on lines, even between stanzas. Writing fifty years later, Finch valued rhythmic polish and accurate rhymes, even in anapestic couplets. Suckling's occasional coarseness, such as his joke about Davenant's venereal disease, would have struck Finch as offensive. Yet coarseness had become a standard feature in successive imitations of Suckling's "Sessions": even harsher satire and obscene humor, particularly regarding women writers, characterized some "Sessions of the Poets" printed during and after the Restoration. One example Finch may have known was printed in *Poems on Affairs of State* (1697),[4] but "The Session of the Poets, to the Tune of Cook Lawrel" must have circulated much earlier, because William D'Avenant, the first contender satirized, died in 1668. The anonymous poet damned Shirley, Robert Howard, Dryden, Buckhurst, Sedley, William Killigrew, Waller, Denham, Samuel Butler, Etherege, and Shadwell, but also Margaret Cavendish, in a particularly crude pair of stanzas. The Duke of Newcastle arrives on behalf of his wife, pulling her writings out of his breeches, "the place where Nature's Posset-maker lives" (92). Apollo advises him to return home "To provide [Margaret] fresh Straw, and a Chamber that dark is" (96).

Women's writing was likewise equated with sexual activity in a "Session"—like its predecessors, in anapestic couplets—printed posthumously as the Earl of Rochester's, although David M. Vieth has suggested Elkanah Settle as its more probable author.[5] Finch might have read "A Session of the Poets" (written c. 1676; printed 1680) in manuscript or in print, since it reflected the harsh critical environment for poets and playwrights of the late Stuart courts. "A Session of the Poets" boldly dismisses potential laureates, advising Dryden to become a priest and his rival Shadwell to concentrate on drinking. Etherege is eliminated because he is too lazy, and Wycherley, no doubt ironically, is eliminated because he is too genteel. Aphra Behn appears among the candidates, boasting both literary and amorous conquests, but is told she is a dozen years too old for either kind of triumph. Apollo's verdict makes Behn's literary achievements contingent on her personal sexual appeal: since her "Black Ace," as "Afra" refers to her private parts, no longer compels masculine desire, Behn no longer compels readers.

While this and the "Session" printed in 1680 are especially cruel, associating women's creativity with madness or sexual promiscuity, women fared only slightly better in such poems when turn-of-the-century values discouraged such outrageous imagery. *The Session of the Poets, Holden at the Foot of Parnassus-Hill, July the 9th, 1696*, an anonymous prose satire, introduces Mary Pix and Delarivier Manley.[6] Each had recently seen her first play produced, and they are described in nearly identical terms. Manley is indicted for having "Sacrilegiously usurp't that Province of Poetry no ways belonging nor appertaining unto her" (39), while Pix is arraigned because she has "unworthily, fraudulently, and sacrilegiously usurpt . . . the Province of Poetry" (46). Manley's "Sentence is, that she must not kiss any Man, nor to be kiss'd by any Person" (48). Pix's sentence is "that she will be desperately in Love with several Persons, but not one of them shall regard but despise and laugh at her Person" (49). Once again, women's writing is associated with sexual activity; Manley and Pix are threatened not with critical disapproval, but with failed love lives if they persist in writing.

In writing "Sessions of the Poets," then, Finch chose a kind of satirical poem that had recently become associated with misogyny and turned it into a woman's tribute to women. She replaced invective with wit, which she defined later in "An Epistle to Mrs Catherine Fleming at Coleshill in Warwickshire but hastily perform'd & not corrected. London October the 18th: 1718":

> True wit is rallery which never flings
> The ridicule but on fantastic things
> The complement insinuated right
> Which sets some talent in its proper light
> And whilst on the possessor it distills
> With conscious pleasure not confusion fills. (72–77)

Finch, whose works are often suffused with irony, despised personal satire such as "Lampoons, and all sorts of abusive Verses," rejecting "both the underhand dealing, and uncharitablenesse which accompanys them" and declaring in "The Preface" to her folio manuscript, "I never suffer'd my small talent, to be that way employ'd" (150–54). "The Circuit of Appollo" demonstrates her preference for graceful compliment, especially praise of talents, as described in her poem to Fleming. Although Finch retained the frame of a legal contest without a winner, she otherwise transformed her "Session" into a vehicle for praising a group of women she deemed the chief poets in Kent.

Besides revising the tone and diction of contemporary "Sessions of the Poets," Finch reimagined the setting of her poetic "trial." Suckling never specifies the location of his court, but his assertion that "the wits of the Town came thither" (5) suggests he is parodying a London court session. Succeeding "Sessions" poems are similarly vague, but the fact that they gather a crowd of poets and playwrights, with increasing emphasis on professional writers, implies that London, the center of the booksellers' trade, is the likely site of Apollo's court in each. Only "A New Session of the Poets" summons the various offending poets to "the Foot of Parnassus-hill," imposing an arduous trek on the defendants. Finch expands the setting in which poets might be found. Apollo is introduced journeying "Throo' the lands of the Muses" (2), a reminder that not all writers are competing for glory in the capital, but are transcribing their works into manuscripts throughout England. Finch's poets are all gentlewomen living on estates or in small villages in Kent; for these writers, a summons to a London court would be a hardship. Neither are they ambitious of print publication, making their appearance near the booksellers or theatres less appropriate than for the competitors in other poems. Rather than summon writers to London, therefore, Finch's Apollo visits the county, a setting more plausible for her contestants. She transforms Apollo into a circuit-rider, a judge who journeys successively to various county towns for periodic sessions to try civil and criminal cases or, in this case, to award the laurel to its rightful claimant.

Having relocated Apollo's court in Kent, where, she claims, most of the poets are women, Finch reveals that only four women have answered his summons. What can Finch's tributes to her fellow Kentish poets tell us about women's writings, milieus, and identities? Despite lingering uncertainty about the identities of the writers who are given pastoral names in the poem, Finch's tributes to living poets offer a glimpse of her manuscript-writing circle in Kent. They suggest insights into, and relationships among, these women's writings. Not least important, they also help confirm the dating of Finch's chief manuscript, a folio volume housed at the Folger Shakespeare Library in Washington, DC.[7]

"The Circuit of Appollo" exemplifies difficulties in identifying women addressed or alluded to, especially by pen names, in all early poems, a problem also addressed by Christine Gerrard and Kathryn King in this volume. Women who wrote when single sometimes become impossible to trace when their names changed, sometimes more than once, due to marriage. Reference books, so useful when researching men, are not always helpful, as even dependable sources like *Burke's Peerage,* George E. Cokayne's *Complete Peerage,* and the *Dictionary of National Biography* sometimes omit the names and date information of men's wives and daughters. Such references can sometimes mislead by, for example, listing only daughters who married prominent men, or by leaving out the names of daughters (and sons) who died young. The only women who can be identified fairly easily today are those addressed or alluded to by their own names and/or those who were noble or, for some other reason, possessed a public identity. In her critical edition of Aphra Behn, for example, Janet Todd can specify most of Behn's women addressees, because Behn often dedicated her writings to noble patronesses or complimented prominent actresses. But when Behn, Katherine Philips, or Anne Finch praise women using pen names, or allude to women who left no or limited historic records, their subjects can remain obscure, unlike the rogues and dunces whom John Dryden, Delarivier Manley, and Alexander Pope "damned to fame" in sensational works that inspired "keys" to specify their victims' identities.[8] This is unfortunate, because unidentified women cannot be studied or placed effectively in relation to a poet's style and writing practices, her ideologies, her personal milieu, and more broadly, her culture, as, for example, Natasha Duquette and Shelley King are able to do in their essays on Helen Maria Williams and Amelia Opie, respectively. Modern readers, whose ideas about gender and publicity are so different from Finch's, must find paradoxical her effort to celebrate her circle as the best poets in Kent while concealing their identities in a poem never intended for print publication.

Much of the difficulty regarding identifications in Finch's verse arises because she was, like Suckling, Philips, Rochester and others, primarily a manuscript poet, with the exception of a number of poems—mostly fables—she apparently wrote specifically for her only printed collection, *Miscellany Poems, On Several Occasions. Miscellany Poems*, published in 1713, contains poems mostly written between 1688 and 1703 but never printed until Finch decided, for complex reasons, to publish her volume. "The Circuit of Appollo" was not included in *Miscellany Poems*, but had been transcribed into Finch's primary manuscript collection, *Miscellany Poems, With Two Plays, by Ardelia*, the folio volume now housed at the Folger Shakespeare Library. "The Circuit of Appollo" is found only in that manuscript; it was never copied or printed in Finch's lifetime, indicating its private nature as a tribute to several women well known to her and presumably to one another and to her intended circle of readers. Despite its intentional obscurity, however, unraveling the mysteries of "The Circuit of Appollo" illuminates a network of women writers located in Kent, recognizing them as poets in a supportive but competitive literary environment. Like Philips's pastoral pen names, Finch's pen names signify familiarity and recognition of a shared enterprise. But while Philips's names concealed the identities of fellow Stuart sympathizers, Finch's pen names signify what was perhaps an equally discreet marker of identity for these Kentish women, their participation in a network of writers.

As for many poems in Finch's folio manuscript, the date of "The Circuit of Appollo" is difficult to specify. Its *terminus a quo* of composition is April 16, 1689, the death date of Aphra Behn, for whom Apollo mourns at the poem's outset (11). The *terminus ad quem* is c. 1701–1702, based on its inclusion in the folio, which was transcribed at that time. The poem contains some clues to its date, but these depend on the concealed poets' probable identities, resulting in a kind of chicken-and-egg puzzle for the interpreter: the dates might confirm the intended poets, but the poets would likewise resolve the poem's date. The poem's manuscript status itself therefore creates difficulties of identification and consequently of interpretation. The poem refuses to name a victor; after considering their respective merits, Apollo confirms his divine wisdom by declining to grant one woman the laurel wreath. He leaves the Muses to decide the controversy, not wishing to make three women his enemies by choosing one. Finch's tone is light and her rhythm jaunty, but her poem acknowledges the competition inherent in contemporary verse-writing. Even among retired women writing manuscript poetry in Kent, verse is appraised, and judgment exercised, by its select group of readers. Finch therefore considers her verse-writing women acquaintances as engaged in a friendly and somewhat covert, but demanding and competitive, enterprise.

Early in the poem, Finch claims that poets are scarce in Kent and are mostly women (4). Finch thus situates herself in a county where poetry is not a widely practiced art, but (perhaps consequently) there are opportunities for women to excel. In particular, Kent was the birthplace of the late Aphra Behn. Finch's first tribute is quite specific: Behn had been superior to all other "Femels" in "fancy, language, or witt" (12–13), but had written "a little too loosly" (14) because her poems stimulated not simply "soft thoughts" but lascivious ideas, causing readers to blush and even commit "faults," either in imagination or by emulating Behn's suggestive verse. Finch's mixed praise and censure of Behn distinguishes her from her famous countrywoman. But it also discriminates between the tastes of Behn's era, and Behn's need for patronage among courtiers and actresses, and the values and needs of Finch's circle. Finch's criticism particularly reflects her personal allegiance to the famously decorous former queen, Mary Beatrice.

Readers need only compare Behn's translation of "The Golden Age" passage from Torquato Tasso's *Aminta* with Finch's to witness the differences between the two poets' cultural ideals. Behn's "The Golden Age," published in her *Poems upon Several Occasions* of 1684, perhaps originated as a tribute to Mary Beatrice when she was Duchess of York, because it derived from a pastoral drama composed by Tasso in 1573 for the court of Mary Beatrice's ancestor, Duke Alfonso II d'Este of Ferrara. In Behn's version of a chorus by Tasso that attempts to talk Sylvia, the drama's heroine, out of her vow of chastity, the golden age predated the hypocritical code of decorum imposing female chastity. Behn's Sylvia is urged by the chorus to indulge her love for Aminta before devotion to honor prevents fulfillment of her youthful desires. Behn's translation was printed in the year of Finch's marriage, when she was beginning her poetic career as a member of Mary Beatrice's court. Finch's manuscript version of fourteen lines from a French translation of Tasso's chorus was also most likely intended as a tribute to her mistress. In stark contrast to Behn's version, Finch's chorus emphasizes the golden age as a time when "innocence, and vertue reign'd" (11). Germaine Greer has discussed the differences between Behn's and Finch's translations at length.[9] Here, I would like to emphasize how the two versions distinguish the two poets' generations, allegiances, and values. Behn, a generation older than Finch, sought patronage chiefly among the members of Charles II's court, including his mistresses. Finch served Mary Beatrice, who encouraged more decorous performances, "to make all hearts beat, without blushes, or faults." Finch's tribute thus summons up the ethos of Mary Beatrice's entourage as well as a cultural climate changed since Behn's generation. With Behn's death, the time is right for a new Kentish laureate.

Among the three contenders Finch praises under pastoral names, the first reminds us of the close ties among prominent families in Kent. Alinda, who begins the contest "with a Song upon Love" (22), was Elizabeth Taylor Wythens (fl. 1685–d. 1708), daughter of Sir Thomas Taylor of Park House in Maidstone,[10] Kent's county town. Wythens was an author of songs and pastoral love poetry who permitted three of her poems to be printed under her maiden name in Behn's *Miscellany* of 1685. She was later described as "Olinda" in Manley's *The New Atalantis*.[11] Finch, or perhaps her amanuensis Heneage, may have misspelled Wythens's pen name, or Manley may have changed it slightly to avoid legal challenges from the family of the by-then recently deceased poet. In any case, the Finches' idiosyncratic spelling does not prevent near-certain identification. Wythens became a scandalous figure, whose story was exploited by Manley: in 1685, the same year her poems were printed, Taylor married Sir Francis Wythens (c. 1635–1704). Soon after her unhappy marriage, she began an affair with a childhood neighbor,

Sir Thomas Colepeper, third Baronet (1656–1723), of Preston Hall near Maidstone, a liaison Finch alluded to sympathetically in another poem, "Ardelia's answer to Ephelia" (182–92). In 1693, Wythens attempted to bankrupt her husband in order to incarcerate him in debtor's prison, which might set the *terminus ad quem* for "The Circuit of Appollo," which contains no hint of public scandal. In "The Circuit of Appollo," the lines of Alinda's love song are described as "easy . . . yet compos'd with such art, / That not one expression, fell short of the heart" (23–24). Since we learned in the previous stanza that the object of poetry is "to stir up soft thoughts, / Yett to make all hearts beat, without blushes, or faults," Alinda's verse fulfills Finch's criteria. Finch herself wrote a number of pastoral poems; indeed, the three poems printed by Behn ("Song" ["Ye Virgin Pow'rs defend my heart"]; "To Mertill who desir'd her to speak to Clorinda of his Love"; and "Song" ["Strephon has Fashion, Wit and Youth"]) resemble Finch's many songs in their chaste but fashionable lyrics about young women determined to avoid seduction by charming rakes, or expressing despair over love denied.[12] Depending on when they became acquainted, Finch and Wythens may have exchanged and critiqued one another's early poems.

The second poet competing for the laurels is "Laura," whose praise of Orinda, the late Katherine Philips's pen name, has impressed Apollo. Laura is most likely Grace Blome (1674–1750) of Sevenoaks, Kent, about twenty miles from Maidstone. After her marriage to Herbert Randolph, Esq., in 1700, she composed, or revised her authorial name in, "An Epistle, From Mrs: Randolph To Mrs: Finch," one of two commendatory poems transcribed at the beginning of Finch's folio volume. Blome-Randolph was primarily a manuscript poet, some of whose poems are preserved at the Bodleian. Another manuscript preserved at the Folger Shakespeare Library as the cookbook of Grace Blome contains not only Blome's family tree, completed after her death with the dates of her birth, marriage, and death, but also a transcription of her only printed poem, an ode on the death of Elizabeth, Lady Oxenden.[13] Lady Oxenden died in 1696, when Blome was still unmarried; she evidently gave permission for the ode's printing under her married name in 1735, the same year that Sir James Oxenden's second wife died, causing confusion about the author's identity and intended subject. We thus glean insight into a culture in which one woman, like Elizabeth Taylor Wythens, might print verse under her maiden name, while another might confidently share her verse in manuscript but refrain from printing, or printing under her name, until after marriage. Blome-Randolph's case in turn complements ongoing discussions about why Finch herself refused to be identified by name in print as a writer until after her husband inherited the earldom of Winchilsea. The three poets' choices suggest a range of options available to genteel women writers who permitted their writings to be printed.

Besides extending our knowledge of Finch's circle, Finch's tribute to "Laura" illuminates Mrs. Randolph's dedicatory tribute at the beginning of Finch's folio volume and, indeed, helps date the Folger folio manuscript itself. Various time sequences have been proposed for the folio's compilation, chiefly W. J. Cameron's supposition, followed by Barbara McGovern in her critical biography, that Heneage began entering poems into the volume around 1696 and concluded with the final poem about King James's death in 1701.[14] We now believe that Heneage transcribed the folio volume in a continuous effort following the death of James, based on evidence within the poems and especially on the analyses of Heather Wolfe, Curator of Manuscripts, and Franklin Maurey, Rare Bindings Specialist, at the Folger Shakespeare Library.[15] Since the folio omits a major poem, Finch's "Ode on the Hurrycane," composed after the Great Storm of 1703, it was most likely planned and completed before that ode was written. A major clue to the date of the folio manuscript is Mrs. Randolph's prefatory poem, which could not have been transcribed before her marriage in 1700. The prefatory poem alludes, and responds generously, to Finch's inclusion of Randolph as a contestant for the laurel wreath, particularly due to her praise of Orinda in a now-lost poem. Randolph returns the compliment:

> A noble Precedent from her you draw
> Who cancell'd great Appollo's Salique Law
> The fam'd Orinda, who had fate contriv'd
> That She our mighty Master had surviv'd
> Had a Poetique Monarchy deriv'd
> In a direct Succession down to You
> Which now by Conquest you begin anew
> In whom their several Perfections meet
> As Cowley strong, and as Orinda sweet. (35–43)

In Randolph's opinion, Finch's Apollo may not have awarded one woman poet the bays, but Finch herself is the rightful heir of Abraham Cowley and Katherine Philips, her "Poetique Monarchy deriv'd / In a direct Succession" (39–40). Randolph would have known her allusion to a legitimate succession would please Finch more than any other, since the Finches were virtually internal exiles in Kent due to their ongoing loyalty to James II.

Randolph's poem completes Finch's "Circuit," since the god coyly refuses to make a decision at the conclusion of "The Circuit of Appollo." While Finch describes herself in the poem (perhaps following Suckling) as a "carelesse" poet, Randolph characterizes her friend's verse as combining the respective gifts of Cowley and Philips, two of women's favorite models. Randolph singles out Finch's "A Pastoral Between Menalcus and Damon on the appearance of the Angels to the Shepheards on Our Saviour's Birth-Day," ensuring that readers will identify Finch as a pious poet whose verse is not only strong and melodious but free from any "looseness." Randolph intimates that Finch has won the crown from not only Cowley and Philips but also Behn, her Kentish predecessor, and is thus entitled by merit and succession to the bays. Randolph's poem is thus in dialogue with Finch's "Circuit," retracing and completing Finch's tribute to her fellow women poets. Her poem evokes a coterie in which manuscripts circulated and poets exchanged and alluded to each other's verse.

The final competitor in Finch's poem is "Valeria," who draws Apollo aside for a private review of her poems. "The Circuit of Appollo" suggests that Valeria shares her poems with very few people but that she is known by her intimates as a serious poet. Several women have been suggested as Valeria's model; the most likely candidate, as the late Ann Messenger and more recently Deborah Kennedy have argued, is Sarah Dixon (1672–1765).[16] Dixon was a Kentish poet with Tory sensibilities who, at the time of Finch's poem, lived in Newnham, about thirteen miles from Finch's home at Eastwell.[17] Dixon's preface to her only printed volume, published when she was sixty-eight, fits Finch's implication that Valeria has shared her verse with very few readers (36–42). In the preface to *Poems on Several Occasions* (Canterbury, 1740), Dixon states, "As to the following Pieces the Reader is to know they were the Employment (an innocent, and, she thinks, no improper Employment) of a Youth of much Leisure. Some little Taste of Poetry, improved by some Reading, tempted our Author to try her Talents, for her own Amusement, and the Diversion of her Friends, in a Country Solitude." Dixon's account is most likely an accurate account of her youthful writing for a coterie that may have included Finch, Randolph, Taylor Wythens, and others.

If, as Messenger and Kennedy believe, Dixon was Finch's "Valeria," the identification helps us to envision a "circuit of Appollo" that really was a circuit or geographical circle, encompassing Newnham, Eastwell, Sevenoaks, and Maidstone, as well as a group of women writers circulating their verse.[18] Dixon's *Poems on Several Occasions*, as Kennedy observed, was influenced by later poets such as Thomas Parnell and Alexander Pope, confirming that

Dixon kept writing throughout her life.[19] But the volume's contents mostly originated in the poetry of an earlier era. Songs abound—there are nine among the 187 poems in the volume—and there are also seven pastorals included, as well as ballads, fables, epistles, hymns, odes, and psalm translations: all verse forms prevalent in Finch's early manuscript volumes as well. As in Finch's manuscripts, there are many biblical and classical allusions, the latter taken frequently from Plutarch's *Lives*.

If, as seems likely, Finch and Dixon were acquainted with one another, Dixon may have emulated the more practiced Finch, and the two were part of a mutually influencing and supportive circle. Dixon's poems include, for example, a "Hymn on Christmas-Day," which may indicate familiarity with Finch's "A Pastoral Between Menalcus and Damon," although both were influenced by Milton's "On the Morning of Christ's Nativity." Dixon's poems also feature pastoral names that, as Messenger commented, would if identified reveal more about her friendship and composition circles. One secure link to Finch's circle is the presence of the first of Grace Blome-Randolph's twelve children, Thomas (1701–1783), on Dixon's subscription list, along with a Miss Randolph and Miss Dorothy Randolph, both of Canterbury and most likely his sisters, since Grace Randolph's husband Herbert (1657–1726) had been the Recorder of Canterbury. If Grace Randolph and Sarah Dixon, or "Laura" and "Valeria," were known to one another as poets, then their participation in Apollo's contest means that the poem does not describe a list of writers Finch knew only individually, but a group well known to one another, perhaps by the poets' pen names, and reading (or sometimes singing) one another their verses as the poem depicts them sharing their writings with Apollo (20). The select readers of Finch's octavo and folio volumes may have included these very women.

Unlike the "sessions of the poets" written by men during the period, Anne Finch's "Circuit of Appollo" concludes on her preferred note of gentle, and general, satire. Apollo refuses to crown the best poet, because what sane man would alienate three out of four women? Within the poem, each of Finch's peers is deemed a worthy contender for the bays, and only his discretion prevents Apollo from naming one as the best poet in Kent. "The Circuit of Appollo" might offer us a view of the writing culture in provincial seventeenth-century England. It hints at a group of women poets writing and circulating their poems in manuscript, perhaps occasionally meeting to read, sing, or otherwise perform their writings. Unlike the subjects of Katharine Kittredge's essay in this volume, Melesina Trench and Mary Leadbeater, their friendship did not enable these women to reinvent, as much as to invent, their own identities as poets. These women would have copied one another's verse, transcriptions that may now be among the few, usually anonymous witnesses of their poems that survive in archives.

Finch's tributes to women in "The Circuit of Appollo" are a mysterious but important record worth attempting to unravel. Through Finch's poem, we can trace the influence of these early women poets on one another, and glimpse a world outside the London print marketplace. In Finch's Kent, women poets competed with, but also supported, one another. Sarah Dixon, like Elizabeth Singer Rowe among the Thynnes and Seymours of Wiltshire, appears to have been esteemed for her well-informed mind despite her lack of wealth. Elizabeth Taylor Wythens was valued for her poetry despite her unhappy marriage and adulterous affair. Though praise of the late Queen Mary II in her elegy on Lady Oxenden indicates Grace Blome-Randolph's political loyalty, her poetry and piety were more important to Finch. In contrast to both of the rowdy "Sessions" poems that portray Apollo as a scornful judge, "The Circuit of Appollo" depicts a circle of women devoted to the god of verse and perhaps, if we can learn more about their identities and relationships, to one another as fellow poets.

Notes

1. See Sir John Suckling, *The Works of Sir John Suckling: The Non-Dramatic Works*, ed. Thomas Clayton (Oxford: Clarendon, 1971), 266–78 for a thorough discussion of Suckling's poem, its form, and the identities of the rival poets. I quote the poem from this edition (71–76).

2. Suckling's biography is derived from Thomas Clayton, "Suckling, Sir John (bap. 1609–1641?)," *Oxford Dictionary of National Biography Online*, www.oxforddnb.com; see also Robert Wilcher, *The Discontented Cavalier: The Work of Sir John Suckling in Its Social, Religious, Political, and Literary Contexts* (Newark: University of Delaware Press, 2007). Wilcher discusses "The Wits" at length (170–80), noting its originality, its folk song-like structure (173), and the relative seriousness and consistency of Suckling's literary judgments, 179–80.

3. Wilcher, *The Discontented Cavalier*, 171–72. Suckling's "A Sessions of the Poets" was first printed in *Fragmenta Aurea. A Collection of All the Incomparable Peeces, Written by Sir John Suckling. And Published by a Friend to Perpetuate His Memory* (London, 1646), 7–10.

4. See Anonymous, "The Session of the Poets, to the Tune of Cook Lawrel," in *Poems on Affairs of State: From the Time of Oliver Cromwell, to the Abdication of K. James the Second* (London, 1697), 206–11.

5. See John Wilmot, *Poems on Several Occasions, By the Right Honourable, the E. of R* (Antwerp, 1680), 111–14. The poem was excluded from the first authorized edition of Rochester's works, Jacob Tonson's *Poems, &c. on Several Occasions: with Valentinian,*

A Tragedy (London, 1691). David M. Vieth discussed the possibility of Elkanah Settle's authorship in *Attribution in Restoration Poetry: A Study of Rochester's Poems of 1680* (New Haven, CT: Yale University Press, 1963), 296–321.

6. Anonymous, *The Session of the Poets, Holden at the Foot of Parnassus' Hill, July the 9th, 1696* (London, 1696). Mary Pix and Delarivier Manley had made impressive debuts that year. Manley's novel *The Inhumane Cardinal* was published and *Ibrahim* premiered in May or June; *The Spanish Wives* would premiere in August. Manley's *Letters by Mrs. Manley* was printed, and *The Lost Lover* and *The Royal Mischief* had premiered in March and April/May, respectively. See William Van Lennep, ed., *The London Stage 1660–1800: A Calendar of Plays, Entertainments and Afterpieces* (Carbondale: Southern Illinois University Press, 1960–68), 1: 459, 461–64.

7. Anne Finch, *Miscellany Poems With Two Plays By Ardelia* (Manuscript Fnb3, Folger Shakespeare Library, Washington, D.C.). Throughout this essay I draw on my research for the explanatory notes to *The Cambridge Edition of the Works of Anne Finch, Countess of Winchilsea*, co-edited with Jennifer Keith (Cambridge: Cambridge University Press, forthcoming). All quotations from Finch's poems are taken from this forthcoming edition and cited by line number(s) within the text.

8. The addressee of Katherine Philips's "A retir'd friendship, to Ardelia. 23d Aug. 1651," the poem from which Finch derived her own pen name, is a good example; Ardelia's identity has not been traced. See *The Collected Works of Katherine Philips, The Matchless Orinda*, vol. 1, *The Poems*, ed. Patrick Thomas (Stump Cross, Essex: Stump Cross Books, 1990), 339, n. 22. John Dryden's "Absalom and Achitophel" (1681) and "Mac Flecknoe" (1682), Delarivier Manley's *Secret Memoirs and Manners of Several Persons of Quality, of Both Sexes, from the New Atalantis, an Island in the Mediterranean* (1709), and Alexander Pope's *The Dunciad* (1728) were among contemporary publications inspiring "keys" to identify their characters.

9. Germaine Greer, "'Alme in Liberte Avvezze': Aphra Behn's Version of Tasso's Golden Age," in *Aphra Behn, 1640–1689: Identity, Alterity, Ambiguity*, eds. Mary Ann O'Donnell, Bernard Dhuicq, and Guyonne Leduc (Paris: Harmattan, 2000), 225–33.

10. Information about Elizabeth Taylor Wythens can be found in Stuart Handley, "Sir Francis Wythens," *Oxford Dictionary of National Biography, Online Edition*, and in Stuart Handley, "Sir Thomas Colepeper, third baronet, of Preston Hall," *History of Parliament Online*, www.historyofparliamentonline.org.

11. Delarivier Manley narrates the history of "Olinda" in *Secret Memoirs and Manners of Several Persons of Quality, of Both Sexes. From the New Atalantis, an Island in the Mediterranean*, ed. Rosalind Ballaster (1709; London: Penguin, 1992), 2: 260–63; see 304, n. 512 for Ballaster's identification of Olinda as Elizabeth Taylor Wythens.

12. For the poems by "Mrs. Taylor," see Aphra Behn, ed., *Miscellany, being a Collection of Poems by Several Hands* (London, 1685), 69–73.

13. Grace Blome Randolph, *The Cookbook of Grace Blome* [1697], Manuscript V.b.301, Folger Shakespeare Library, Washington, D.C.

14. William J. Cameron, "Anne, Countess of Winchilsea: A Guide for the Future Biographer" (PhD diss., Victoria College, 1951), 75–77, 120; Barbara McGovern, *Anne Finch and Her Poetry: A Critical Biography* (Athens: University of Georgia Press, 1992), 70.

15. Heather Wolfe, Curator of Manuscripts, and Franklin Mowery, Rare Bindings Specialist, are both at the Folger Shakespeare Library in Washington, D.C. My co-editor, Jennifer Keith, and I were privileged to consult with them while sharing an NEH-funded fellowship at the Folger in Spring 2011. I wish to thank the NEH, the Folger Shakespeare Library, and everyone on the Library's staff for their invaluable assistance with our work on *The Cambridge Edition of the Works of Anne Finch, Countess of Winchilsea*.

16. Ann Messenger recovered details of Dixon's biography in *Pastoral Tradition and the Female Talent: Studies in Augustan Poetry* (New York: AMS, 2001), 136–41; Deborah Kennedy supports and extends her proposal that Dixon was Valeria in *Poetic Sisters: Early Eighteenth-Century Women Poets* (Lewisburg, PA: Bucknell University Press, 2013), 127–29.

17. Kennedy, *Poetic Sisters*, 128.

18. Messenger proposes that Dixon was close to Lord Teynham's family at Lynsted Park near Newnham. Lord Teynham had eight daughters, one of whom may have been the "Stella" addressed in Dixon's poems (*Pastoral Tradition and the Female Talent*, 137–38). That Finch would most likely have known Lord Teynham's family is suggested by his biography: a former Page of Honor to Queen Catherine, the Roman Catholic Christopher Roper, fifth Baron Teynham, was appointed Lord Lieutenant of Kent by James II in October 1688 but fled England during the Glorious Revolution. He died in Brussels in 1689. His next two heirs, sons John (d. 1697) and Christopher (d. 1699) also died overseas. Not until his third son Henry became eighth Baron Teynham in 1699 did the head of the family resume a sustained presence in Kent; Henry conformed to the Anglican faith in 1716 and took his seat in the House of Lords, although he committed suicide in 1723. Of the fifth Baron's daughters, three—Penelope, Winifred, and Ann (perhaps the youngest children)—were given a pass to travel to France with their nurse, presumably to join their parents. Finch would at least have heard of the Roper family's travails due to their continuing loyalty to James, and would most likely have been acquainted with the members of this prominent family still resident at Lynsted Park. See G. E. Cokayne, *The Complete Peerage*, ed. Geoffrey H. White, 13 vols. (London: St. Catherine Press, 1953), 12.1: 682–83.

19. Kennedy, *Poetic Sisters*, 145 (Parnell); 159 (Pope); see also Messenger, *Pastoral Tradition and the Female Talent*, 139–40.

"Those Stately Palaces"
Tribute and Estates in the Work of Anne Finch and Jane Barker

NICOLLE JORDAN

Land may seem an obscure or elusive index for women writers' tributes to other women, and yet, by focusing on women's literary texts that venerate landed property, we may appreciate how such tributes expose the male prerogatives that operate through literary convention. These conventions—country house poetry in particular—express women's typical (though not exclusive) status as objects rather than owners of property. This proposition prompts questions about the shaping as well as expressive qualities of convention; that is, literary convention not only depicts but also perpetuates women's exclusion from the privileges of property ownership and stewardship. In this essay, I investigate two instances of female tribute through the lenses of two genres: country house poetry and the book dedication. My tribute texts include a poem by Anne Finch, Countess of Winchilsea (1661–1720), entitled "To the Honorable the Lady Worsley at Long-leate" (c. 1690), and a book dedication by Jane Barker (1652–1732) entitled "To the Right Honourable the Countess of Exeter," which accompanies the novel *The Amours of Bosvil and Galesia* (also known as *Love Intrigues*) (1713/1719). Both texts express the writers' material and emotional dependence on the recipients of their tributes, who have given them much-needed access to land—that is, to a home or a substitute home. As we will see, Finch bears the burden of convention more decisively than Barker does, though both texts illuminate their authors' intertwined struggles with authorship and ownership. Despite the obstructions of convention, however, both Finch and Barker demonstrate the transgressive potential of female appropriation of a typically male preserve. In opposing ways, Finch's poem and Barker's dedication illuminate women writers' efforts to attain the prerogatives of ownership despite the forces of exclusion, whether literary or material. That both writers pursue these ends specifically in the context of paying tribute to another woman suggests that engagement with their own gender may have provided a congenial context in which to challenge these obstructing forces.

In "To the Honorable the Lady Worsley at Long-leate," Finch fuses an occasional poem honoring her niece to the venerable tradition of country house poetry, thus elevating Lady Worsley by locating her in the privileged precinct of a famous estate. The poem expresses gratitude to the eponymous figure for offering solace and hospitality during a particularly difficult time in the Finches' trials as non-jurors. As Stuart loyalists, Anne and her husband Heneage suffered considerable losses during the so-called Glorious Revolution. Their refusal to swear loyalty to the new Protestant monarchs left them disenfranchised and deprived of the opportunity to acquire their own home, given that their resources and the means to acquire them were severely limited by their non-juring status. The poem in question is one of several in which Finch managed her predicament in part by availing herself of country house poetry's hospitality rhetoric in works she addressed to her hosts and hostesses. Among such hosts were the Thynnes of Long-leat, in Wiltshire, the home of Heneage Finch's sister Frances Thynne, Viscountess Weymouth (the mother of the poem's Lady Worsley). As Barbara McGovern has demonstrated, Finch's intimacy with the Thynnes evolved over many years and several generations of the family. Poems such as "A Description of One of the Pieces of Tapistry at Long-Leat" and "A Letter to the Hon:ble Lady Worseley at Long-Leat, Lewston August the 10th 1704" evidence the recurrence of this estate in the poet's oeuvre.[1]

Unlike these poems, however, "To the Honorable the Lady Worsley" is haunted by the speaker's sense of affliction. It begins on a decidedly gloomy note. The autobiographical speaker, writing "from some obscure and lonely recesse," takes up the pen to honor her niece, Frances (Thynne) Worsley, who is now married.[2] This biographical orientation is explicit in the headnote: "Who had most obligingly desired my corresponding with her by Letters." The speaker's dejection, evident in the first lines, suggests that Finch may have written the poem at a time when her afflictions were particularly acute. Recent scholarship dates the poem's composition most likely to some time between August and November of 1690.[3] At this time, Heneage Finch was being held in London under suspicion of treason for having attempted to aid his monarch's escape to France, and Anne was staying at Godmersham, a priory near the Finch family estate at Eastwell (which was presided over by her nephew Charles Finch, third Earl of Winchilsea). She thus had ample reason to describe her "recese" as "Fitt only for the Wretch opress'd by Fate" (4).[4]

The foregoing circumstances intimate how, in the midst of such domestic turmoil, Finch would have been drawn to the idealizing rhetoric of country house poetry. "To the Honorable the Lady Worsley at Long-leate" constructs a paradise of sorts, where natural beauty and familial contentment distract the speaker from her travails. Ironically, though, the estate named in the poem's title upstages its hostess, for the poem treats landscape improvements as more worthy of praise than the generosity of the woman who—though by proxy—gives the speaker access to them. What begins as appreciation for a female relative morphs into a celebration of a famous estate and its improver, Thomas Thynne, first Viscount Weymouth. The displacement of Lady Worsley by her father in this poetic tribute is, I would argue, a consequence of the fact that though she is the source of solace, Lady Worsley does not occupy the position of owner or mistress and therefore cannot assume the responsibility or praise for the estate's comfort and luxury. The synecdoche that conventionally links estate and owner cannot operate in Lady Worsley's case, and so her father inadvertently usurps the glory meant for her.

The poem's structure and the extent of its hyperbole echo the preponderance of male over female influence. For instance, of its 111 lines, only twenty-three focus on the eponymous figure of Lady Worsley. These twenty-three lines occur near the beginning (13–36), and feature dazzling images of Utresia (the speaker's name for her niece), "Who like the Sun in her Meridian shows / Surrounded with the Lustre she bestows" (26–27). Utresia emerges as source of beauty, compassion, and "chear" (32). In figures of visuality that refract the pleasure experienced and created by Utresia, the poem first renders her as a bright spectacle, and then turns its gaze on her surroundings. There is, however, a transitional moment when the speaker suggests that the pleasure of looking at and being in the company of Utresia extends to the inspirational impact of her letters:

> Cou'd but the Witt that on her paper flows
> Affect my Verse and tune itt to her Prose
> Through every line a kindly warmth inspire
> And raise my Art equal to my desire
> Then shou'd my Hand snatch from the Muses store
> Transporting Figures n'ere expos'd before
> Something to Please so mouing and so new
> As not our Denham or our Cowley knew. (36–43)

Just as the light shining on and from Utresia illuminates those around her, so too her Prose sings to them, providing a musical model that enables the speaker to sing her own praises to the muse-like Utresia. A singular moment in the poem, here the speaker explicitly expresses gratitude for Utresia's letters in particular. The lines conjure an image of Finch sitting alone at Godmersham, holding the paper on which Lady Worsley wrote to her and spiriting herself to Longleat and into the company of her dear relatives. Though the subsequent lines show the speaker being swept up in the glory of Utresia's home and its creator, here we witness a unique expression of the value of an epistolary relationship.

The lines echo a similar rapport elucidated by Laura Tallon (see her essay in this volume), in which Anna Letitia Barbauld invokes the muses as she pays poetic tribute to her friend Mary Priestley. Disrupting the conventional poetic relationship between a male poet-speaker and a female muse, both Finch and Barbauld transform a neoclassical trope into a means for valorizing female friendship rather than male virility. The strategy exemplifies how women writers resist their objectification in literature by reimagining the dynamics of poetic inspiration, making verse the product of communion with a fellow woman rather than the fruit of erotic intrigue. Indeed, by figuring herself as a thief ("Then shou'd my Hand snatch from the Muses store"), Finch reinvents the creative process as something that women may engage in outside of the traditional mode of poetic inspiration. Stealing from one muse to give to another, as it were, Finch breaks open the typical two-way circuitry of creative stimulation and introduces a third party to the proceedings who further extends the possibilities for poetic communion.

In broader terms, however, I have been suggesting that Finch's choice of poetic tradition—country house poetry—stymies the tribute she seeks to deliver. Two telling allusions in the foregoing lines attest to the anxiety of influence within which she operates, and to the standards she feels she must meet and even surpass. By naming her poetic predecessors John Denham and Abraham Cowley, whose versifications of country life she clearly admires, Finch intimates her sense of being an interloper in a male domain. Just as she feels compelled to steal from the muses, so too she professes an awareness that her work will be evaluated according to a male standard. Though her intention to concoct figures of which men are incapable ("As not our Denham or our Cowley knew") expresses admirable ambition, it may also disguise a subtextual fear of inadequacy. When assessed alongside the poem's dominant presence, Lord Weymouth (discussed hereafter), the allusions to male poets strengthen the impression that country house poetry is uncongenial territory for female poets wishing to re-craft the form as a celebration of female friendship. The poem's male-authored intertexts resonate with its most prominent figure—the father—thus affirming the masculine influence dominating this ostensibly female tribute. There is, I am suggesting, a broader, literary-historical explanation for the way in which men and masculinity upstage Lady Worsley in this poem. Operating within a poetic tradition that emerged from and perpetuated these circumstances, Finch confronts obstacles to her attempt at female tribute that appear, from this historical perspective, insurmountable.

The manner in which the poem contends with its successive objects of admiration and inspiration offers further evidence of how male influence weighs heavily on the speaker despite the lightness she derives from Utresia. Dazzling as Lady Worsley may be, she cannot compete with the supernatural feats subsequently attributed to her father, Viscount Weymouth. Indeed, an accumulation of statements about the difficulty of the speaker's tasks implies, effectively, that it is easier to describe Utresia than to limn the wonders of Longleat or its famed improver. After professing a desire to surpass Denham and Cowley, the speaker suggests that she faces an even greater challenge in the attempt to capture Longleat's beauties in verse: "Or shew (the harder labour to compleat) / The real splendours of our fam'd Long-leate" (45–46). The following lines depict soaring fountains and sprawling cascades, which provoke the gods to play with these earthly waterworks ("Th' amazed Clouds now feel the Rains ascend / Whilst Phoebus as they tow'rds his Mantion flow / Graces th' attempt and marks them with his Bow" [56–58]). Such images reveal that the speaker is up to the challenge, but they also indirectly diminish the impact of the ostensible object of admiration: Utresia.

Likewise, just as the speaker falters before describing the estate, so too does she balk at the notion of describing its creator rather than his accomplishments:

> But Oh! Alas! cou'd we this Prospect give
> And make itt in true lights and shaddows live
> Ther's yet a Task att which 'twere vain to Strive
> His Genius who th'original improv'd
> To this degree that has our wonder mov'd
> Too great appears and awes the trembling hand
> Which can no Colours for that Draught command. (69–75)

Though perhaps using hyperbole as a way to amplify an already outsized spectacle of wondrous proportions, Finch may also be deliberately choosing rhetoric that gives precedence to the lord rather than to his creations. Whereas the poem's initial progression from lady to estate harmonizes their alluring effects, here the lord's "Genius" threatens to overshadow these preliminary delights. As a result, Utresia fades into the background, behind

Lady Worsley's more towering father and his creations. Treating the estate and its creator as greater artistic challenges than the celebration of Utresia, the speaker weakens the significance of her putative muse. Though the implied ease of portraying Utresia may testify to the speaker's greater affinity for and comfort with her niece, these are minor considerations when it comes to assessing how stature affects representation in literature. In other words, Finch's fondness for her niece cannot mitigate country house poetry's propensity to reward and perpetuate male superiority.

Not only does the poem elevate Finch's brother-in-law Lord Weymouth above his daughter, Lady Worsley, but it also avails itself of the hyperbole that is typical of country house poetry in such a way as to vest Weymouth with god-like qualities. In fact, Finch could be said to violate this convention insofar as its earliest exemplars honor their patrons by affiliating them with monarchs and religious luminaries, while Finch does not. In "To Penshurst" (1616), Ben Jonson pays tribute to his patron Sir Robert Sidney by alluding to King James's visit to the renowned estate; likewise, in "The Description of Cooke-ham" (1611), Aemelia Lanyer honors her patron Margaret Clifford, Countess of Cumberland, by suggesting that her ladyship walks her "sweet woods" in the company of Christ, his Apostles, and Moses.[5] Finch's speaker disavows the need for external support in order to portray Lord Weymouth, rendering him *sui generis* as a model for

> his future Race [. . .] Who from abroad shall no Examples need
> Of men Recorded or who then Exceed
> To urge their Virtue and exalt their Fame
> Whilst their own Weymouth stands their noblest Aime. (88, 90–93)

From line forty-five on, the speaker is thus swept up in the hyperbole of country house poetry rhetoric, in which house and lord mirror one another in complementary splendors that cast a long shadow over Utresia. She becomes a comparatively modest figure in a more illustrious home and beside an even more illustrious father. Finch surely intended to honor her niece by associating her with a renowned estate and its owner; yet the dictates of a form that treats estate and lord as mutually affirming seemingly allots only marginal space to peripheral figures like Utresia.

Thus far we have seen how the first part of "To the Honorable the Lady Worsley at Long-leate" uses Utresia to prepare the way for the grounds of her childhood home, and then subsequently treats those grounds as an extension and manifestation of their lord. There is a comparable shift in gender dynamics when the speaker turns her gaze upon the man presiding over

Longleat, whereby sympathetic femininity cedes to awesome masculinity. At first, then, the speaker derives comfort and inspiration from her contemplation of a fellow woman, engaging in a process of identification that fortifies her creativity.[6] Filial affection no doubt also motivates the speaker's shift of attention to her brother-in-law, and it is fair to acknowledge that the praise bestowed on each family member serves to elevate the other. But once the speaker begins to describe Lord Weymouth, no other figures of femininity appear in the poem, as if his entrance on the scene has stifled such fancies. The speaker may be playful rather than in earnest when suggesting that she trembles to sketch her lord ("His Genius [. . .] Too great appears and awes the trembling hand" [72–74]), yet there is a daunting aspect to this portrait of a man who prompts the speaker to profess her inferiority, however solicitous such gestures may be. Thus, she declares,

> No syllables the most sublimely wrought
> Can reach the loftier Immage of his thought
> Whose Judgment plac'd in a superior hight
> All things surveys with comprehensive sight
> Then pitying us below stoops to inform us right
> In Words which such convincing Reasons bear
> We silent wish that they engraven were. (76–82)

Awed respect is one thing, but one has to wonder why Finch feels compelled to place Weymouth on a higher plane than herself and others (including, presumably, Utresia). Whereas previously, contemplating her niece made the speaker "Soften our Cares and grow enlighten'd too," here Finch is cast down rather than raised up when figuring her relation to her brother-in-law.

No historical evidence suggests that he was a particularly overbearing man, and McGovern's biography, though noting no specific interactions between Finch and Lord Weymouth, describes a warm and long-lasting friendship between the Thynnes and the Finches.[7] The above tribute to Lord Weymouth therefore strikes me as a lighthearted yet deeply respectful gesture—but one that also, perhaps subconsciously, propels Finch into a realm of female self-denigration in spite of herself. The sentiment presents a striking contrast to the arresting proto-feminist statements found elsewhere in Finch's oeuvre, notably the mournful declaration in "The Introduction": "How are we fal'n, fal'n by mistaken rules? / And Education's, more than Nature's fools."[8] The conventions of country house poetry would seem to partake of, and perpetuate, these "mistaken rules" by hobbling Finch's effort to honor her niece in the glorious setting of a rural estate. A similar dynamic of marginalized—even "disappeared"—femininity appears to be at work in Anna Seward's poetic tribute to Lady Eleanor Butler and Sarah Ponsonby, the subjects of "Llangollen Vale." As Susan Lanser argues in her essay in this volume, "the burden of tribute leads to an erasure of the very couple who are the objects of praise," though in this case, anxiety about same-sex desire, rather than male literary prerogative, is the culprit. Lanser's study makes for a provocative counterpart to the present one insofar as she too elucidates the perplexing ways in which literary depictions of female stewardship of land—inadvertently, perhaps—effect the evacuation of women therefrom. Hewing to literary tradition in "To the Honorable the Lady Worsley at Long-leate," Finch constructs a patriarchal household and places Lord Weymouth squarely at its center. But, as we have seen, abiding by tradition necessitates that women be relegated to the margins, leaving us to ponder the other consequences—literary, material, or otherwise—that result from forms that encode male privilege.

The two editions of Jane Barker's book dedication to which I now turn offer evidence of women's authority over land, thus contrasting the incontrovertibly male stewardship that dominates Finch's poem and renders female stewardship unimaginable. Barker's tribute is explicit in "To the Honourable the Countess of Exeter," which accompanies *Love Intrigues* (1713), and slightly more so in "To the Right Honourable the Countess of Exeter," which precedes *The Entertaining Novels of Mrs. Jane Barker* (1719), wherein the renamed novel, *The Amours of Bosvil and Galesia*, appears. The shift from "the Honourable" to "the Right Honourable," the proper honorific for a countess, displays Barker's meticulous attention to decorum, which, as we will see, she was at pains to recuperate following the unauthorized first edition of the novel and dedication. The 1719 paratext invests Barker's patron and landlady, Elizabeth Cecil, with all the prerogatives and privileges of a mistress of the estate, in this case, Burghley House, in Lincolnshire. Thus Barker claims, "Was it not Burleigh-house with its *Parks*, *Shades*, and *Walks*, that form'd in me the first idea of my SCIPIO's Country Retreat?"[9] Though referring to her second novel, *Exilius, or, The Banish'd Roman* (1715), Barker might just as well name Galesia, the heroine of her three other novels, here, as she embraces estate management with the same vigor that Barker attributes to her patron.

Yet, the dedication's repeated reference to *Exilius* demands consideration; after all, Barker directly links Burghley House to this novel and not to the other one in the collection (*The Amours*). An intricately woven text (subtitled "A New Romance in Two Parts"), *Exilius* does not thematize land, landscape, or stewardship in the ways that its companion in *The Entertaining Novels* does. Though its layered plots speak to contemporary concerns, particularly female sexual desire, it nevertheless offers little in the way of thematic resonance with the concerns relating to land and property that interest me here.[10] I therefore pursue a more capacious interpretation of the dedication, finding that its lionization of the noble Lady illuminates aspects of *The Amours*—and even of its sequel—which legitimate and celebrate female landed authority. In this light, we may better appreciate how the countess becomes a model for "the noble Ladies, who inhabited those stately Palaces, amongst whom none has been a greater Ornament to this noble Family than your Ladyship."[11] A reference to the noble ladies and stately palaces of *Exilius*, this line nevertheless establishes the standard by which other noble ladies in Barker's fiction may be measured. Candidly honoring female authority in both her dedication and her fiction, Barker proves less hobbled by tradition than her near-contemporary Anne Finch apparently was. Idiosyncratic in so many ways, Barker—and her heroine Galesia—defy convention by treating female estate stewardship as not only fathomable but especially praiseworthy precisely because it is exceptional.

A few biographical preliminaries will illuminate Lady Exeter's inspirational role in the Galesia trilogy. For over fifty years, the Barker family leased property in Wilsthorpe, Lincolnshire, from the family into which Elizabeth née Brownlow had married, the Cecils, "whose great Burghley House and vast estate had provided a model of rural excellence" (see fig. 1).[12] (The house had been built between 1555 and 1587 for William Cecil, First Lord Burghley, chief advisor to Queen Elizabeth). Though scholars warn us not to conflate Barker with her fictional avatar, Galesia, I believe the resonance between Barker's depiction of her patron in the dedication and her portrait of an estate-stewarding heroine in *The Amours* is significant. The language of landscape appreciation that Barker uses to honor Lady Exeter in the dedication also appears in the voice of Galesia as she describes how natural scenery salved her broken heart. Thus, words and images from the dedication praising "Burleigh-house with its *Parks, Shades,* and *Walks*" echo in the novel, wherein Barker's heroine declares, "Sometimes I endeavour'd to divert my Chagrin, by contemplating, in these shady Walks, the wonderful Works of the Creation."[13] I do not mean to suggest that Galesia is a fictional rendition of Lady Exeter (or of Barker for that matter); rather, I am interested in how the shady walks of Burghley House infiltrate Barker's imagination as she conjures a scene of rural solace for her heroine. The similar

Figure 1. View of Burghley House, engraved and published by Robert Havell, 1819, after Frederick Mackenzie. (Stapleton Collection/Bridgeman Images)

language in these texts suggests that Lady Exeter modeled the practice of landscape appreciation and estate stewardship that later became the hallmark, and the solace, of the fictional character.

One might expect an estate as famous as Burghley House to have generated a rich historical record of its illustrious inhabitants, and that these sources would corroborate or otherwise illuminate Barker's treatment of Lady Exeter (see fig. 2). But it so happens that her husband John Cecil, the sixth Earl of Exeter, inherited the debts but not the renown of his father, who traveled to Europe at least four times to acquire artwork and other finery with which to embellish his home. In the company, and with the fortune, of his wife, heiress Anne Cavendish, the fifth Earl of Exeter undertook an expansion and redecoration of the house that contributed significantly to its current reputation as one of the finest stately homes in England. "Little is known of [the sixth] Earl," according to Lady Victoria Leatham, "although it might be suspected that he spent his whole life worrying about the enormous debts left behind by his father. He married twice, [. . .] the second time to Elizabeth Brownlow, who bore him five sons and one daughter."[14] Here ends the entry on the sixth Earl of Exeter in Leatham's catalogue of the Cecil dynasty. From the paucity of information on Elizabeth in comparison to the detailed rendering of her predecessor's shopping sprees in

Italy, we may infer that she adequately stewarded Burghley House and the Cecil family but did not distinguish herself through extravagant purchases. She lives on primarily in the names of her son Brownlow, the eighth Earl of Exeter, and his son Brownlow, the ninth Earl of Exeter.[15]

Barker's dedication to the Countess of Exeter serves as a counterweight to the family histories that privilege glamour and patrilineal succession.[16] Despite the lack of a historical record to bolster Barker's depiction of the Countess as a great "Ornament to this noble Family," the dedication testifies to her performance of the quotidian aspects of stewardship, such as the modeling of an appreciation for nature. The Countess's exemplarity possibly extends no further than her performance of the expected duties of a noble lady presiding over a fine estate; even so, Barker makes that performance honorable by praising it in her dedication. And, as we have seen, she has Galesia emulate "the noble Lady," savoring as she does in *The Amours* "the wonderful Works of the Creation." I argue, moreover, that Barker's indirect emulation of her noble benefactor signals a commitment to hierarchical order that overlaps with patriarchy while nevertheless containing a parallel class of feminine nobility with significant appeal to writers like Barker. In this light, it becomes possible to read Lady Exeter as a kind of avatar for Elizabeth Montagu, estate steward *extraordinaire,* who inspired writers such as Helen Maria Williams to honor her patron's hospitality and generosity in ways that echo Barker's tribute to Lady Exeter (see Natasha Duquette's essay in this volume).

The "tyranny of genre" that might be said to operate in Finch's poem does not quite obtain in Barker's dedications. Indeed, the looser confines of the novel allow for an array of gentlewomen and noblewomen to emerge in whom traces of Lady Exeter may be detected. Furthermore, the book dedication may be less hide-bound than country house poetry in the sense that dedication protocol does not exclude women from the ranks of dedicatees in the way that estate poetry excludes—or at least marginalizes—the ladies of the house. Kathryn R. King's essay in this volume offers complementary evidence for this claim, in the example of an anonymous dedication of an anonymous novel to "the Incomparable Mrs. Eliza Haywood." Despite such beguiling ambiguity, King demonstrates how dedications to novels may provide insight on people about whom little other contemporary biographical information exists (as is also the case for Elizabeth Cecil). Barker invokes a tradition of female patronage in her dedication to the countess of Exeter by naming the countess of Pembroke as the model with whom she would associate her benefactress in soliciting sanction for the ensuing novels.[17] The

Figure 2. Portrait of Elizabeth Brownlow, Lady Exeter, by Godfrey Kneller, c. 1699. (Burghley House Collection)

appearance of another countess (Lady Mary Herbert née Sidney) in Barker's dedication suggests the latter author's acute sensitivity to the subtleties of her culture's patronage system.

Indeed, the history of this particular dedication offers a test-case for the punctilios of literary patronage. The first, anonymous, edition of *The Amours of Bosvil and Galesia*—and the first dedication—appeared in 1713 without the author's permission, under the title *Love Intrigues*. As Kathryn

King has argued, the publication of a dedication intended only for a small coterie audience surely caused Barker considerable embarrassment, an insight that leads King to track the differences between the first and second (approved) edition of the novel.[18] The deletion of a comment that discloses the novel's autobiographical orientation particularly catches King's attention; the first edition expresses the hope that the countess's daughter (then a young girl) "never intangle her Noble Person in the Levities and Misfortunes the ensuing Treatise describes me unhappily to have struggled with."[19] Noting that Barker would never have included such self-revelations in a novel that she intended for print, King exposes the politics of book dedication in ways that inform my own interpretation of the relationship between Barker's dedications and her novels. Conformity to the social hierarchy weighs heavily upon Barker, who therefore apologizes in the second dedication for the apparent presumption of publishing a dedication without her patron's permission.

Despite the revisions that impose proper distance between client and patron, Barker's so-called *Galesia Trilogy* still contains traces of the female community in which it originated, as King persuasively suggests: "The 'corrected' 1719 dedication, which *was* intended for print, is wholly devoid of self-reference, never mind the tone of woman-to-woman intimacy so striking in the original version, and is swollen instead with praise of the countess. Comparing these dedications one gets the strong sense that in its earlier form the story of Bosvil and Galesia was written for, and meant to circulate within a small, select, sympathetic, and almost certainly feminine circle of élite readers."[20] By "swelling" her dedication with praise for her patron, Barker not only makes amends for an accidental peccadillo but also signals her unswerving commitment to a strict social hierarchy, a matter of personal principle that informs her Jacobite political allegiances.[21] In this light, the text's high-flown sycophancy registers less as mere flattery and more as a fundamental index of Barker's identity. She maneuvers in both the dedication and the novels to align herself with noble women, and always in ways that naturalize and genuflect to social difference. In this sense, her tribute to the countess of Exeter also functions as a tribute to royalist ideology. Deriving dignity and a sense of purpose from her affiliation with Lady Exeter, Barker celebrates female nobility in the dedication and then uses her novels to enact the social order over which she sees noblewomen rightly presiding.

We may find evidence for these claims by looking in more detail at the inspirational role that Barker's patron plays in the plots concocted for her heroine. As I have previously suggested, Lady Exeter serves as a model for the estate stewardship practiced by Galesia in the first novel of the trilogy and, as I will demonstrate hereafter, the countess also exemplifies the hospitality extended to the heroine in the second, entitled *A Patch-Work Screen for the Ladies* (1723). As both steward and hostess, the noblewoman exercises authority over land, making decisions over how it is maintained and who is invited to preside there, and these roles clearly constitute—as evidenced by both the dedication and the novels—key components of her identity. These facets of Lady Exeter, I argue, infiltrate Barker's novels and may therefore be read as subjects of her tribute, locating author and patron in the female network that King identifies in the first dedication—a network firmly planted, if you will, in landed property.

The most decisive evidence that Lady Exeter's example informs the plotting of Galesia's life appears near the end of *The Amours*, when the heroine embraces the role of estate steward. In the dedication, Barker asserts, "Your Ladyship's Virtue and Prudence hav[e] gain'd so absolute an Empire over the Hearts of the World, that none can reject what you are pleas'd to approve."[22] In the novel, the lovelorn Galesia explains: "I retir'd into myself, and return'd to my Studies; the Woods, Fields, and Pastures, had the most of my Time, by which Means I became as perfect in rural Affairs as any *Arcadian* Shepherdess; insomuch, that my Father gave into my Power and Command all his Servants and Labourers; it was I that appointed them their Work, and paid them their Wages; I put in and put out who I pleas'd, and was as absolute over my Rusticks, as the Great *Turk* over his Subjects."[23] The language of absolutism that these texts share intimates Barker's unshaken devotion to hierarchical social relations.[24] More remarkable, however, is her placement of women at the top of the hierarchies referenced in both her dedication and her novel. The countess reigns over an "Empire," Galesia, over her "Rusticks." Both women, as I have suggested, derive authority from the land over which they reign in some capacity. Their authority may be provisional because it is implicitly subordinate to their respective lords (Lord Exeter in the dedication; Galesia's father in the novel). Nevertheless, ample evidence in Barker's oeuvre suggests that the path to female authority wends through a landed estate. Barker's tribute to the countess hinges upon her stewardship of the land; and, in turn, Lady Exeter inspires another heroine—Galesia—whose authority over land makes female authority seem both plausible and laudable.

In addition to modeling an appreciation for beautiful landscapes and other virtues worthy of emulation, Lady Exeter also emerges as a paragon of hospitality when we scrutinize her role as Barker's landlady. By essentially providing shelter for her client, she is linked in a metonymic chain to another hospitable woman, one who figures prominently in *A Patch-Work Screen*. In this, the second Galesia novel, a kind Lady rescues the heroine from circumstances that are both dire and yet lightheartedly rendered. The novel begins with the narrative frame of a stagecoach journey in which Galesia and four fellow passengers exchange stories to pass the time as they travel north from London. The journey goes awry when the coach and Galesia, as the last passenger, are overturned into a river. Thankfully unhurt, she finds much-needed though scanty assistance in a nearby village, only to get lost while making her way to the stagecoach's inn the next day. Finding herself in "a fine Park, amongst Trees, Firs, Thickets, Rabbet-burrows," and at a loss for what to do, she listens to the birds, which seem to speak to her and, hearing the sounds of a hunt underway, muses in gratitude for its benefits. The Lady of the estate, meanwhile, who is participating in the hunt, "resolv[ed] to walk home over the Park, it being a fine smooth Walk betwixt two Rows of Lime trees, planted and grown in exact Form, agreeable to the Eye, pleasing to the Smell, and making a most delightful Shade."[25] Landscape appreciation implicitly aligns Galesia with the Lady of the estate, even before she extends the invitation that establishes her exemplary hospitality. Echoing the walks, trees, and shades that punctuate the first Galesia novel and its dedication, this arboreal prelude to the second novel's successive "Leaves" links the historical and fictional women in the congenial realm of the rural retreat. Behaving in ways that signal their conformity to a social order inhering in landed property, Galesia and the Lady admire the park, respect the hunt, and move through their days accordingly.

The rural delights that initiate Galesia's fortuitous rescue also foretell the commodious accommodation that one would expect from a Lady who so wisely stewards her property. The subsequent description of the Lady's home and conduct reinforces her status as a model hostess and estate steward:

> The Lady most courteously and charitably took [Galesia] along with her to her House, which was a Noble Structure, situate in the midst of that Park. Here she entertain'd her very kindly; assuring her of all Assistance to convey her to the Place to which she was design'd, when she had rested and recover'd her Fatigue. In the mean Time, she diverted her, by shewing *Galesia* her Gardens, House, and glorious Appartments, adorn'd with rich Furniture of all Sorts; some were the Work of hers and her Husband's Ancestors, who delighted to imploy poor Gentlewomen, thereby to keep them from Distress, and evil Company, 'till Time and Friends could dispose Things for their better Settlement.[26]

As a recipient of the Lady's charity, Galesia effectively joins the ranks of the "poor Gentlewomen" who participate in the making of that "rich Furniture." The eponymous *Patch-work* refers, of course, to the Leaves that Galesia contributes to the unfinished Screen among the Lady's sumptuous handiworks, "most curiously composed of rich Silks, and Silver and Gold Brocades." Galesia joins the estate's micro-economy by agreeing to help complete the Lady's screen, settling upon "Pieces of *Romances, Poems, Love-Letters,* and the like" when her trunk spills these out instead of the "Wearing Cloaths" she had intended to offer.[27] Her writing thus becomes part of the accoutrements of a country house, and situated as these are within an elegantly designed landscape park, they jointly comprise a privileged domain not unlike the one that Barker honors in her dedication—Burghley House. Echoing the dedication's "stately Palaces; amongst whom none has been a greater Ornament to this noble Family than your Ladyship," Barker links the Lady's luxurious estate to her virtue in ways that reiterate the author's idealization of female nobility and stewardship. A novel's dedication, it would seem, makes it fathomable for a Lady to adorn her home as an ornament and effectively become a synecdoche for her estate in ways that Finch did not achieve within the confines of country house poetry.

Barker's dedications differ from Finch's female tribute by linking women to the land in ways that do not subordinate them to men, as Finch's "To the Honourable the Lady Worsley" ultimately does. I would not, however, go so far as to attribute Barker's seemingly progressive orientation to the equally progressive novel form. Her retrograde political commitments, harking back to a time of putatively greater social stability, make such an interpretation untenable, especially in light of the Jacobite inflections of her work. Especially germane here is King's observation that Barker was "unable to reject received views of the 'natural,' divinely sanctioned subordination of women."[28] But perhaps the inadvertently feminist implications of Barker's tribute to her patron and landlady make it all the more compelling as an instance of female tribute. Barker recognizes the link between estate stewardship and female authority, and implicitly acknowledges that woman's status in society depends upon her relationship to landed property. Finch's poem, meanwhile, does not categorically negate the capacity for country house poetry to honor female stewardship, as the example of Lanyer's "Cooke-ham" amply demonstrates. Rather, "To the Honourable the Lady Worsley" may be said to historicize how the male prerogative became entrenched—partly through the agency of this poetic genre—and thus to document the discursive production of gender inequality. Together, Finch and Barker illuminate both the limiting and enabling aspects of literary convention, and thus both the confines and the potential of women's tributes to women.

Notes

1. Barbara McGovern, *Anne Finch and Her Poetry* (Athens: University of Georgia Press, 1992), 112–17.

2. Anne Finch, "To the Honorable the Lady Worsley at Long-leate," in *The Poems of Anne Countess of Winchilsea,* ed. Myra Reynolds (Chicago: University of Chicago Press, 1903), 52–55, l. 1. Subsequent citations will be to this edition and will give line numbers in the text.

3. *The Cambridge Edition of the Works of Anne Finch, Countess of Winchilsea, Volume 1,* ed. Jennifer Keith and Claudia Thomas Kairoff (New York: Cambridge University Press, forthcoming).

4. For details about Godmersham, see McGovern, *Anne Finch and Her Poetry,* 61.

5. Ben Jonson, "To Penshurst," in *The Poems of Ben Jonson,* ed. George Burke Johnston (Cambridge, MA: Harvard University Press, 1985), 76–81; and Aemilia Lanyer, "The Description of Cooke-ham," in *Salve Deus Rex Judaeorum* (London: Printed by Valentine Simmes for Richard Bonian, 1611), 81–86, 81.

6. Jennifer Keith elaborates on this process of female identification in the work of Behn, Finch, and Mary Leapor (among others). See *Poetry and the Feminine, from Behn to Cowper* (Newark: University of Delaware Press, 2005), especially 20–21.

7. McGovern, *Anne Finch and Her Poetry,* 112.

8. Anne Finch, "The Introduction," in *The Poems of Anne Countess of Winchilsea,* 4–6, lines 51–52.

9. Jane Barker, *The Galesia Trilogy and Selected Manuscript Poems of Jane Barker,* ed. Carol Shiner Wilson (New York: Oxford University Press, 1997), 3. Wilson uses the 1719 edition of *The Entertaining Novels of Mrs. Jane Barker.*

10. Eleanor Wikborg, "The Expression of the Forbidden in Romance Form: Genre as Possibility in Jane Barker's *Exilius,*" Genre 22 (Spring 1989): 3–19.

11. Barker, *The Galesia Trilogy,* 3.

12. Carol Shiner Wilson, "Introduction," *The Galesia Trilogy,* xxx.

13. Barker, *The Galesia Trilogy,* 13.

14. Lady Victoria Leatham, *Life at Burghley: Restoring One of England's Great Houses* (Boston: Little, Brown, 1992), 90. Leatham is the daughter of the sixth Marquess of Exeter.

15. See the Cecil family tree in Lady Victoria Leatham, *Burghley House* (Derby, UK: English Life Publications, 2000), 17.

16. For further evidence of this tendency, see Reverend Mark Noble, *A Biographical History of England Vol. 1* (London: Richardson, et. al., 1806), 323.

17. Barker thus explains the motive for her dedication: "I was encourag'd by casting an eye on that great Wit, worthy of his Time, Sir PHILIP SIDNEY, whose Steps with awful

Distance, I now take Leave to trace; and beg this may find the same acceptance thro' your Goodness, as his found thro' its own Merit; and then I am sure my *Roman* Heroes will be as safe in the Protection of the Countess of *Exeter*, as his *Arcadians* were in that of the Countess of *Pembroke*." *The Galesia Trilogy*, 2–3.

18. Kathryn R. King, *Jane Barker: Exile* (New York: Oxford University Press, 2000), 182–83.

19. *Love Intrigues* (London: Printed for E. Currl, 1713), sig. A. For the full text of the first dedication, see *Popular Fiction by Women 1660–1730*, eds. Paula R. Backscheider and John J. Richetti (New York: Oxford University Press, 1996), 82.

20. Kathryn R. King, *Jane Barker: Exile*, 185.

21. Ample scholarship exists on this dimension of Barker's oeuvre; see, for example, Toni Bowers, "Jacobite Difference and the Poetry of Jane Barker," *English Literary History* 64 (1997): 857–69; Leigh A. Eicke, "Jane Barker's Jacobite Writings," *Women's Writing and the Circulation of Ideas: Manuscript Publication in England, 1550–1800*, eds. George L. Justice and Nathan Tinker (New York: Cambridge University Press, 2002), 137–57; and Kathryn R. King, *Jane Barker: Exile*, especially chapter four.

22. Barker, *The Galesia Trilogy*, 3.

23. Ibid., 35.

24. Constance Lacroix notes the shift in dedicatees, from the Countess in *The Amours* to "THE READER" in its sequel, *A Patch-Work Screen for the Ladies*. She attributes the shift to the latter text's depiction of the ascendance of tradespeople, who "surpass the rural gentry and aristocracy. [. . .] The aristocratic dedicatee of *Love Intrigues*—the countess of Exeter—is accordingly replaced in the allegorical forewords of the more democratic miscellanies by anonymous 'readers,' a 'Throng of People of all ages, Sexes, and Conditions . . . rejoicing at a wonderful Piece of Patch-work they had in Hand.'" Space constraints prevent me from attending to the dedications to the second and third Galesia novels (the latter being *The Lining of the Patch Work Screen* [1726]). Yet Lacroix affirms Barker's royalist orientation, and compellingly tracks how a coterie writer such as Barker was obliged to accommodate commercial print culture. See Lacroix, "Wicked Traders, Deserving Peddlers, and Virtuous Smugglers: The Counter-Economy of Jane Barker's Jacobite Novel," *Eighteenth-Century Fiction* 23 (2010–2011): 269–94.

25. Barker, *The Galesia Trilogy*, 72, 73.

26. Ibid., 74.

27. Ibid.

28. King, *Jane Barker: Exile*, 55.

Martha Fowke's Tributes to Mary, Lady Chudleigh, 1711 and 1726

CHRISTINE GERRARD

When the distinguished poet Mary, Lady Chudleigh, died after a long illness on December 15, 1710, her death seems to have passed almost unnoticed by both the general public and by other writers. Such absence of tribute seems ironic given Chudleigh's own reputation not just as the author of the well-known *The Ladies Defence* and "To the Ladies," but also as a moving elegist who paid eloquent public tribute to the lives of other women. In her *Poems on Several Occasions* (1703), Chudleigh published three distinctive elegies under her own name, "On the Death of his Highness the Duke of Glocester," "On the Death of my Honoured Mother Mrs Lee: A Dialogue between Lucinda and Marissa," and "On the Death of my dear Daughter Eliza Maria Chudleigh: A Dialogue Between Lucinda and Marissa."[1] Anne K. Mellor has described Chudleigh as a superlative elegist, who in "three extraordinarily powerful and perceptive elegies . . . defines the conventions of the elegy as intuitive grief-work."[2] In her tribute to the Duke of Gloucester, who died aged eleven in 1700, Chudleigh unashamedly showed maternal grief as a far more powerful and obsessive emotion than paternal grieving, attributing to Princess Anne an overwhelming sensation of drowning in despair at the loss of her last surviving son. Chudleigh herself lost several children in early infancy, including her son Richard. But the double blow of her daughter Eliza's death aged around eight or nine, following the death of her own mother Mary Sydenham Lee the previous year, inspired her two deeply personal elegies, "On the Death of my Honoured Mother Mrs Lee" and "On the Death of my dear Daughter Eliza Maria Chudleigh." Like her elegy on the Duke of Gloucester, Chudleigh's elegy to Eliza dwells painfully on the tension between hope and despair, the sense of helplessness as the mother watches her own child die. These two elegiac dialogues dramatize Chudleigh's grieving process, and her struggle to reconcile her deep sense of loss with a state of stoic acceptance and Christian consolation.

Yet who was left to write an elegy on Mary, Lady Chudleigh? No one, it seems, rushed into print. "On the Death of Lady Mary Chudleigh: An Ode," by Chudleigh's friend and protégé Elizabeth Thomas, may have been written soon after her death, but it did not appear in print until Thomas's *Miscellany Poems* of 1722.[3] The only obvious immediate tributes to Chudleigh were a new map of Europe published by local Devon scholar and cartographer John Reynolds, dedicated to the "Illustris Maria Chudleigh" as the "*Sappho Anglicanus,*" praising her "*Ingenis, & Eruditione clara*" (intelligence and famous learning),[4] and—the subject of this essay—a poem by an unknown author, one "Mrs Fowke," entitled "An Epitaph on the late Excellent and Ingenious Lady, the Lady Chudley, of Aston in Devonshire."

Fowke's epitaph on Chudleigh is interesting for a number of reasons. It was one of the very first poems to have been published by the hitherto unknown Martha Fowke, or "Clio," as she later became known, and it was published almost nine years before anything else of hers appeared under her own name in print. It was published in a slightly unlikely volume—the April 1711 edition of *Delights for the Ingenious*, a periodical published by Coventry mathematician and bookseller John Tipper. The popularity of Tipper's *Ladies Diary*, which included mathematical puzzles and riddles, inspired him to try a monthly version, *Delights for the Ingenious,* to which he invited his readers to submit both puzzles and original verse, promising to add the authors' names if they so desired. Women figured strongly as contributors of both the puzzles and the poems he published. Martha Fowke, a young and unknown writer at this time, unmarried, living in London with various friends and relatives following the deaths of both her parents, presumably sent in the poems and agreed to her name being used. In the April 1711 issue, Tipper published three poems by "Mrs Fowke," "On a Silk-Paper at a Fair Lady's Bosom" and "The Billet-Deaux Answer"—a pair of witty, light-hearted amorous pieces—and the very different "An Epitaph on the late Excellent and Ingenious Lady, the Lady Chudley."[5] At the age of twenty-one, Fowke would have had few, if any, connections in the London publishing world to promote or patronise her writing. By submitting the Chudleigh epitaph, in addition to the two playful pieces (the periodical's usual fare), Fowke may have hoped to show herself not only as a witty and urbane poet, but also as a serious and ambitious one, sufficiently skilled to write within the elegiac mode so popular in the period, especially among women poets.[6]

Fowke clearly admired and read Chudleigh's poetry, and may also have been personally moved by her death. The two women poets were distantly related and may have known each other in London literary circles. Even more intriguing is the fact that Fowke completely rewrote her early Chudleigh poem some fifteen years later, for republication in Richard Savage's *Miscellaneous Poems and Translations* (1726). The later version, "On Lady Chudleigh," was almost an entirely new elegiac poem—shorter, and in a different style—and one of the last poems she published before she disappeared from the London literary scene following a spate of attacks on her reputation by her rival within Aaron Hill's circle, novelist Eliza Haywood. Fowke's two tributes to the memory of Mary, Lady Chudleigh, separated by some fifteen years, act as bookends to her poetic career. They show how Chudleigh's reputation helped sanction and validate Martha Fowke, first, in 1711, as a young and unknown poet venturing onto the literary scene, and later, in 1726, as a way of reminding readers that she could also be a serious-minded poet of piety and probity, as well as the playful, flirtatious, passionate, and provocative "Clio" of many of her post-1720 poems, when her name had unfortunately become associated less with fame than with infamy.

In December 1710, Mary, Lady Chudleigh, was buried without inscription or monument in the family vaults of the Church of St. John the Baptist, Higher Ashton, Devonshire. The plainness of her burial may have reflected Chudleigh's personal wishes. Although married to an Anglican, Chudleigh was raised in a devout Puritan family, the daughter of Richard Lee and Mary Sydenham Lee, and considered the paraphernalia of funereal pomp as a display of worldly vanity.[7] Chudleigh's own first work in the elegiac mode testifies to this love of simplicity—a short epitaph inscribed on a headstone to her infant son Richard Chudleigh: "I will sing of the Mercies of the Lord" (1688). Yet Fowke may have wished to redress the absence of a physical monument to Chudleigh with her own poetic tribute. She thus deliberately entitled her poem an "Epitaph"—a poem written from the site of the grave itself—rather than an elegy, a form more fitting for a female poet. Few women poets wrote formal epitaphs. Fowke rather boldly drew on a masculine tradition of epitaph writing, when one (male) poet writes an epitaph on another recently deceased (male) poet, lamenting the neglect of that poet after his death. Pope's complaint that Dryden lies buried beneath a "rude and nameless stone" seems to lie behind Fowke's own lament on Chudleigh's lack of a physical memorial.[8]

Fowke opens her epitaph by contrasting Chudeigh's fame as a writer with the obscurity of her burial. Though "famous" during her life, now in death, she is "undistinguish'd" and "sleeps among the vulgar throng" (1–4). Fowke's meditations on the universality of death draw on a seventeenth-century tradition of graveyard poetry that was to become increasingly popular, exemplified by Thomas Parnell's "A Night-Piece on Death" (1722). However,

Fowke's emphasis on the grotesque, almost baroque aspects of corporeal disintegration have a darkly Marvellian cadence that links it to seventeenth-century poetic practice: "Tho' Sawcy Worms will feed upon this Scull, / As well as on the Stupid, and the Dull" (5–6). Fowke's dismissive collocation of "stupid" and "dull" has a Rochesterian ring to it, as does her praise of Chudleigh as a woman "who ne'er wrote, nor spoke a foolish Thought" (35)—an unconscious echo perhaps of the Earl of Rochester's lampoon on Charles II, "who never said a foolish thing, / Nor ever did a wise one." The epitaph's frequent references to Chudleigh's "wit" also anchor the poem in a seventeenth-century context that pays tribute to Chudleigh's lively intellectual as well as moral qualities. "If thou a Lover art of Sacred Wit" (9); "Yet here the God of Wit did once resort" (7); "A sprightly Wit, a Judgement sound and strong" (31). The poem contains a run of triplet rhymes, a distinctively Restoration-era rhyme pattern. The epitaph is designed to show Chudleigh's strengths as a writer as well as a wife and mother: "The Glory, and the Envy of her Kind, / Not to be match'd by those she's left behind, / Tho' all their strongest Forces were combin'd" (11–13). The poem also draws strongly on Chudleigh's own neoplatonic writings, which repeatedly emphasize the disparity between the corporeal "Lump of Dirt," and the noble soul that wishes to escape. In her final days, Fowke observes, when Chudleigh was racked with rheumatism, "Her Soul and Body seem'd unfitly join'd, / As one grew brighter, t'other still declin'd" (19–20).

In writing this tribute, Fowke was clearly drawing on her knowledge of Chudleigh's own poetic works as well as other late seventeenth-century poems. Her description of Chudleigh's body as a "Case" of "brittle Clay" from which her distinguished soul escapes into the light (15–16) echoes Chudleigh's poem "Solitude," which celebrates the moment when "the confining Clay / Falls off, and nothing's left behind / Of drossy Earth."[9] Fowke clearly read and admired Chudleigh's work, but she may also have known Chudleigh personally. They were distantly related, through the Sydenham family—Chudleigh's mother, Mary Jeffries Sydenham, was a cousin of the Fowkes.[10] Chudleigh spent her later winters in London escaping from the Devonshire damp that exacerbated her severe and crippling rheumatism. Fowke, who moved to London with her family at the turn of the eighteenth century, and was already writing poetry in her very early teens, might have been on the fringes of Chudleigh's literary circle.[11] The *Epitaph* praises Chudleigh as a generous poetic mentor and a maternal figure. "Yet she would oft her brighter Beams confine, / And silent sit, to let some other shine" (36–37). Fowke lost her own mother Mary Chandler in 1704, aged sixteen. She then lost her beloved father Thomas Fowke four years later. Her epitaph on Chudleigh echoes, in many of its lines, Chudleigh's own epitaph on the death of her mother. Just as Chudleigh praised Mary Sydenham Lee as "The best of Wives, of Mothers, and of Friends,"[12] so Fowke praises Chudleigh as "A tender Mother, and a faithful Friend" (29). Just as Chudleigh praises her mother's angelic nature: "All you cou'd wish she was; as Angels kind, / As Nature lib'ral, of a God-like Mind;"[13] so Fowke praises Chudleigh as "An Angel's Mind cast in a Humane Mould" (43).

Whether she knew her personally or not, Chudleigh was evidently a powerful formative influence on the young Martha Fowke. Fowke admired Chudleigh as a successfully published female poet whose *The Ladies Defence* (1701), *Poems on Several Occasions* (1703), and *Essays Upon Several Subjects in Prose and Verse* (1710) had secured her a lasting reputation within the final decade of her lifetime. Chudleigh's interest in neoplatonic thought, particularly Lucretian atomism, inspired by her friendship with the Cambridge platonist Richard Norris, resonates in Fowke's later verse.[14] Although many poets at the turn of the century were influenced by neoplatonic thought, Fowke was, by the 1720s, probably the only woman poet who still drew repeatedly on the vocabulary of atomism: "No solid lead is in my atoms mix'd"; "From Heaven itself my Passion came, / In ev'ry Atom of my frame"; "There is no atom in this frame / That does not talk to thee."[15]

Yet Martha Fowke became a very different kind of poet from Mary, Lady Chudleigh. In 1716, she first adopted the pseudonym or nom-de-plume "Clio" when she published three poems in William Tunstall's *Ballads and Some Other Occasional Poems: by W—— T—— in the Marshalsea*, addressed to William Tunstall and Charles Logan, who had been brought down from Preston to London prisons after their involvement in the Jacobite rebellion of 1715.[16] "Clio" is a confident, even jaunty poet, who aligns herself with Waller and the cavalier tradition, and complains playfully to Tunstall, "How many *Lovers* have I lost / With thoughts of my distress." In 1720, Fowke confirmed her identity as "Clio" in the poems she had published in Antony Hammond's *A New Miscellany of Original Poems, Translations and Imitations*, not least in the poem that became her signature piece, "Clio's Picture." "Clio's Picture. To Antony Hammond Esq; By Mrs Fowke," is a poetic self-portrait of an unconventional, passionate, frank, amatory female poet, one comfortable with physicality and sensuality:

> My Hair dark brown wants not Bucelia's Aid,
> Flows in the Wind, nor of the Comb afraid.

> Beneath my Waist in natural Rings descends,
> Or pliant to the artful Finger bends,
> When it betides that Dress and I are Friends.[17]

Fowke's most successful publication, *The Epistles of Clio and Strephon*, also published in 1720 and co-authored with William Bond, blends neo-platonic idealism with the love letter form in a series of letters exchanged between correspondents who had never met. Yet, as Phyllis Guskin notes, this tradition of romantic and platonic love led Fowke into a more sexually charged mode of writing, one that drew more on the libertine tradition of "frank physicality and sexual freedom."[18] Fowke's poem "The Innocent Inconstant," which answers Richard Savage's charge of female inconsistency with a radical defence of "inconstancy," seems to draw less on the idea of a platonic equality of souls than upon the kind of "inconstancy" that both Donne and especially Rochester described.

> I search—but rarely meet an equal Taste,
> Then I grow weary, and I change in haste;
> Where I discern, that heavy Earth prevails,
> I leave the Lumber, and I shift the sails.[19]

Fowke's emphasis on female seductiveness and attraction may have been linked at one level with the popularity of female amatory fiction (Fowke herself makes an unflattering appearance in several of Haywood's romans-a-clef).[20] But her concern with her own image in "pictures" and "portraits" also seems shaped by an agenda set by male poets such as Matthew Prior, Parnell, Pope, and Swift in which female appearance, beauty, and specular images of women prevail.[21] Fowke's defence of her own "inconstancy" and her almost brutal eagerness to jettison men whose tastes fail to meet her own might represent a riposte to female commodification, a feminist stance in its own right. However, such frankness explains, in part, why Fowke is today a relatively unknown poet, despite publishing at least 160 poems, whereas Mary, Lady Chudleigh, has received significant critical attention and a scholarly edition.

Unlike the work of other more familiar women poets—Chudleigh, Anne Finch, Mary Barber, Mary Jones, Mary Leapor—Fowke's poems were never collected in one volume, either during her own lifetime or afterward. She was not devoid of literary connections, but (perhaps for reasons similar to those that hindered Laetitia Pilkington) she could never have succeeded in launching a subscription publication because her reputation was too scandalous.[22] Unlike Leapor or Jones, she had no close female friends who would support her or take charge of publishing her poems for posterity. Fowke could not draw on a reputation for respectability, piety, female friendship, or maternal virtue—all the familiar "modesty topoi" for a woman "stepping out of her province" and venturing into print. Thus it is that Fowke's very extensive poetic output, in common with that of many largely unknown female poets, is dispersed across poetic miscellanies or embedded within longer mixed-genre prose/poetry works and "patchwork" novels.[23] A whole tranche of Fowke's verse appears to have traveled to Barbados with one of her lovers, Nicholas Hope, to be published in the *Barbados Gazette* and subsequently in the 1741 miscellaneous collection *Caribbeana*.[24] No subscription could be raised for a volume of poems by a lady "once too well known."[25] As one of the central figures of Hill's circle, "Clio" was praised and adored by male authors such as Hill himself, John Dyer, David Mallet, and James Thomson. Eliza Haywood also depicted her memorably as a sexually predatory female bent on seducing younger men, "as many as her now almost antiquated Charms have powers to seduce" (Fowke was thirty-six at the time).[26] Fowke's reputation in her own time and in the decades that followed was undoubtedly sunk by scandal and diluted by miscellany publication. When it was finally published in 1753, *Clio: Or, a Secret History of the Life and Amours of the Late celebrated Mrs S—N—M,* the long love letter in manuscript that Fowke wrote in 1723 to her mentor and possible lover Aaron Hill when she was heavily pregnant, but married to a man she hated, was marketed as a scandal memoir, rather than a work of passion and poetry.

With this image in mind, it is now helpful to return to Fowke's second, shorter version of the Chudleigh epitaph, one of nine poems by "Clio" that appeared in Savage's 1726 *Miscellaneous Poems and Translations,* the last large group of her poems printed during her lifetime. Savage's *Miscellany* contains poems by members of the Hill circle, such as Savage himself, David Mallet, John Dyer, Edward Young, Benjamin Victor, Eliza Haywood, and Margaret Hill—poems both by and about the male and female members in the group. The new, completely reworked "On Lady Chudleigh by Clio" is now no longer an "Epitaph," and it is attributed not to "Mrs Fowke," but to "Clio." There are several reasons why Fowke may have rewritten this poem completely and included it in the *Miscellany.* New editions of Chudleigh's work in 1713 and especially 1722 testify to the enduring popularity of Chudleigh as a poet. Furthermore, in 1722, Chudleigh's protégé Elizabeth Thomas finally published her own *Miscellany Poems,* which contained three poems on Lady Chudleigh, "To the Lady Chudleigh: The Anonymous Author of the Ladies' Defence;" "To the Lady Chudleigh: On her printing her Excellent

Poems," and "On the Death of the Lady Chudleigh: An Ode."[27] Given that the contents of Savage's *Miscellany* were almost completely assembled and ready to print by the end of 1724,[28] it is tempting to see the 1722 publication of Thomas's tributes to Chudleigh as the immediate spur to Fowke's competitive reworking of her earlier poem.

Both of Fowke's poems on Chudleigh were more accomplished than Thomas's "Ode on the Death of the Lady Chudleigh." Thomas imagines a ghostly visitation from a seraphic, larger-than-life "Marissa." The ambitious ode form did not come naturally to Thomas, whose poem is full of awkward bathetic twists: "I've come, she cried, to bid a *long Adieu!* / And had a Mind to let you know, / I must a *wond'rous Journey* go." Thomas's ode is interesting less for its level of poetic skill than for what it tells us about another female poet's nostalgia for the loss of a matrilineal heritage of female poetic mentors—first "pious *Sulpitia*" (Katherine Philips, or possibly Anne, Lady De La Warr), then "charming Musidora snatched by death" (her friend Diana Bridgeman), then "good *Marissa*": "*Marissa* from her Marble *Urn*, / Can ne'er to *Life* return."

Fowke's second Chudleigh poem, in contrast to Thomas's "Ode," is a masterpiece of controlled feeling and minimalism. Fowke might have rewritten the poem because she no longer had access to a copy of her previous version and was unable to recall the original text. Yet it seems more likely that Fowke made a conscious decision to revisit and reframe her praise of Chudleigh. Only twenty-four-lines long, as opposed to the original's forty-seven lines, the second Chudleigh poem functions as a powerful reminder of an earlier strong woman poet, appropriate for a miscellany volume designed not only to promote Savage's cause, but also to showcase female literary talent. Savage ostentatiously dedicates *Miscellaneous Poems and Translations* to another literary "Lady Mary"—Lady Mary Wortley Montagu, patron, poet and enlightenment thinker: "Our Country has been honour'd by the Glory of your *Wit*, as Elevated and Immortal as *Your Soul*. It no longer remains a Doubt, whether your Sex have Strength of Mind, in proportion to their Sweetness."[29] Included in the volume is Aaron Hill's poem on Lady Mary's introduction of a smallpox vaccine and Savage's poem on the talented actress Anne Oldfield, as well as a poem congratulating Eliza Haywood on her novel *The Rash Resolve*. The volume contains not only nine original poems by "Clio," but also numerous poems addressed to her by the male poets in the Hill group, as well as a sequence of poems by other pseudonymous women poets, often addressed to each other, including poems by "Evandra," "Aurelia," and "Miranda." As with Chudleigh's 1703 *Poems on Several Occasions,* a number of the women writers included in Savage's *Miscellaneous Poems* of 1726 have yet to be identified under their classical pseudonyms, though we know that Hill's wife Margaret was "Miranda."

One of the largest differences between the female presence in this later coterie volume and Chudleigh's 1703 *Poems* is the almost complete absence of the sense of female solidarity and literary community that characterises Chudleigh's intimate poems to her female writing friends. Whereas Chudleigh's "The Inquiry: A Dialogue between Cleanthe and Marissa" shows women agreeing with each other to ridicule male affectation, the dynamics of Savage's *Miscellaneous Poems* are very different. There is only one poem that suggests that the Hill circle inspired in its female writing members a sense of mutual support, "To EVANDRA, on seeing some poems of her writing."[30] Many of the other poems hint at secret jealousies and suspicions between female members, others at rivalry for the favors of their male mentor Aaron Hill. "Clio" plays a number of different roles in this volume. She is the bewitching and erotically intriguing poetess of "To Lady E—H—," showing us "how in verse to hunt a lover," the Horatian recluse of "Invitation to a Country Cottage," at home in her cottage in Fulham with her dogs and books. She is the easily bored but passionate libertine of "Innocent Unconstant." She is the object of male adoration in poems by John Dyer and Benjamin Victor. She is admired, coveted, modest, boastful, in rivalry with her female poets over other men, the target of their sexual jealousy. But she is not primarily a lofty, intellectual, or devotional poet.

The second Chudleigh poem thus supplies a very different image of Fowke: not as the subject of the poetic gaze, of male painters' and poets' portraits (a common theme in the volume as a whole), but as a high-minded and platonic poet linked in memory to an earlier admired female mentor. "To Lady Chudleigh" lacks the biographical immediacy of the earlier "Epitaph ... on the Lady Chudley." Instead, Fowke reimagines Chudleigh as an exemplary, romantic, iconic, almost austere and solitary figure, in the vein of Pope's Eloisa: "Methinks I see, yet weeping o'er her Cell." Yet she is also feminised as this "soft Fav'rite, of the gentler Kind," and contrasted with masculine strength, here reattributed to the male "SONS of Apollo" who display "great numbers and their force is strong" (4). Fowke replaces her earlier Restoration emphasis on female "wit" with a celebration of female "Genius." Chudleigh is now a naturally inspired genius who transcends male poetic rules:

> Man look'd with Envy, and laid Learning by,
> And let his useless Books neglected lie:
> Her inborn Genius ask'd no foreign Aid,
> A Muse may be *improv'd*, but never *made*. (6–10)

This proto-romantic prioritization of female "inborn Genius" over masculine "useless Books" and "Learning" shapes many of Fowke's poems. In a lively poem first published in the *Barbados Gazette*, "On being charg'd with Writing incorrectly," Fowke celebrates her "freeborn Thoughts" and disparages male educational rules that attempt to stifle female poetic creativity:

> No, let my Genius have its Way,
> My Genius I will still obey;
> Nor with their stupid Rules, control
> The sacred pulse that beats within my soul.[31]

Most striking of all in this later version of the Chudleigh tribute is Fowke's awareness that Chudleigh the feminist poet managed to transcend scandal, "Scandal, that common shade of Womankind / Dimmed not the Candor of her glitt'ring Mind" (15–16). The word "Scandal"—the wrong kind of fame—reverberates throughout the coterie poems in Savage's *Miscellaneous Poems*, in poems both by and addressed to Fowke: "Scandal wou'd listen with relenting Heart"; "Here, out of hated Scandal's noisy Sound."[32] Fowke retains only one similar couplet from the earlier Chudleigh poem, the couplet that praises Chudleigh's generosity to other women in her literary circle. Lines 35–36 in the 1711 version read, "Yet she would oft her brighter Beams confine, / And silent sit, to let some other shine." These become, in 1726, "She check'd the Reins of Wit, and wou'd confine / Her brighter Thoughts, to let Another's Shine" (13–14). By 1726, generosity toward and from other women poets would have had a much stronger resonance for Martha Fowke, who already in her unpublished *Clio* of 1723 voiced her fear of the power that "scandal" might have to destroy her, particularly when spread by the writings of the "Scorpion *Haywood*" "who darts the Poison of her Pen" and "who delights in my Misfortunes, and pursues me in all that is dear and sacred to me, my Friends, my Reputation, my Parents."[33]

The Chudleigh elegy is very different from the other female-authored poems in Savage's *Miscellany*. It transcends the poetic exchanges between Fowke and other writing women within Hill's circle—poems that were part of a tangled contemporary web of personal and sexual relationships and of literary rivalries and jealousies. It is a tribute poem shaped by admiration, nostalgia, and longing for past female literary greatness. It also suggests that by the mid-1720s, it was far less easy than it had been in 1711 to praise other women for their strength, wit, and masculine force. The two different versions of the Chudleigh epitaph reflect Fowke's transition from a young and unknown female poet, part of a turn-of-the-century feminist writing movement, to a celebrated yet scandalized poet of the 1720s whose notoriety damaged her literary reputation in irreversible ways. Chudleigh's blend of Puritan piety and exemplary stoicism, and her ability to mock misogyny from a feminist perspective while retaining a respectable reputation as a wife and mother, may have seemed to Fowke—and perhaps to other poets of her generation—a rare and enviable combination.

> An Epitaph on the late Excellent and Ingenious Lady, the Lady Chudley, of Aston in Devonshire.
> By Mrs. Martha Fowke
> From *Delights for the Ingenious,* April 1711, 129–30
>
> With Pious Reverence these Ashes tread,
> Nor dare to trample on this famous Head:
> For tho it sleeps amongst the vulgar throng,
> And undistinguish'd must decay e're long;
> Tho' Sawcy Worms will feed upon this Scull,
> As well as on the Stupid, and the Dull;
> Yet here the God of Wit did once resort,
> And here the Muses us'd to keep their Court.
> If thou a Lover art of Sacred Wit,
> On bended knees approach this dark Retreat;
> The Glory, and the Envy of her Kind,
> Not to be match'd by those she's left behind,
> Tho' all their strongest Forces were combin'd.
> Oh who that does her charming Verse survey!
> Wou'd think the Case where such a Treasure lay,
> Was form'd, like one of us, of brittle Clay!
> If we poor humble Shrubs of short-liv'd Grass,
> Might on great Nature's Works our Judgments pass,
> Her Soul and Body seem'd unfitly join'd,
> As one grew brighter, t'other still declin'd,
> And like a dying Taper faintly shin'd.
> At last, alas! It so transparent grew,
> That her fine Soul was seen to sparkle through;
> For that cou'd all the Storms of Life engage,
> The Frowns of Fate, and Death's approaching Rage.
> For while below, Mortality she wore,
> None suffer'd better, and none suffer'd more.
> She'd ev'ry Grace to Charm, and Recommend,
> A tender Mother, and a faithful Friend,

Free from those Faults that on her Sex attend.
A sprightly Wit, a Judgment sound and strong,
Fit for the Sallies of Poetick Song,
A charming Pen, and an unerring Tongue.
Which with such Goodness, and such Sense was fraught,
That she ne'er wrote, nor spoke a foolish Thought.
Yet she would oft her brighter Beams confine,
And silent sit, to let some other shine.
True to her Friends, nay Generous to those
Whom Envy and Report had made her Foes.
No Satyr in her Heav'nly Lines was found,
But all with Charity and Goodness Crown'd.
Such, such, she was, and more than can be told,
An Angel's Mind cast in a Humane Mould.
But whilst her own Immortal Works remain,
All that our Tongues, and Pens can say, is vain;
There, there, a lasting Monument You'll have,
Which fears not Death, nor the devouring Grave.

On Lady Chudleigh
By Clio
From *Miscellaneous Poems and Translations by Several Hands* (1726), 213–14

Methinks I see, yet weeping o'er her Cell,
The Vertues, in her Breast once known to dwell.
Apollo mourns not for a *Son,* so long,
Great are their Numbers, and their Force is strong:
But this soft Fav'rite, of the gentler Kind,
Scarce left Her Likeness, in Her Sex, behind.
Man look'd with Envy, and laid Learning by,
And let his useless Books neglected lie:
Her inborn Genius ask'd no foreign Aid,
A Muse may be *improv'd,* but never *made.*
Goodness still soften'd her superior Sense,
She knew not Affectation or Offence
She check'd the Reins of Wit, and wou'd confine
Her brighter Thoughts, to let Another's shine.
Scandal, that common Shade of Womankind,
Dimm'd not the Candor of her glitt'ring Mind.
Not on her Friends alone she smil'd, but Those,
Whom Ignorance, or Envy, made her Foes.

Her Soul and Body seem'd unfitly join'd;
The Frame so weak, so nobly strong the Mind!
But, when she languid, and more feeble grew,
The ill-cas'd Diamond seem'd to sparkle through.
As if it struggled for it's native Light,
And scorn'd th'adhering Earth, that clogg'd its Flight.

Notes

1. See *The Poems and Prose of Mary, Lady Chudleigh*, ed. Margaret Ezell (New York: Oxford University Press, 1993), 47–60; 129–35; 135–40. All references to Chudleigh's work are to this edition.

2. Anne K. Mellor, "'Anguish No Cessation Knows': Elegy and the British Woman Poet, 1660–1834," *The Oxford Handbook of the Elegy*, ed. Karen Weisman (Oxford: Oxford University Press, 2010), 445.

3. Elizabeth Thomas, "On the Death of Mary Chudleigh. An Ode," *Miscellany Poems on Several Subjects* (London, 1722).

4. John Reynolds, *Pomponii Melae de situ Orbis* (Exeter, 1711), Plate 4.

5. The "Epitaph" is reprinted above, taken from *Delight for the Ingenious: or, A monthly entertainment for the curiosity of both sexes* (April, 1711), alongside the later version in Savage's *Miscellaneous Poems and Translations* (1726). *Delights for the Ingenious* is mistakenly catalogued in the Bodleian Library, Oxford as "Delights for the Ingenuous."

6. See Ralph Houlbrooke, ed., *Death, Ritual and Bereavement* (London: Routledge, 1989), 12, for the popularity of the elegy. Esther Schor, *Bearing the Dead: The British Culture of Mourning from the Enlightenment to Victoria* (Princeton, NJ: Princeton University Press, 1994), 27, argues that between 1700 and 1730, the majority of printed elegies were written by women.

7. For Chudleigh's Puritan upbringing, see Julie Sampson, ed., *Mary, Lady Chudleigh: Selected Poems* (Exeter, UK: Shearman Books, 2009), 9. See also Barbara Olive, "The Fabric of Restoration Puritanism: Mary Chudleigh's *The Song of the Three Children Paraphras'd*," in Laura Lunger Knoppers, ed., *Puritanism and its Discontents* (Newark: University of Delaware Press, 2003), 124.

8. Alexander Pope, "Epitaph: Intended for Mr Rowe in Westminster Abbey," *Minor Poems*, ed. Norman Ault and John Butt (London: Routledge, 1993), 208.

9. *The Poems and Prose of Mary, Lady Chudleigh*, 126.

10. Martha Fowke's uncle, the Rev. Richard Fowke, married Joyce (Elizabeth) Sydenham. See *Clio: The Autobiography of Martha Fowke Sansom (1689–1736)*, ed. Phyllis J. Guskin (Newark: University of Delaware Press, 1997), 19.

11. Ibid., 66.

12. *The Poems and Prose of Mary, Lady Chudleigh*, 131.

13. Ibid., 132.

14. See Margaret Ezell, Introduction to *The Poems and Prose of Mary, Lady Chudleigh*, xxx. For Fowke's interest in the cult of platonic love, see Earla Wilputte, *Passion and*

Language in Eighteenth-Century Literature: The Aesthetic Sublime in the Work of Eliza Haywood, Aaron Hill and Martha Fowke (New York: Palgrave Macmillan, 2014), 60–61.

15. "The Innocent Unconstant," line 3, in *Eighteenth-Century Poetry: An Annotated Anthology*, eds. David Fairer and Christine Gerrard, 3rd ed. (Oxford: John Wiley, 2015), 236; "On Reading Dr Donne's Poems," line 30, and "To *****," line 9, in *A Letter to My Love: Love Poems by Women First Published in the Barbados Gazette, 1731–1737*, ed. Bill Overton (Newark: University of Delaware Press, 2001), 46–47.

16. See "To Mr Tunstall, and his Friends, in the Marshalsea," in William Tunstall, *Ballads and Some Other Occasional Poems* (London, 1716), 12–14. This was the first occasion on which Fowke adopted this name in print.

17. Antony Hammond, ed., *A New Miscellany of Original Poems, Translations and Imitations* (London, 1720), 257–60.

18. *Clio*, 27.

19. Savage's "Unconstant" and Fowke's response, "The Innocent Inconstant," appear in *Eighteenth-Century Poetry*, 234–35 and 236–37.

20. See Christine Gerrard, *Aaron Hill: The Muses' Projector, 1689–1750* (Oxford: Oxford University Press, 2003), 88–96; Kathryn R. King, "Eliza Haywood, Savage Love, and Biographical Uncertainty," *Review of English Studies* New Series 59, no. 242 (2008): 722–39; and King, "New Contexts for Early Novels by Women: The Case of Eliza Haywood, Aaron Hill, and the Hillarians, 1719–1725," in *A Companion to the Eighteenth-Century Novel and Culture*, eds. Paula R. Backscheider and Catherine Ingrassia, (Malden, MA: Blackwell, 2005), 261–75.

21. See Kathryn R. King, "The Constructions of Femininity," in *A Companion to Eighteenth-Century Poetry*, ed. Christine Gerrard (Chichester: John Wiley and Sons, 2014), 431–43.

22. For Pilkington's failure to launch a subscription edition of her poetry, see A. C. Elias Jr., *The Memoirs of Laetitia Pilkington*, 2 vols. (Athens: University of Georgia Press, 1997), I, xxii-xxv.

23. I am currently working on a complete edition of the poems of Martha Fowke, with Phyllis Guskin and Kathleen Keown. So far we have located over 160 separate items.

24. See *A Letter to My Love*, and Phyllis Guskin, "'Not originally intended for the Press'; Martha Fowke Sansom's Poems in the *Barbados Gazette*," *Eighteenth-Century Studies* 34.1 (2000): 61–91.

25. Karen E Davis, "Martha Fowke: 'A Lady Once Too Well Known,'" *English Language Notes* 23.3 (1986): 32–36.

26. Eliza Haywood, *Memoirs of a Certain Island Adjacent to the Kingdom of Utopia* (London, 1725), 184.

27. Elizabeth Thomas, *Miscellany Poems on Several Subjects* (London, 1722), 288–95.

28. In the *Plain Dealer*, November 30, 1724, Savage claimed that "the *Book* is now off the Press, and will be published as soon as it can be *printed off.*"

29. Savage, *Miscellaneous Poems and Translations*, v.

30. Ibid., 253–54.

31. *A Letter to My Love*, 60.

32. Savage, *Miscellaneous Poems and Translations*, 263, 289.

33. *Clio*, 82.

Eliza Haywood, Fame, and the Art of Self-Homage

KATHRYN R. KING

The view of Eliza Haywood (c. 1693–1756) as mere hack has fallen out of favor (and good riddance), but literary history has yet to reckon with the force of her literary ambitions. Her desire for Fame, however, was sufficiently well known among her contemporaries to be the target of good-humored satire, notably in Bonnell Thornton's *Spring-Garden Journal* (1752). "No Woman can be deaf to applause," writes Priscilla Termagant, the fictive essayist partly modeled on Haywood, "The vast Reputation which I have acquired by my Wit, Vivacity, and happy Turn of Thought, cannot fail to give me the most pleasing Reflections."[1] *Spring-Garden Journal* features three installments of "The New Female Spectator," a mock-solemn parody of the manner and matter of Haywood's widely read periodical the *Female Spectator* (1744–1746).[2] "Fame is an alluring Object," its author pronounces, "it is this inspires the Muse; this is the Idol, to which every Genius burns his Incense; it is this enlarges our Ideas, and fills the Soul with Raptures of Divinity."[3] Haywood usually wrote better than this, but she did write, and often, about Fame. Early on, she decried the "Difficulties a *Woman* has to struggle through in her Approach to *Fame*"—envy and contempt chief among them—and pleaded for the "Encouragement" that might raise her own genius "to a Praise-worthy Height."[4] (Just such envy and contempt was expressed by Richard Savage a few years later when he jeered at her as one who "pants" for "Stage-Renown.")[5] Much later, Haywood sold books and pamphlets out of a shop in the Great Piazza of Covent Garden at the sign of Fame, which was represented as a classically draped woman blowing a trumpet. Encouragement, noble emulation, and literary excellence are recurrent themes in Haywood's long career as writer, and I will show that these themes are enmeshed in widely shared classical understandings of Fame, or "just admiration," as a stimulant to civic virtue and artistic merit. Ambition for just admiration propels authors to strive for praiseworthy heights, to perform brilliantly.

Haywood's hunger for Fame is overshadowed today by her reputation for literary and sexual ill fame. The disrepute has perhaps been exaggerated, but Betty Schellenberg is right to characterize Haywood's position in the London literary community at mid-eighteenth century as dubious.[6] She had been in the 1720s an object of abuse for several of the era's towering satiric writers—Savage, Jonathan Swift, and above all, of course, Alexander Pope, whose unpleasant attack in *The Dunciad* (1728) still reverberates. Pope's swollen-breasted "Eliza," sexually wayward and intellectually vacant, would not be challenged by women writers until Clara Reeve's well-intentioned but problematic rehabilitation in *Progress of Romance* (1785). Indeed, from the late 1730s, Haywood provided a generation of self-consciously virtuous women writers with a ready signifier of a licentious female writing past against which to define themselves. She was, in well-known phrase, the poison to which Bluestocking-styled writers were the antidote.[7] Even today, the whorish hack of Pope's imagination can be a student's first encounter with Haywood, and too often the last. Literary history has made much of the bespattered Haywood but has mostly ignored the counter-current of praise that brings needed depth and complexity to the image of Haywood handed down by hostile contemporaries.

The discussion that follows performs a classic feminist recovery on several levels. Women writers *did* praise Haywood, I will show, and if relatively few specimens of homage have survived, they deserve to be known. They illustrate how, in the case of Haywood, literary history has disproportionately represented men's views, especially when they take the form of slurs, while underplaying almost *anything* positive from women. I attempt a more subtle correction of the historical record, as well, by seeking to recover the neoclassical ideal of Fame as noble emulation that informed women's understanding of themselves as writers and shaped their homages to one another—and, in Haywood's case, to herself. Haywood began her writing life as a coterie poet proudly avowing her desire for renown. She soon found herself obliged to live by the pen, however, and the noble pursuit of Fame was a luxury a marketplace writer could ill afford. By the end of her career, she was publishing anonymously and practicing "the little arts of fame," that is, the career-promoting self-advertisement required of professional writers. The trajectory of her career, then, traces a shift in models of authorship obscured by the oft-applied but seldom helpful phrase, "grubstreet hack." We are reminded that, as Schellenberg neatly puts it, "the writer as respectable professional, rather than as either cultivated amateur or disreputable hack, was a model in the making over the course of the long eighteenth century."[8]

I identify what I take to be an homage to a nostalgically conceived poet-self that surfaces in one of her late-career writings, *Epistles for the Ladies* (1748–50). For this work, Haywood created a poetic surrogate, a talented but self-effacing manuscript poet to whom she gave the name Ardella, a variant on the pen name used by the leading gentlewoman-amateur of the first half of the century, Anne Finch. I conclude with some polemical words on how literary history might benefit from an expanded understanding of the cultural functions of praise in the long eighteenth century.

Fame

First, some words on Fame. To modern ears, *fame* may conjure notions of shallow and even tawdry celebrity, but in the Augustan period the word, although already picking up negative connotations, still pulsated with classically derived meanings clustering around the core idea of just and enduring applause for distinguished achievement. Ovid in Dryden's translation of "The Poet Concludes" equates Fame with a poet's "nobler Part"; it "shall reach the Skies, / And to late Times with blooming Honours rise."[9] The redoubtably learned Elizabeth Carter imagines enduring renown for her poetic precursor Katherine Philips: "Sweet may her Fame to late Remembrance bloom."[10] Carter is sometimes said to exemplify the virtuous poet of the publicity-eschewing school, one of the "so-called 'private' writers," as Norma Clarke wryly puts it, so her open avowal of emulative ambition is worth noting. She signed a 1739 magazine poem on the death of Mrs. Rowe with her full name, declaring that to join it with Rowe's constituted her "best attempt for fame."[11] Ambition for fame rings loud and clear in Aphra Behn's well-known Preface to *The Lucky Chance* (1687): "I prize fame as much as if I had been born a hero."[12] It entwines Martha Fowke's passionate yearning for a life of the mind with a complaint about the limitations imposed by gender: "The *Name* [Woman] does Immortality prevent. / Yet, let me stretch, beyond my Sex, my *Mind*, / And, rising, leave the flutt'ring Train behind."[13] It shapes the exalting if finally bittersweet boast-poem by Ovid's follower, the poet and amateur physician Jane Barker, who, rejoicing that the "*Sturdy Gout*" that had withstood "all Male-Power" is vanquished by her "soft Female Hands," pretends that the praise of learned men is sufficient pretext for self-celebration: "For since the Learn'd exalt and own our Fame, / It is no Arrogance to do the same."[14] All these poets—and many other examples could be adduced—testify to the inspiration that women poets as different as Carter, Behn, Fowke, and Barker found in the idea of Fame.

Haywood's early work abounds in statements of desire for recognition and renown. An address to the reader prefacing her first printed play, *The Fair Captive* (1721), expresses disdain for writers who seek money rather than applause: "But without a Prospect of some Applause, I shou'd never imagine, if the Example of many Authors did not convince me, that any meaner Views cou'd wing the Poet's Flight."[15] She would soon be constrained by the "meaner Views" of the professional writer, and, as Patrick Spedding observes, her "rapid adaptation to full-time authorship" would extinguish "her aristocratic disdain for writing popular works," novels and the like.[16] But she continued to identify herself with the prestige genre of poetry. In the late teens and early 1720s, she was one of a group of poets who orbited around the eminent literary figure Aaron Hill, whom Haywood considered a beloved friend, mentor, and fellow poet of the Longinian sublime.[17] Emulation of Hill represented her "best Plea for Fame." The phrase comes from "To Mr. Walter Bowman," one of a handful of verses from this period to have survived, in which she credits herself with giving Hill his coterie name of Hillarius. This act of naming kindles a "boastful Pride"—not unlike that evinced by Barker in the gout poem cited earlier—which she celebrates in lines of expansive self-appreciation:

> A Pride, so vast, as Empire could not give!
> Far as Creation reaches, shall the Name
> *Eliza* chose, tune the whole Voice of Fame;
> The wafting Air shall bear the Accents round,
> And all the wide Expanse echo the rapt'rous Sound.[18]

This pride is vast indeed—coextensive with "Creation" itself and orchestrating "the whole Voice of Fame"—and bears out Earla Wilputte's perception that the coterie verse "makes a bold statement about her writing and the aesthetic effects of art."[19] Haywood affirms her identity as a poet of the sublime in "The Vision," a tribute to Hill that showcases her own ecstatic expressivity ("My staggering Reason, into Flights I run! / With incoherent Extasies am fir'd, / Such, as of old, the *Bacchanals* inspired!"[20]). Verse exchange with Hill "allows her not only to experience Hill's sublime but to appropriate it to the extent that she becomes a poet herself," according to Wilputte, and poems such as "The Vision" provide a platform on which to perform her own claim to poetic greatness.[21]

The Admiring Twenties

During the remarkable five or six years starting in 1719 when *Love in Excess* took the polite reading world by storm, it is hard to find anything but acclaim for Haywood's writings. Even Jane Brereton, who lumped her in with the "Behns, the Manleys," authors "Politely lewd and wittily profane," was forced to concede the beguiling charm of Haywood's "soft, seducing style."[22] The verse tributes by men reprinted in the Broadview edition of *Love in Excess* have attracted some attention, but tributes by women from the 1720s remain little studied. The first of two I shall consider comes from Elizabeth Boyd, a fascinating but under-examined poet who professed herself "*urg'd on by Nature to defend my Sex.*"[23] In addition to poems, she published a novel with a Haywoodesque title, *The Unhappy Unfortunate* (1732), the commendatory lines to which herald her as a "*new* Elisa" poised to topple our Eliza's ascendancy ("Yeild *Heywood* yeild, yeild all whose tender Strains, / Inspire the Dreams of Maids and lovesick Swains").[24] In 1745, while Haywood was publishing her monthly periodical essay the *Female Spectator*, Boyd conducted a periodical whimsically entitled the *Snail; or, The Lady's Lucubrations*. She may have aspired to be a playwright for she named Susannah Centlivre as the inspiration for her "youngling Muse."[25] The work of greatest interest for students of female commemoration is her first published poem, *Variety* (1727), a jaunty two-canto celebration of movement, of the need to seek variety and change, to "rove" and make one's own female way in the flux of circumstance and occasion. *Variety*, described in one of very few commentaries as a "witty and paradoxical defence of inconstancy," is remarkable as well for its "original, discriminating praise for women's writing," offering appraisals of Behn, Delarivier Manley, and Centlivre, in addition to Haywood.[26]

Boyd admires Haywood, but with reservations. Her mixed tribute of twelve lines begins on an unequivocally positive note—"Sweet, *Haywood*, and immortal are thy Lines: / Smooth as the God, that in thy Novels shines"—and the adulation is sustained in the rhetorical question that follows, which positions Haywood as the leading figure in the present field of women writers: "What modern She hath grasp'd such true Desert / Who does not envy thee thy charming Art?" But a doubtful note enters. Addressing Haywood directly, Boyd urges her to "take this Truth, and take it from a Friend," from, that is to say, a well-disposed sister author (although the possibility that they were actual friends cannot be discounted). She would have Haywood send "a kinder Envoy" to women:

> To your own Sex a kinder Envoy send;
> Let not a Woman's Writings blur her Sex,
> Whiles too, too charming she their Faults dissects;

ELIZA HAYWOOD, FAME, AND THE ART OF SELF-HOMAGE

> O *Haywood!* ever fear the Coxcomb Croud;
> Of Woman's Errors critically proud.[27]

The word "blur" is evocative. To blur is to stain, sully, blot, or blemish the beauty of anything; it is to smear as with ink, asperse, defile. Boyd's reservation about Haywood's propensity to asperse women points to a persistent pattern of ambivalence in the history of Haywood's critical reception by women, a tough, hard-to-digest *something* about her that results in mixed, almost grudging responses to her work and in efforts to recast her in more acceptable guises—Reeve's reformed fallen woman being the best-known example. In addition, Boyd thinks the charm of the fictions are tainted by Haywood's tendency to adopt male points of view (those of the "Coxcomb Croud") that disparage, injure, and generally dishonor womankind. Haywood could indeed be severe in her treatment of female characters, especially those modeled on actual women in personally motivated secret histories and scandal chronicles. Haywood is sometimes described today as a champion of her sex, but Boyd's rendering of a male-identified writer whose work "blurs" the dignity of womankind may partly explain why women later in the century regarded her as anything but their champion.

A second tribute, a warm appreciation of Haywood as a gifted novelist and cherished friend, is found in the dedication to *The Prude* (1724), a novel by an unknown author who signs herself MA. A., a "young Lady." In period usage, that elastic phrase covers a goodly range of authorial possibilities—possibly representing a woman no longer young, a cross-dressing man, or conceivably Haywood herself—but I shall take MA. A. at her word and proceed as if the dedication is what it seems, a friend's homage, at once heartfelt and strategic, to the "extraordinary Merits" of Haywood's writing and character, and one that illustrates Nicolle Jordan's point elsewhere in this volume that the dedication to a novel can lend itself to unusual forms of commemoration.[28] *The Prude* is a tale of amatory intrigue somewhat in the manner of Haywood. The complicated courtship plot contains none of Haywood's signature languors or grassy-bank seductions, but it does deliver an entertaining exposure of the coarse libertinism of the titular prude, Elisinda, who, among other excesses, shares the person of a comely footman with a female friend until they exhaust him into a fatal consumption. There was doubtless an element of commercial savvy in MA. A.'s choice of "the Incomparable Mrs. Eliza Haywood" as dedicatee. Women writers later in the century "strenuously avoided associations" with Haywood, as is well known, but Sarah Prescott has shown that, at least until

1732, her name had "considerable market value."²⁹ The Haywood dedication was made a selling point in the fairly extensive advertising campaign for the first part of *The Prude*: it was announced at the top of every advertisement to appear in the London papers.

Haywood's bibliographer Patrick Spedding, noting that the dedication provides "one of a very small number of contemporary descriptions of Haywood," thought it important enough to reprint in part,³⁰ but it has attracted little attention, perhaps because MA. A.'s picture of the "excellent Good-Breeding" of a polite and elegant Haywood is at odds with her usual low image. The dedication opens with an approving discussion of the recently published *The Rash Resolve* (1723). The troubles of the heroine, Emanuella, an unmarried mother, are "represented with so forcible, so natural a Delicacy" as to arouse "generous Pity" for vulnerable young women caught up in the harsh realities of male sexual predation.³¹ MA. A.'s Haywood is less a novelist than a lyric poet of great power and musicality, and this genre-elevating maneuver is bolstered with a reference to Sappho, the classical poet associated with the intensities of lyric poetry as well heterosexual (and, sometimes, lesbian) desire. She predicts, with "prophetick Boldness," that a play she has read in manuscript will make Haywood's "Fame as immortal, tho' in a different way, as the never-dying *Sapho*."³² She also likens Haywood to Orpheus, the mythological musician-poet fabled for the power of his song to uproot trees, move rocks, and make even the animals weep.³³

Tributes by men also applaud the musicality and emotional force of Haywood's language: "As music fires, thy language lifts the mind," one has it; another says her voice "too divinely sings" and "mov'st the heart."³⁴ But only MA. A. compares her "easy flowing Stile" to "*Orpheus's* Harmony" and finds in his legendary ability to beguile even stones an analogy for the power of her language to rouse the dullest minds "to (till then) unknown Pleasures, or generous Pity."³⁵ Light social verse of the period used the Orpheus reference to compliment a lady's singing or playing, the conventional "young lady singing motif," but MA. A. may be hinting at something akin to the Renaissance idea of "Orpheus the civiliser," which continued to have "some serious resonance" into the eighteenth century.³⁶ The suggestion that Haywood's lyrical novels have a civilizing function, that they serve to refine the sensibility of her readers and foster in them more generous sympathies—fellow-feeling, for example, for the sufferings of an unwed mother—invites speculation that Haywood played a more important role than has been recognized in the emergence of the literature of sensibility. At the very least, the references to Orpheus and Sappho confer authority upon her artistry. It is probably not relevant but wonderful all the same to consider that in Ovid's version of the Orpheus story, the poet's "singing head washes up on the shore at Lesbos, where Sappho's song begins."[37]

The remarkable behind-the-scenes portrait of Haywood's character in the final paragraph is so unlike anything else recorded about Haywood that it deserves quotation in full: "All I have mentioned of your Perfections, is already conspicuous to the World, but the affable Politeness of your Conversation, is what only can be known, and enjoy'd by an *Intimate*; and indeed that excellent Good-Breeding so apparent in your Writing, adds an uncommon Lustre to your other good Sense, which is still greater, by being joined to such an open Candour and Sincerity, by which the Rough and Unpolish'd often endeavour to atone for their want of that Accomplishment."[38] It is a pity that we know nothing about the identity of the woman who signed herself MA. A., but there is reason to suppose that her friendship with Haywood survived into the next decade. In 1733, the "author of The Prude" published another novella in the Haywood line, a tale of amatory intrigue in a French aristocratic setting. *The Female Politician: or, the Statesman Unmask'd* is the story of two female friends, confidantes, each married happily to the man of her desires. One of the friends—beautiful, virtuous, possessed of superior discernment—may have been an homage to Haywood. She is given the name Amiana, the same name Haywood gave to the sparkling character in *The Tea-Table: or, A Conversation between some Polite Persons of both Sexes* (1725–26) who stands in for her creator in discussions of contemporary literary affairs, delivering (among other things) exquisitely polite slurs on her friend-turned-adversary Savage. That no other use of the name Amiana is captured by *Eighteenth Century Collections Online* is suggestive. MA. A.'s affectionate account of her friend, her tribute to the good-breeding, genteel demeanor, and affable politeness of a sister writer she claims to know intimately, stand as a reminder of the extent to which our perception of Haywood's "scandalous" reputation in the 1720s hinges on the smears of her literary enemies.

The Little Arts of Fame

As a professional author, Haywood accepted that it was part of the job to assist her publishers in making a market for her works. The expectation that periodical essayists, for example, would puff their own publications was so settled by mid-century as to become a matter for jest. In 1753, the fictitious editor of the *World,* Adam Fitz-Adams, disingenuously declared himself above "such little arts of fame," but earlier he had asked, "by what rule of reason should a man expect the good word of another, who has nothing to say in favour of himself?"[39] In the *Spring-Garden Journal,* Priscilla Termagant defends the "noisy Panegyricks" that attend "Authorism." "An Author must eat," she shrugs, and since respite from hunger requires brisk sales, why should she "be debarred the Liberty of Puffing? Why deprived of assuring the Publick, that my Book contains all the Sense, all the Wit, and all the Learning, that is, has been, or ever will be in the World?"[40] Haywood seldom indulged in self-mocking "Authorism," preferring to affect an earnest moralism more Doctor Johnson than Bonnell Thornton, Termagant's creator, but in *Female Spectator,* she was not above using the complimentary openings of what may have been self-composed letters to tout the merits of her periodical. One such letter begins: "*Dear Female Sage,* I have a vast Opinion of your Wit. . . ." Another addressed the fictive "authors" of that periodical: "*Ladies,* or *Gentlemen, Madam,* or *Sir,* Whether you are a single or collective Body; whether *Female,* as you pretend, or *Male,* as the Strength and Energy of your Writings tempts me rather to believe. . . ."[41] Haywood took pleasure in dangling gender ambiguities before her readers, as she did in one of her last works, *The Invisible Spy* (1755), when her narrator-protagonist taunts, "whether I am even a man or a woman" will prove "as difficult to discover as the longitude," and at all points of her career she drew upon the device of androgynous praise to craft her authorial image, as will be seen.[42]

For evidence of Haywood's aptitude for self-promotion we can consider the publicity around her stage comedy *A Wife to be Lett.* A notice in the *Daily Post* for August 10, 1723, announced that she would be playing the lead role of Mrs. Graspall, claiming, implausibly, that the last-minute substitution was owing to the "indisposition" of the original actress. The notice puffed play and author in fairly restrained terms: "If we may judge by her writings we may reasonably expect she will bid fair to entertain the Town very agreeable."[43] But the comedy fizzled after three nights and, two years later, Haywood turned to the papers to try to get it revived. Writing as "Mrs Graspall," she took out space in *Mist's Weekly Journal* to urge the Drury Lane management to mount the play: if they will do so "within ten Days"—the unrealistic timeframe is hard to explain—"they will oblige her and a great many of the Quality to whom she communicates her Design."[44] The management declined to take up the proposal. Her most flamboyant gesture on her own behalf is the Prologue to *Wife to be Lett,* which deploys to memorable effect the convention of androgynous praise. The playwright is a "dangerous *Woman-Poet,*" fierce, fearless, and undaunted by the critics—"More than your Match, in every thing, but Railing"—who already has under her belt an impressive body of work. Her *"known novels"* blend masculine and feminine strengths: "Measure her Force, by her *known novels*, writ / With manly Vigour, and with Woman's Wit."[45] The neoclassical convention of androgynous praise would go out of fashion later in the century, but Paula Loscocco has shown that since at least the middle of the seventeenth century, it had served as a means to honor women poets of exceptional power, most notably in the torrent of adulation for Katherine Philips, "the matchless Orinda," released by her early death. Abraham Cowley famously celebrated Orinda's artistry using a synthesis of manly strength and womanly sweetness: "than Man more strong, and more than Woman sweet."[46] Hill's praise of Haywood in "The Vision" echoes Cowley: "all that's manly, joins with all that's sweet."[47] Interestingly, Haywood's Prologue to *Wife to be Lett* replaces the feminine sweetness commended by Cowley and Hill with a more bracing reference to "Woman's Wit," and I would like to think this departure from convention amounts to deliberate self-fashioning on Haywood's part.

The Prologue is unsigned—not even the indispensable "Friend" or "Person of Quality" is conjured for the occasion—and absent attribution, one is permitted to presume Haywood's likely authorship.[48] *Invisible Spy* ridicules self-promotion of this sort when Mr. Invisible takes a swipe at a certain author who thinks it "proper to bespeak [the public's] favour by a pompous prelude, and sounds his own praises, like a trumpet at the door of a Puppet-shew."[49] The unnamed target is Henry Fielding, a sometime puppeteer, but Haywood knew as well as Fielding that it was only good business to trumpet one's own praises. It was she, after all, who hung the image of Fame blowing her trumpet above the door of her Covent Garden pamphlet shop.

Haywood achieved great commercial success over a career spanning nearly four decades as a more or less continuously employed editor, adapter, translator, and original author who could boast a successful periodical franchise and a host of titles still in print at mid-century, to say nothing of a mid-career swerve into acting and playwriting at the edgy Haymarket, and, for a spell, a sideline as a publisher and print retailer in Covent Garden. But none of this is the same as achieving Fame. From the 1730s most of her work was issued anonymously, and her questionable status in the literary community precluded her leaving a positive legacy for the generation of culturally ambitious women who followed her. One looks in vain for tributes to Haywood from women at mid-century. Unless, that is, one seeks them in Haywood's own work. Eve Tavor Bannet argues convincingly that *Invisible*

Spy shows Haywood "making a point about her own contributions to literature, history, and politics ... at a moment when she rightly feared that this was likely to be forgotten."[50] Something similar seems to have occurred in *Epistles for the Ladies*. By means of the figure of Ardella, an amateur poet introduced late into the network of exchanges that constitute this generically elusive epistolary fiction, Haywood revisits and boldly reimagines a version of the authorial self we encountered earlier: the ardently self-affirming poet of the sublime whose emulation of Hill was her best plea for Fame. Haywood loved disguises, and in the reading developed in the next section, I will propose that Ardella represents a concealed homage to self that was conceived at a juncture when the aging author had occasion to think more seriously than ever before about her legacy as a woman writer.

Epistles *and Self-Homage*

Epistles for the Ladies, written in the interval between the publication of *Clarissa* (1747–48) and *Sir Charles Grandison* (1753–54), is Haywood's fullest statement on the regenerative powers of public-spirited female virtue. It deserves study as a late-life rethinking of her identity as a woman writer, including, perhaps, the way she would like to be remembered by a new generation of women writers should she, fantastically enough, contrive to seize control of her image. Haywood was fifty-seven or thereabouts when she completed *Epistles* in 1750. Midway through its serial publication—it was originally intended, like *Female Spectator*, to be issued in monthly "books"—she fell gravely ill. In a poem inserted toward the end of *Epistles*, she likens her recovery to being "Snatch'd from Eternity's tremendous Brink."[51] It is hardly surprising that the work, the final books especially, should be preoccupied with thoughts of death, the afterlife (in religious and worldly senses), and the image Haywood would pass on to posterity.

Ardella, a complexly layered stand-in for Haywood's poetic self, serves as a focus for these concerns. She is a manuscript poet, as Haywood was in the days of the Hill circle, but in other ways Ardella, diffident and self-effacing, is an image-in-reverse of the assertive, self-affirming, and boastful poet we encounter in the surviving coterie verse. Possessed of an almost debilitating "Excess of Modesty,"[52] Ardella would never own her desire to "tune the whole Voice of Fame" as Haywood does, exuberantly, in "To Walter Bowman." Ardella, interestingly, incarnates the view of Haywood embodied in Hill's "The Vision," a companion piece to Haywood's piece of the same title, in which he depicts her as one "Blind to her Worth" who "despises Fame!"

(Really? Haywood?) The poem closes with a strangely self-contradictory image of the "lovely Eliza" "hid in Bay-Leaves" in which acclaimed achievement ("Bay-Leaves") is superimposed upon a leaf-obscured and all but invisible Eliza. Wilputte is surely right to say that Haywood would have rejected Hill's vision of "a modest poetess awaiting discovery by the male gaze and words."[53] How intriguing then that decades later she would style her poetic stand-in as just that, a retiring poetess who could not be more unlike the dangerous woman-poet of the 1720s who all but shouted her desire for Fame. What is going on here?

It is probably significant that Hill had died in February 1750, around the time a shaken Haywood returned to her work on *Epistles*. His death, on top of her own recent illness, may have released memories of their verse exchange three decades earlier. If nothing else, it freed her to repurpose his verse for her own uses in ways that tighten for us the Haywood-Ardella links. She reprinted without acknowledgement two poems that Hill had addressed to her, the most important of which, "The Vision," is inscribed to Ardella.[54] In addition, Ardella is credited with an ode on the birth of a son to the Welsh Jacobite Sir Watkin Williams Wynne that can be attributed to Haywood. It opens with an autobiographical glance at her recent illness, and an asterisked note informs the reader that the "Authoress was just recovered from a long and dangerous Fit of Sickness, when she wrote these Verses."[55] Consciousness of mortality and of the imminence of death pervades *Epistles*,[56] and it makes psychological sense that, at this time, the contours of a poetic alter ego would emerge in Haywood's mind as a kind of bridge to the younger self who wrote and exchanged coterie verse back in her day. What gives the Ardella self-inscription its especially interesting character is the way in which Haywood recrafts the authorial self to align with the model of respectable female authorship emerging at mid-century: a Blue-tinctured ideal that united piety, virtuous intellect, and service to society.

In her final appearance, Ardella is imagined as an exemplar of the culturally sanctioned female poet endorsed by the rising self-consciously virtuous generation of women writers. This refashioning takes place in Epistle CXLIII to Ardella from Eusebia, a friend writing *"in Praise of some Verses she had seen, of her composing."* Eusebia urges Ardella to turn her poetic talents in a new direction, toward religious poetry, and proposes as subject matter the biblical story of Mary Magdalene's return to the sepulcher, an episode "so often mentioned in the Gospel, to the Honour of our Sex."[57] First, though, Eusebia pays tribute to Ardella as one possessed of "the most perfect Purity of Heart, with the most exalted Ideas of Gratitude, and

Love" and an ability to express "the utmost Delicacy of Sentiments, and Eloquence of Style." These attributes fit her for the creation of verse of the highest order, namely, that "in the religious Strain"; no other strain is "worthy of such a Pen as yours, or [able to] afford so lasting a Satisfaction to a reasonable Mind."[58] Thus is the dangerous woman-poet of earlier days reinvented as a religious poet perfectly suited to face off against members of the younger generation, an Elizabeth Carter for example, on their own virtuous ground.

The rejection of Haywood by other women writers can conveniently be dated to 1737, when Carter, just twenty at the time, published in *Gentleman's Magazine* the first of two elegies to the impeccably credentialed Mrs. Rowe. "On the Death of Mrs. Rowe," as Susan Staves observes, "constructed a history of women's writing as an earlier dark age of licentiousness and misogyny, of female wits enthralled by 'Th' intriguing novel and the wanton tale."[59] Carter signed it "Eliza," is if to displace the wanton novelist whose name she shared. By mid-century, Haywood was so thoroughly repudiated that even the wit Laetitia Pilkington, who one might have thought an ally, mocked her for exchanging her "former luscious Stile" for "the insipid," sniping that her *Female Spectators* are a Collection of trite Stories, . . . bless'd Revolution."[60] Eusebia's luxurious evocation of the Magdalene story could be said to represent on Haywood's part an oblique counter-reformational move: part reaffirmation of her identity as a poet of the sublime, part moving on with the times to compose "to the Honour of our Sex," and part ur-Haywood, a lyricism of the senses. The retelling of the Magdalene story focuses upon powerful sublime feeling—her terror and grief succeeded by amazement at the sight of the angels and holy raptures when she is addressed by the resurrected Jesus. The passionate expressivity of the scene recalls Haywood's earlier experiments in the poetic and the amatory sublime, and the proposed treatment of "this lovely Saint" speaks to Haywood's lifelong fascination with sensuous experience: Eusebia would have Ardella show how the Magdalene "shone the Pride of *Herod*'s Court,—the Idol of a vain luxurious Age:— How every Joy, that vicious Wit and Fancy can invent, filled her each Sense:—How every Step she took was to some new Delight." It is an audacious piece of self-fashioning, this reimagining of the authorial self as the chronicler of a "pious Penitent," and is eerily prophetic of Reeve's rewriting of Haywood as a reformed woman who had the "singular good fortune to recover a lost reputation, and the yet greater honour to atone for her errors."[61]

Implications

Feminist theory provides important insights into the way women's tributes to women belong to an economy of commemoration that served to resist presumptions of male superiority and foster female solidarity, but there is another story here as well, one that touches on the themes of patriotism, national identity, and symbolic femininity developed in scholarship by Harriet Guest and Emma Clery, among others. For this story we need to return to the pre-Enlightenment conceptions of Fame that underpin many of the tributes examined earlier. The classical scholar Robert von Hallberg argues on the basis of his study of Ancient Greek and Hebrew choral traditions that poetry derives its authority from encouragement: the "deepest power" of poetry comes "from praise."[62] A poetry of praise consists of more than "referential statements about particular people, events, or things." It has crucial community-building functions. Praise in Ancient Greek and Hebrew traditions "circulates through a culture, justly binding people in a network of obligations"; it "produce[s] general value for a wide audience to share," serving as a kind of "medium of exchange whereby general values" acquire "communal meanings."[63] Adopting his argument to the subject of this volume, we might say that women's tributes to women functioned not only to honor female literary excellence—"she that writt best, with a wreath should be crown'd," as Finch puts it in "The Circuit of Appollo"[64]—but also to disseminate more general values associated with what Clery describes as the process of "feminization," the growing perception in eighteenth-century England that women's gains in status and influence were cause for pride, at least in progressive quarters, "as an index of increasing refinement or civility."[65] Women's tributes to women, in this view, invite members of the reading public to associate themselves with the laudable achievements of literary ladies, to share in their Fame, and in this way to celebrate with and through them the civilized progress of the nation.[66]

The "extreme activity of mind" that in Virginia Woolf's perdurable phrase energized female life at the end of the eighteenth century was preceded by a period of extreme activity of praise and commemoration. Writing women in the first half of the long eighteenth century together, as if by shared instinct, applauded the female pursuit of Fame. Hill's wife, the former Margaret Morris, is a case in point. Writing as Miranda, she praises the poetic accomplishments of her sexual rival Martha Fowke with outwardly generous, if perhaps ironic, warmth:

> Thou! great Redeemer of thy Sex's Fame,
> Outblazest Manhood with thy tow'ring Flame;

> Ages to come, the wide-spread Light shall see,
> And worship Womankind in Praise of thee.

To Evandra, a friend, she writes: "A Woman's Fame, methinks, all Women share:/ And Policy shou'd make her praise their Care." Evandra praises Miranda in return: "While she obliges, she instructs me too,/ Fame, by Her great Example, to pursue."[67] In popular and emerging forms such as plays, novels, journalism, and periodical publications, praise often takes the distinctively modern form of puffing, branding, and self-promotion intended to attract an audience and boost sales. But coexisting alongside these new "arts of fame"—publicity, in the modern sense of the term—was an older conception of Fame linked to classical and Renaissance ideals of civic virtue, literary excellence, and noble emulation, especially in relation to the still-revered genre of poetry, and the rhetoric of Fame may have seemed to writing women a vehicle for raising women's status within the nation.

Whatever its effect on women's actual lives, a question beyond the scope of this essay, this vibrant culture of commemoration is worth closer study than it has received from scholars of women's writing. If the history of Haywood's critical reception teaches us anything about the biases that shape reconstructions of women's writing pasts more generally, it is this: literary history prefers stories of men's enmity to those of women's amity, of male derogation to female commemoration. The usefulness to feminist historians of outbreaks of male hostility is easy to understand: each retelling of Pope's grossly scurrilous treatment of Haywood in the *Dunciad* provides a tonic reminder of the damaging force and at times sheer malignity of the masculinist pushback an assertive woman of wit could expect if she chose to go public as a writer. But a history skewed toward abuse comes with a cost. Awareness of MA. A.'s homage to a refined and elegant Haywood, an intimate friend at that, invites us to ponder the largely unconscious pattern of distortion that produced, especially among those with only passing knowledge of Haywood, endlessly recycled accounts of a sexually tarnished low-life outlier.

Feminist scholars are familiar with the recurring bouts of cultural amnesia that sometimes go by the name the Great Forgetting, that process by which women once celebrated by their contemporaries disappear rapidly from cultural memory. Norma Clarke has called it "an astonishing fact" that a writer widely read "over thirty-seven years of intense literary activity, whose name was a byword for a certain kind of writing, who was embedded in London networks of writers, theatrical companies, booksellers and printers, could later be as obscure as Eliza Haywood."[68] Haywood never vanished entirely, of course; she persisted as a cautionary tale or as a figure of disrepute of one sort or another. But knowing what we do about Haywood's professional achievements over nearly four decades, about her admirable pursuit of recognition, and about the tributes she garnered from many quarters when she published under her own name early in her career, it is an insult to her and embarrassment to literary history that the likes of Savage and Pope be given the last or loudest word on her. Women's homages to women and, as in Haywood's case, their homages to themselves, propose for our consideration an archive more worthy of critical attention.

Notes

1. [Bonnell Thornton], *Spring-Garden Journal* (London, Nov–Dec 1752), 69; henceforth *SGJ*. Termagant is the *Journal*'s eidolon.

2. So far as I know, these three "New Female Spectators" remain undiscussed. No. I (*SGJ*, 38–41) reflects on sexual difference; No. II (*SGJ*, 55–58), burlesques her cautionary tales by way of the story of a writer, Lovewit, who loves his own wit, writes badly, and dies "a short Time after"; No. III (*SGJ*, 77–80) dead-pans what is represented as Haywood's habit of making obvious moral discriminations.

3. Ibid., 56.

4. Eliza Haywood, dedication to *Memoirs of the Baron de Brosse* (London: Browne and Chapman, 1725), v; ital. reversed.

5. Richard Savage, *The Authors of the Town; A Satire* (London: J. Roberts, 1725), 10.

6. For a concise summary of Haywood's position, see Betty A. Schellenberg, "The Professional Female Writer," in *The Cambridge Companion to Women's Writing in Britain, 1660–1789*, ed. Catherine Ingrassia (Cambridge: Cambridge University Press, 2015), 44–46.

7. Famously, Richardson to Lady Bradshaigh in *Selected Letters of Samuel Richardson*, ed. John J. Carroll (Oxford: Clarendon Press, 1964), 173.

8. Schellenberg, "Professional Female Writer," 37.

9. "The Poet Concludes," trans. John Dryden in *Ovid's Metamorphoses in Fifteen Books* (London: Tonson, 1717), 589.

10. Elizabeth Carter, "Occasioned by an Ode written by Mrs. Philips," in *Poems on Several Occasions* (London: Rivington, 1762), 16.

11. Norma Clarke, *The Rise and Fall of the Woman of Letters* (London: Pimlico, 2004), 93. Elizabeth Carter, "On the Death of Mrs. Rowe," *Gentleman's Magazine* 9 (Mar. 1739), 152.

12. Aphra Behn, preface to *The Lucky Chance*, in *The Works of Aphra Behn*, ed. Janet Todd (Columbus: Ohio State University Press, 1996), 7: 217.

13. "To Mr. John Dyer, of Carmarthenshire" in *Miscellaneous Poems and Translations*, ed. Richard Savage (London: Chapman, 1726), 210; henceforth *Miscellany*.

14. "On the *Apothecaries* Filing my *Recipes* amongst the *Doctors*" is in Jane Barker, *A Patch-Work Screen for the Ladies* (1723), in *The Galesia Trilogy and Selected Manuscript Poems of Jane Barker*, ed. Carol Shiner Wilson (New York: Oxford University Press, 1997), 117, 119.

15. Eliza Haywood, "Advertisement to the Reader," *The Fair Captive: A Tragedy* (London: Jauncy and Cole, 1721), xi.

16. Patrick Spedding, *A Bibliography of Eliza Haywood* (London: Pickering & Chatto, 2004), 100.

17. Seven poems from this period that presumably had first circulated in manuscript were published as *Poems on Several Occasions*, henceforth *POSO*, appended to the final volume of the four-volume *The Works of Mrs. Eliza Haywood* (1724): see Spedding, *Bibliography*, 139. For a detailed discussion of the coterie verse, see Earla Wilputte, *Passion and Language in Eighteenth-Century Literature: The Aesthetic Sublime in the Work of Eliza Haywood, Aaron Hill, and Martha Fowke* (New York: Palgrave Macmillan, 2014), 98–113.

18. "An Irregular Ode, *To* Mr. Walter Bowman, *Professor of the* Mathematics. *Occasion'd by his objecting against my giving the Name of* Hillarius *to* Aaron Hill *Esq*," *POSO*, 4.

19. Wilputte, *Passion and Language*, 98.

20. Haywood, *POSO*, 13.

21. Wilputte, *Passion and Language*, 99.

22. Jane Brereton, "*Epistle to Mrs Anne Griffiths. Written from London, in 1718*," in *Eighteenth Century Women Poets: An Oxford Anthology*, ed. Roger Lonsdale (New York: Oxford University Press, 1989), 80.

23. Elizabeth Boyd, *Variety: A Poem, In Two Cantos* (Westminster: Warner and Creake, 1727), [76].

24. "On *Louisa's* NOVEL, call'd, *The Happy-Unfortunate*," in Elizabeth Boyd, *The Happy-Unfortunate; or, the Female-Page: A Novel* (London: T. Edlin, 1732), n.p.

25. Boyd, *Variety*, 64.

26. "Elizabeth Boyd," in *Orlando: Women's Writing in the British Isles from the Beginnings to the Present*, eds. Susan Brown, Patricia Clements, and Isobel Grundy (Cambridge: Cambridge University Press Online, 2006), http://orlando.cambridge.org/, accessed August 24, 2016.

27. Boyd, *Variety*, 62.

28. See Nicolle Jordan's essay in this volume. The attribution to "a Young Lady" may be a marketing ploy: see Sarah Prescott, *Women, Authorship and Literary Culture, 1690–1740* (New York: Palgrave Macmillan, 2003), 81.

29. Prescott, *Women, Authorship and Literary Culture*, 83; for Haywood's importance in "niche marketing" of amatory fiction by women, see 80–83.

30. Spedding, *Bibliography of Eliza Haywood*, 653.

31. MA. A., dedication to *The Prude: A Novel*, by a Young Lady (London: J. Roberts, 1724), iii; ital. reversed.

32. Ibid., iv. Haywood had published a play in 1723, her second, *A Wife to be Lett*, but it failed to secure her immortal fame.

33. For the Orpheus myth, see Geoffrey Miles, ed., *Classical Mythology in English Literature: A Critical Anthology* (New York: Routledge, 1999), 61–74. For Orpheus and lyric

poetry, see Heather Dubrow, *The Challenges of Orpheus: Lyric Poetry and Early Modern England* (Baltimore: Johns Hopkins University Press, 2008), 18–26.

34. Richard Savage, "To Mrs. Eliza Haywood, on Her Novel, called *The Rash Resolve*" (1724); James Sterling, "To Mrs. Eliza Haywood on Her Writings" (1725). They are reprinted in Eliza Haywood, *Love in Excess; or, The Fatal Enquiry*, ed. David Oakleaf, 2nd ed. (Peterborough, ON: Broadview, 2000), 271, 278.

35. MA. A., *The Prude*, iii.

36. Miles, *Classical Mythology*, 67.

37. Robert Von Hallberg, *Lyric Powers* (Chicago: University of Chicago Press, 2008), 15.

38. MA. A., *The Prude*, iv.

39. Edward Moore, ed., *The World, for the Year One Thousand Seven Hundred and Fifty Three* (London: R and J. Dodsley, 1753), 1: 79, 8.

40. *SGJ*, A2, 4.

41. Eliza Haywood, *Female Spectator*, eds. Kathryn R. King and Alexander Pettit, in *Works of Eliza Haywood*, ed. Alexander Pettit (London: Pickering & Chatto, 2001), II, 2: 285, 233.

42. Eliza Haywood, *The Invisible Spy*, ed. Carol Stewart (London: Pickering & Chatto, 2014), 7.

43. See Kathryn R. King, *A Political Biography of Eliza Haywood* (London: Pickering & Chatto, 2012), 206, n. 12.

44. *Mist's Weekly Journal*, November 6, 1725.

45. Eliza Haywood, prologue, *A Wife to be Lett: A Comedy* (London: Browne and Chapman, 1724), v; ital. reversed.

46. Paula Loscocco, "'Manly Sweetness': Katherine Philips among the Neoclassicals," *Huntington Library Quarterly* 56, no. 3 (Summer 1993): 259–79; Cowley qtd. on 266.

47. Aaron Hill, "The Vision," in Savage, *Miscellany*, 75. Savage used the trope of androgynous praise in "*To Mrs. Eliza Haywood, on Her Novel, called The Rash Resolve*": "The sciences in thy sweet genius charm, / And, with their strength, thy sex's softness arm"; reprinted in Oakleaf, *Love in Excess*, 271.

48. My thanks to Sarah Creel and Diana Solomon for counsel on the question of unattributed prologues.

49. Haywood, *Invisible Spy*, 241.

50. Eve Tavor Bannet, "The Narrator as Invisible Spy: Eliza Haywood, Secret History and the Novel," *Journal for Early Modern Cultural Studies* 14, no. 4 (Fall 2014): 157.

51. Eliza Haywood, *Epistles for the Ladies*, ed. Christine Blouch and Alexander Pettit, in *Selected Works of Eliza Haywood*, ed. Alexander Pettit (London: Pickering & Chatto, 2000), I, 2: 430; hereafter, *Epistles*.

52. Ibid., 430.

53. Wilputte, *Passion and Language*, 112.

54. "THE VISION. Inscribed to the incomparable *Ardella*," *Epistles*, 391–93, was first published in Savage's *Miscellany*, 71–76, and written earlier still, possibly in the teens. The other poem, "On the excellent *Clarismonda's* intending a *Voyage* to Spain," *Epistles*, 394, was published in Savage's *Miscellany*, 90, as "To *Eliza*, on her design'd Voyage to Spain."

55. *Epistles*, 430. For the Wynn ode and Haywood's illness, see King, *Political Biography*, 168–69.

56. *Epistles*, 430. For Haywood's mid-century religious turn, see Kathryn R. King, "The Pious Mrs. Haywood; or, Thoughts on *Epistles for the Ladies* (1748–1750)," *Journal for Early Modern Cultural Studies* 14, no. 4 (Fall 2014): 187–208.

57. *Epistles*, 438, 439.

58. Ibid., 438.

59. Elizabeth Carter, "On the Death of Mrs. Rowe," *Gentleman's Magazine* 7 (1737): 247; Susan Staves, *A Literary History of Women's Writing in Britain, 1660–1789* (Cambridge: Cambridge University Press, 2006), 227.

60. A. C. Elias, Jr., ed., *Memoirs of Laetitia Pilkington* (Athens: University of Georgia Press, 1997), 1: 227.

61. *Epistles*, 439; Clara Reeve, *The Progress of Romance* (1785), reprinted in Oakleaf, *Love in Excess*, 285.

62. Hallberg, *Lyric Powers*, 40.

63. Ibid., 48, 47, 42.

64. Myra Reynolds, ed., *The Poems of Anne, Countess of Winchilsea* (Chicago: University of Chicago Press, 1903), 92.

65. Emma J. Clery, *The Feminization Debate in Eighteenth-Century England: Literature, Commerce and Luxury* (Houndmills, Basingstoke, UK: Palgrave Macmillan, 2004), 1.

66. For relations between representations of learned women and national identity at mid-century, see Harriet Guest, *Small Change: Women, Learning, Patriotism, 1750–1810* (Chicago: University of Chicago Press, 2000), esp. chapter 2, "The Female Worthies."

67. "Miranda to Clio," "*To* Evandra, *on seeing some Poems of her writing*," "*On the Incomparable* Miranda's *commending what I writ*," in *Miscellany*, 265, 253, 256.

68. Clarke, *Rise and Fall*, 93.

In the spirit of tribute, I want to express my gratitude to the editors of this volume and especially to the reader for the press, Susan Staves, for their engaged reading of this essay. Their comments and suggestions improved it immeasurably.

"Who Praises Women Does the Muses Praise"

Mary Barber, Laetitia Pilkington, and Constantia Grierson's Poetic Tributes

CATHERINE INGRASSIA

"A Friend so gen'rous, ardent, and sincere" is how Constantia Grierson describes Mary Barber in her tribute poem *To Mrs. Mary Barber, under the Name of Sapphira: Occasion'd by the Encouragement she met with in England, to publish her Poems by Subscription*. "Her Breast with every Grace inspir'd," Barber merits admiration not "only for her Lays," but also for her passion and sense of social justice.[1] Focusing on Barber's poetic prowess and her personal qualities, Grierson signals a relationship with her based on respect, encouragement, and reciprocity. In an earlier poem to Laetitia Pilkington, Grierson also celebrates their friendship, praising the poet's "Wit" and "Beauty" while lamenting her temporary absence from Dublin: "O hasten to Town! and bless the longing Eyes / Of your Constantia."[2] Written before her death in 1732, the tributes by Grierson capture the optimism and energy of the three women who were part of a lively Dublin poetic circle for about a decade beginning roughly in 1724.[3] The tributes illustrate how poetic skills and personal friendship intertwine within a feminocentric group, a circle with shared but distinct literary and scholarly abilities.

Yet Grierson never published those poems, or any poem, during her lifetime; they appeared only within Mary Barber's volume *Poems on Several Occasions* (1734) and Pilkington's *Memoirs* (1747), contexts that complicate their meaning.[4] The posthumous use of Grierson's poems memorializes the late poet—publication itself serving as a form of tribute—and, in the process, simultaneously elevates the surviving poets trying to capitalize on Grierson's affection, praise, and residual cultural currency. For Pilkington and Barber, both increasingly beset by financial and reputational challenges after 1734, Grierson functioned as an unequivocally distinguished (and distinguishing) figure. With her reputation as a scholar, printer, and poet, all inviolate after death, Grierson was a valuable commodity whose memory invoked moments of potential success for the women. By publishing Grierson's poems, Barber and Pilkington each sought to control her legacy (poetic and otherwise) as a way of claiming a greater degree of intimacy with the late poet. Their strategic inclusion of her poems, like their narrative treatment of her, also continued a subtle, ongoing competition between Pilkington and Barber. Their use of Grierson's tribute poems, like their own tributes to her, reveals a relationship between the two women that began as collaborative (if at times contested) but, after the death of Grierson, devolved into an overt rivalry. Thus, while the tribute poems themselves represent the supportive dynamic among these women poets, their subsequent circulation and placement within the published volumes of others reveals a more complicated and nuanced hierarchy among the women.

"A Scotch Booksellers wife," who "is a very good Latin and Greek Scholar, and hath lately published a fine Edition of Tacitus, with a Latin Dedication to the Lord Lieutenant," Constantia Grierson (1704/5–1732) possessed unusual classical knowledge as well as a privileged position within Dublin's print trade. Swift described Grierson to Pope as "both a Scholar and Poet,"[5] noting that she "writes *carmina Anglicana non contemnenda*."[6] Grierson never published her poems in English, her *carmina Anglicana;* her classical editions also appeared without her name, "not even Latin dedications for the Tacitus or the Terence."[7] A. C. Elias suggested that Grierson, not much caring "to be read, or at least be personally appreciated" beyond her Dublin circle, "made few of the usual efforts to make herself known, either to a wider circle or to posterity."[8] However, Grierson's abilities and activities were extraordinary. "A prodigy, a busy and productive figure working in a bewildering range of areas," Grierson attended not only to her own literary work (translation, editorial work, and the creation of her own poetry) but also had extensive involvement in her husband's printing business.[9] The *Journals of the House of Commons* contains her husband's petition for a better patent for the King's Printer's post, detailing how Grierson "in a more particular Manner, applied herself to the correcting of the Press, which she performed to general Satisfaction; insomuch, that the Editions corrected by her have been approved of, not only in this Kingdom, but in Great Britain, Holland, and elsewhere, and the Art of Printing, through her Care and Assistance, has been brought to greater Perfection than has been hitherto in this Kingdom."[10] Her widely praised, diverse activities within the print trade complemented what was an unimpeached character marked by "Virtue and Piety"; "she was too learned to be vain, too wise to be conceited, too knowing and too clear-sighted to be irreligious" writes Barber in the Preface to her volume.[11] Grierson's character, her reputation as a classicist, and her professional savvy in the print trade distinguished her.

Mary Barber (c. 1685–1755), introduced to Swift by Dr. Patrick Delany or possibly Grierson, was "a Woollen-drapers wife, declind [sic] in the world., [with] . . . a knack at versifing."[12] Described by Swift as "our chief Poetess, and upon the whole hath no ill Genius," he distinguished her as "a Poet only, but not a Scholar,"[13] a persistent distinction between Grierson and Barber. Dr. Delany described her as "one who hath laboured more years than Duck hath lived in a course of upright, obliging, well guided, and unwearied, though unsuccessful industry." The reference to the thresher-poet Stephen Duck suggests Barber's non-elite cultural status and her often precarious financial position. "[O]n the verge of fifty, with an hereditary gout, cough, and asthma, with a load of four children," continued Delany, although "excellently educated" and "perfectly well-disposed," Barber, Swift's "Citizen Housewife Poet," remained "utterly unprovided for."[14] Barber describes herself as "destin'd to a low Estate."[15] By contrast, Laetitia van Lewen Pilkington (1712–1750), the daughter of prominent Dublin physician John van Lewen (1684–1737) initially enjoyed a genteel upbringing and elevated family connections until her 1725 marriage to clergyman and aspiring poet Matthew. Pilkington's vivacity, persistence, and poetic skills quickly made her "a bosom friend of Dean Swift's."[16] Swift famously referred to Matthew and Laetitia Pilkington as "a little young poetical parson" and his "littler young poetical wife."[17] Subsequently, Pilkington's *Memoirs* served as the first biography of Swift.

Sharp differences in social status, geography, and education did not limit the intimacy of these three women. Grierson knew Pilkington since roughly 1722 when she lived in the van Lewen household while apprenticed as a midwife to Pilkington's father; during that period they were, in Pilkington's words, "seldom asunder."[18] She also provided a meeting place for Laetitia and Matthew before their marriage. Grierson and Barber served as sponsors to Pilkington's son Jack upon his christening—Mrs. Grierson gave "learning," and "Mrs. Barber, poesy."[19] Barber's biography of Grierson in the Preface to her poems offers an intimate portrait of her life and personal qualities, supporting Elias's assertion that Grierson was Barber's "closest friend in the editorial group."[20] This female writing circle fostered creativity. As Paula Backscheider notes, "the poetry of each woman gives permission, enables the poetry of the others." Grierson and Barber particularly "had been encouraging each others reading and writing for some time."[21] Despite this supportive culture, the group of aspiring poets—which included Matthew Pilkington—also vied for Swift's approbation in a careful dance of collaboration and competition.

The most pointed competition arguably existed between Barber and Pilkington. Initially, Pilkington "looked on Mary Barber with becoming deference, as something of a patroness in her own right," which proved accurate when Barber "arranged for a copy of Matthew's *Poems* to be presented to the newly appointed Lord Lieutenant of Ireland."[22] In fact, Pilkington describes how Mary Barber "was with me at my first meeting with the Dean," likely facilitated either by Barber herself or by Dr. Delany who knew Pilkington's father at Trinity College. However, "Mrs. Barber's work came so late in her life and Mrs. Pilkington was so precocious," wrote Myra Reynolds, "that they were in effect poetical contemporaries" and, I would add, poetical rivals.[23] Elias characterizes Barber as "a rival protégée" to Pilkington.[24] Perhaps Pilkington's generally competitive nature fueled her own sense of the rivalry. In her *Memoirs*, she suggests at times that she had been "excluded from the Delight and Instruction" of the group surrounding Swift because "truly they were envious, and would not let me see the Dean, knowing how much I surpassed them all."[25] Pilkington also infrequently mentions Grierson and Barber and often presents herself as the only woman in Swift's circle: "I believe there never was any Set of People so happy in sincere and uninterrupted Friendship, as the Dean, Doctor Delany, Mr. Pilkington, and myself; nor can I reflect, at this Hour, on any thing with more Pleasure, that those happy Moments we have enjoyed!"[26] She fashions herself as *prima inter pares*.

In the 1730s, Pilkington may have resented Barber's emergent success as a published poet, advanced in no small part by Swift's concerted assistance. Four of Barber's pieces had appeared individually as broadsides between 1725 and 1728, and several others were published in miscellanies between 1724 and 1733. Recognizing that "there was a Great Combat between her modesty and her Ambition," Swift used his own connections—and engaged Pope's assistance—to help her publish her collection of poems.[27] Although it took nearly four years, Swift's efforts coupled with her own dogged persistence secured Barber 913 subscribers. *Poems on Several Occasions* was published in 1734; it was reissued with some additional poems in 1735 and 1736. "Barber's was among the first collections of poems by a woman to appear by subscription," notes Adam Budd, "It would have appeared to be an enormous triumph for her."[28] Unlike Barber, Pilkington never published a volume of poems although poetry remained her highest ambition: "I was charmed and ravish'd with the Sweets of Poetry; all my Hours were dedicated to the Muses." For her, poetry was an "incurable disease."[29] While she wrote poetry throughout her life, Pilkington's personal situation was not conducive to her literary aspirations. In Matthew, Pilkington found a poetically ambitious and personally indifferent husband who resented her prodigious skills. Despite her associations with Swift, the initially Dublin-bound (and child-burdened) Pilkington did not have many options for publishing her work. After her public, acrimonious divorce in 1738, spurred by Matthew's accusations of adultery, Swift and much of Dublin society repudiated Pilkington. The subsequent years found her ghost-writing poems for pay simply to sustain herself.[30]

Unsuccessfully circulating a proposal for a volume of poems by subscription in the early 1740s, Pilkington ultimately published her *Memoirs* by subscription in 1747. Although she included all of her own poems within her *Memoirs,* that proved small consolation and obviously lacked the status of a dedicated volume of verse.[31] Certainly Pilkington had her champions; Colley Cibber, who encouraged her to write the *Memoirs,* believed that "under all the Rubbish of your Misfortunes ... your Merits sparkle like a lost Jewel."[32] Despite her poetic precocity and promising relationship with Swift, however, after 1738, Pilkington grappled with a deteriorating reputation, precarious financial situations (including brief homelessness), and engagement with the more disreputable elements of print culture.

Barber does not mention Pilkington by name in the Preface to her volume of poems. However, immediately before she begins her tribute to Grierson, she alludes to an incident with which Pilkington is associated. Explaining the delay in publishing her volume "as soon as I ought to have done," Barber cites her "want of Health" and "the Affairs of my Family" as contributing factors. But she also refers to "a new Perplexity [that] hath obliged me to trespass further upon" the patience of subscribers: "misfortunes that should not be imputed as my Fault."[33] The "Perplexity," well known at the time to those familiar with her and her circle, was Barber's arrest and imprisonment in England in January 1734. In late 1733, Barber traveled to England with Pilkington's husband Matthew to deliver three poems written by Swift (*On Poetry, An Epistle to a Lady,* and *On Reading Dr. Young's Satires*). As Elias details, the Government, "stung by mockery of the Walpole ministry in On Poetry and the Epistle to a Lady ... retaliated by harassing those responsible with King's Bench prosecutions."[34] Matthew informed on Barber, revealing her possession of the poem, which led to her arrest.[35] Elias suggests that, following the arrest, Barber's publishing delays may also have resulted from "last-minute changes ... writing the Pilkingtons out of" the text.[36]

That breach of trust associated with Pilkington arguably informs the tone with which Barber treats Grierson. Barber's Preface includes a biographical notice of Grierson as well as a syntactically and conceptually complicated passage that explains why Barber's volume includes some of Grierson's poems. Grierson's lines "written in my Commendation," details Barber, "do Honour to the Female Sex in general, as they are a strong Proof that Women may have so much Virtue, as, instead of depreciating, to endeavour to raise the Character of each other."[37] The terms "depreciating" and "raise" implicitly capture the subtle competition between and literary economy of the members of their poetic circle. Grierson's words add value to Barber's poems. "The Poems written in my Favour by Mrs. GRIERSON, will, I think, be allow'd to" evince the potential for women's supportive and collaborative relationships, doing "Honour to the Female Sex in general."[38]

Barber details the intimacy of her "known Friendship" with Grierson, which resulted in her role as the guardian of Grierson's poetic legacy: "To her known Friendship for me, the Reader must attribute the great Partiality she has there shewn; nothing else could have thus bias'd her Judgment: which I am so conscious of, that those Poems should never have appeared in this Collection, but that from her abundant Regard to me, she made me promise, a little before her Death, to publish them upon this Occasion."[39] "[K]nown Friendship" reiterates the public dimension of their relationship. The "great Partiality" Grierson felt for Barber "bias'd her Judgement" enough for her to give Barber her heretofore unpublished poems. The inclusion of Grierson's poems does not mark Barber's esteem for Grierson but rather Grierson's "abundant regard" for Barber. That regard contrasts with the apparent indifference Grierson had for her own poems. "She wrote several fine Poems in *English*," continues Barber, "on which she set so little Value that she neglected to leave Copies behind her but of very few."[40] Grierson, in Barber's telling, was not interested in seeing all her poems published, only those that pay tribute to Barber, what Elias calls "the tribute of true sincerity from a tragic figure." The inclusion of Grierson's poems functions as a mutual form of tribute. Not only does Grierson's request that Barber include her poems suggest her certainty that Barber's volume would in fact be published, but it also subtly diminishes the significance of Grierson's friendship with Laetitia Pilkington and emphasizes Pilkington's dimmer prospects for publication. Grierson entrusted Barber alone with her work. Publishing Grierson's poems distinguished Barber as someone not competitive with her (now dead) friend but, more importantly, actively working to preserve her poetic legacy.

Barber's biography of Grierson (subsequently used almost verbatim by George Colman and Bonnell Thornton in *Poems by Eminent Ladies* [1755]) continues the laudatory tone and functions as a eulogy cum obituary. "[O]ne of the most extraordinary Women that ... this Age ... ever produced," Grierson was an "excellent Scholar," an "Eminence in Learning" she achieved "merely by the Force of her own Genius, and continual Application."[41] By ignoring Grierson's poetic abilities, Barber again avoids any competition between the two women. Indeed, Barber's forecast for Grierson, "if Heaven had spared her Life," is that she would have been a great figure "as any of her Sex are recorded to have done" in "the learned World," not the poetical one.[42] Additionally, Barber specifically describes Grierson as someone fully supportive of other women and envious of no one: "As her Learning and Abilities raised her above her own Sex, so they left her no Room to envy any; On the contrary, her Delight was to see Others excell [sic]." Mutuality and reciprocity shaped their friendship: "She was always ready to advise and direct those who apply'd to her; and as willing to be advis'd."[43] While Barber's tribute doubtless stemmed from her warm personal relationship with Grierson during her lifetime, notably, it also advances her praise of her patron Lord Carteret. As part of Barber's tribute to Grierson, she specifically notes Carteret's own generous act toward Grierson: "when He was Lord Lieutenant of *Ireland*, He obtained a Patent for Mr. Grierson her Husband to be the King's Printer, and to distinguish and reward her uncommon Merit, had her Life inserted in it."[44] Describing this gesture allows Barber to conclude the dedication with a final encomium about Carteret (not Grierson): "It was truly a Nobleman so eminent for Learning and great Abilities, to distinguish those Excellencies wheresoever He found then, as He did remarkably in many Instances during his Administration in *Ireland*."[45]

Grierson's tribute poem to Barber, written January 5, 1732, appears in the Preface separate from Barber's poems in the volume.[46] Its position frames the reader's engagement with Barber's body of work. This poem, written in anticipation of the volume's publication, celebrates the reciprocity and intimacy between the women in which poetry played the central role. As Elias observes, Grierson writes with "an ardent sincerity, an unreserved admiration for special friends" like Barber.[47] Her praise focuses both on Barber and, as the title notes, on her successful search for subscribers; the poem is "Occasion'd by the Encouragement She met with in *England*, to publish her poems by Subscription." Rhetorically, then, Grierson both positions Barber as an appropriate object of charity for her subscribers and, in turn, praises the subscribers' discerning taste and beneficence: "Modesty conceal'd [Barber's works] in Night" until "generous Britons"—the subscribers—brought them "to Light." The use of the term "Britons," like the flagging of "England" in the title, marks the apparent solidarity between the Irish and the British, reinforcing, perhaps, the volume's dedication to an Englishman like Carteret, who served as a colonial governor in Ireland. This unity is underscored earlier by Barber's own pointed gratitude in the dedication for Carteret's "great Goodness" when he "condescended to distinguish me, when I was a Stranger in *England*" and then, subsequently, his "bounteously" "enrich[ing]" her "in *Ireland*, at a Time when my Want of Health made your Generosity the more valuable."[48] In her tribute poem, Grierson casts these "gen'rous Britons" not simply as benefactors, but also as "the Arbiters of Sense": "Long may your Taste, and long your Empire stand, / To Honours, Wit, and Worth, from every Land."[49] Just as Barber's preface simultaneously praises Grierson and Carteret, so too Grierson's tribute poem—while primarily focusing on Barber—also incorporates fulsome praise of the subscribers as well.

In distinguishing Barber, the subscribers have chosen, as Grierson details, a worthy poet. Grierson marks Barber's poetry as distinctly not classical in subject or form. While "the Warrior's and the Lover's Fire" have long "employed the Poet," Barber's verses offer "Far different themes . . . alike sublime, and new / . . . [and] . . . but for Thee, almost unknown to Song." She singles out the originality of Barber's poems; Barber uses her verse to describe social ills and to spur charitable actions (a result the volume's most well-known poem, "The Widow Gordon's Petition," handily achieved). As Backscheider notes, "many women poets recognized the kinds of innovations their friends were making."[50] Her poems strive "to ease those Wants, with which the Wretched pine." The preoccupation with charity within Grierson's poem serves as a lesson to the subscribers themselves, reminding them that they too should enact such a purpose. The accessibility of Barber's poems might also increase the likelihood for their effectiveness. The "wise Reflections" of her "Lays," "Elegant" and "Refin'd" sentiments, appear in simple language: "No florid Toys, in pompous Numbers drest; / But justest Thoughts, in purest stile, exprest." Her poems are "tuneful Labours," a term that perhaps suggests (as Pilkington later does in her *Memoirs*) that Barber's poetic prowess is hard-earned, but that also recognizes the work that goes into literary production.

Barber's personal qualities—her altruism, empathy, and sense of justice—further embellish Grierson's portrait of Barber as a worthy object of charity. She inventories Barber's "silent virtues," although laments that her own "conscious Muse" cannot "fully trace" these admirable qualities:

> How much her Heart, from low Desires refin'd;
> How much her Works, the Transcript of her Mind;
> Her tender Care, and Grief for the Distrest;
> Her Joy unfeign'd, to see true Merit blest;
> Her Soul so form'd for every social Care;
> A Friend so gen'rous, ardent, and sincere.

In reiterating Barber's characteristics, particularly her focus on "the Distrest" and commitment to "social Care," Grierson reinforces altruistic qualities the subscribers should locate in themselves. While Grierson's poem implicitly betrays an awareness of the differences in class, education, and socio-cultural standing between the two women, that, in many ways, only makes Barber a more worthy object of attention. Barber's evident social purpose, her attempt to "imitate Beneficence divine," distinguishes her work from other contemporaneous verse and elevates her within the hierarchy the poem establishes.

The distinction between simple and "florid" verse, and the poetic merits of Barber, shapes another poem that appears in the volume, "Upon my Son's speaking Latin in School to less Advantage than English: Written as from a Schoolfellow." The attribution of this poem bears note. In Barber's 1734 volume, this poem is identified as written "By Mrs. Grierson." Colman and Thornton modify the title of the poem to read "Upon *Mrs. Barber's* Son speaking Latin," to clearly identify Barber's son "Con" as the young man in question, and also attribute the poem to Grierson. Cambridge's *Orlando* database insists that attribution, however, "must be a mistake," although that assertion seems to assume that Grierson is writing about her own son rather than Barber's (a situation the Colman and Thornton modification of the title corrects).[51] Elias's careful examination of Grierson's manuscript book, which includes many of her other poems in draft, does not locate this poem there, perhaps substantiating the assertion in *Orlando*. Bernard Tucker, in his 1992 edition of Barber's poems, omits it.[52] The poem's preoccupation with poets who can (or cannot) write in Latin might have caused the attribution to the classicist Grierson. Regardless of its attribution, the poem demonstrates the dynamic within these feminocentric tribute poems, the relationship between the two women, and the climate in which the women wrote.

The poem ventriloquizes "a schoolfellow" of Barber's son Constantine, "Con," whose deception has been "twice detected" by his now "undeceiv'd

Companions." His stellar "*English* verse," in which "ev'ry Line" has been "echo'd with Applause," are not his own. Rather, "The Muse, thy Mother, only speaks in thee." His inferior Latin verse, which reveals the deception, might have been improved if his mother "In learned Languages had . . . been skill'd." The poem details how Barber's ignorance of classical languages stems from Phoebus's jealousy when he sees each (female) Muse, "with endless Pains, / Forming the curious Texture of her Brains." They are responsible for her "no uncommon Gifts." Yet, when the Muses seek "to inspire / A double Portion of celestial Fire"—that is, to provide Barber with facility in the classical languages—Phoebus, "Grown jealous for the Honour of the Dead" male poets such as Virgil and Ovid, denies her "their universal Tongue." Had she been granted that gift, "Their matchless Fame, thro' *many* Ages won, / (Her Sex might boast) would be in *one* out-done."[53] The poem points to poetic competition between male and female poets (both in the present moment and in posterity), suggesting that perhaps the playing field is not level. Although lavishly praising Barber and her poetic skills, the poem does hinge on the limits of her education and her consequent lack of the "universal tongue." (For some readers within the women's circle, the poem might implicitly have elevated Grierson's absent compositions in Latin above those of Barber's contained within the volume.) Although the two tribute poems specifically point to Barber's more modest education and plain-style poetry, these qualities serve to intensify rather than diminish her achievements. That small detail, born perhaps of Grierson's own sensitivity to classical education, provides a more nuanced context in which to understand this network of poetic exchange.

Like Barber, Pilkington establishes her "long Friendship and Familiarity" with Grierson and consolidates her two tribute poems near the beginning of her *Memoirs*. Directly addressing the publication status of the late poet's work, Pilkington questions "Whether it was . . . her own Desire, or the Envy of those who survived her" that caused the poems to remain private. Pilkington subtly attributes envy to Barber, who is most closely identified as Grierson's poetic executor. "[O]f her various and beautiful Writings," continues Pilkington, "except one Poem of her's in Mrs. Barber's Works; I have never seen any published."[54] (Pilkington ignores the fact that six Grierson poems appear in Barber's volume, not one.) This lack of publication, like the origins of her classical knowledge, remains a lingering mystery surrounding Grierson. Nevertheless, the poems strategically establish the credibility of Pilkington, representing her and Grierson as peers and intimates. Grierson lived with Pilkington's family while apprenticing with her father,

Dr. van Lewen, who "gave her a general invitation to his Table." Grierson and Pilkington were confidantes "seldom asunder." Noting that Grierson's "Piety was not inferior to her Learning," Pilkington observes how her parents were "well pleased with our Intimacy." Grierson's "extraordinary Talents"—"She was Mistress of *Hebrew, Greek, Latin* and *French;* understood the *Mathematicks,* as well as most Men"—distinguish her, her talent both mysterious ("I could never obtain a satisfactory Account from her" on "such great and excellent Acquirements") and nearly divine: "her Learning appeared like the Gift poured out on the Apostles, of speaking all Languages, without the Pains of Study; or, like the intuitive Knowledge of Angels." Pilkington basks in the reflection of Grierson's refinement and elevated knowledge, and insinuates herself into that realm as a near-equal. "The most delightful Hours I ever past [sic]," writes Pilkington, "were in the Conversation of this female Philosopher."[55] This intimacy was not just intellectual, however. Pilkington later remarks that Grierson helped facilitate meetings between her and her then-suitor Matthew at her lodgings, a gesture that simultaneously enhanced their friendship and also, in retrospect, advanced what would be a disastrous marriage.

Although the friendship itself ennobled Pilkington, her poetic relationship with Grierson brought the real currency. Pilkington concedes that the poems "might not be agreeable to the present Taste," since Grierson's "Turn was chiefly to philosophical or divine Subjects." In these poems, Grierson's "heavenly Muse descend[s] from its sublime Height to the easy epistolary Stile, and suit[s] itself to my then gay Disposition." While Pilkington feigns reluctance to share the laudatory poems, "I must also beg Pardon for publishing the Compliments paid to me in them, which I really would omit were it possible," its praise of Pilkington in her youth, as the "Miss Laetitia Van Lewen" to whom the poems are inscribed, is in fact her primary motivation.[56] They provide insight into a vivacious and youthful Miss van Lewen and speak, almost nostalgically, to a more hopeful moment in Pilkington's life. Certainly, Pilkington's reflective positioning of these poems is significant, striving both to best Barber and to capitalize on Grierson's largely unimpeachable reputation.

The two epistolary poems, written from Grierson in Dublin to Pilkington while she was "in a Country-Town at the Assizes Time," construct a refined, educated, and charming Pilkington superior to her rural environs and its people. Grierson imagines Pilkington passing the day "gravely" discussing mundane agrarian issues—"Possets, Poultices, and Waters still'd"—with "some serious Matron," and then dining "with a great Crowd, choice Meat, and little Wit." "[N]ot a Mortal" there has the refinement to appreciate Pilkington: "they'd a Cock or Hare, / To thee in all thy blooming Charms prefer." Pilkington's rarified qualities, as Grierson fashions them, require the stimulation of the city both as a contributor to and recipient of its urban delights and inhabitants. Grierson imagines Pilkington's reaction, "Methinks, I see Displeasure in your Eyes," and establishes herself as the preserver of Pilkington's image, "O my Laetitia, stay no longer there, / You'll soon forget, that you yourself are fair." Without Grierson to reflect her beauty and wit, Pilkington will lose the sense of self reinforced by female relationships. Away from the comfort of her witty writing circle, Pilkington will be surrounded by "Discourse" she must "despise." Grierson likens Pilkington's absence to almost a form of hoarding as she keeps "us, from all that's gay, / There in a lonely Solitude to stay?" Grierson urges her to "O haste to Town! and bless the longing Eyes."[57] Although the poems praise Pilkington's wit generally rather than her poetry specifically, their appearance advances Pilkington's goals in publishing her *Memoirs* to control or reframe the narrative of her life, and, perhaps most important, to repair her reputation to the degree possible.

Pilkington and Grierson's intimacy is also forged by their shared role as editors of Barber's work in a meeting of the so-called "Senatus Consultum . . . frequently held" by Doctor Delaney. Elias describes the Senatus Consultum as "a literary subcommittee . . . meeting by special invitation."[58] The gatherings "at which were present sometimes the Dean (in the Chair), but always Mrs. *Grierson*, Mr. *Pilkington*, the Doctor, and myself," writes Pilkington, were devoted to editing or "correcting" the work of another member. In a letter by Swift published in the prefatory materials of Barber's volume, he characterizes her as someone "ready to take advice, and submit to have her verses corrected, by those who are generally allow'd to be the best judges."[59] Pilkington details the editing or "correcting" of what she describes as the "undigested materials" of Barber, "whose Name at her earnest Request, I omitted in my first Volume" of *Memoirs*. Barber's poems, "dull as they were, they certainly would have been much worse" without the group's efforts. The description of the Barber editing session positions Pilkington as the editor, one of the "Best judges" to which Swift refers.[60] To reiterate her superior, indeed exclusive, status, she includes a poem by Patrick Delany summoning the group to the Barber edition session: "One Day that he had appointed for this Purpose, we received from him the following Lines, which, as they contain a Compliment to me, from so eminent a Hand, I must insert."

> ... a solemn Senatus I call,
> To consult for Saphira, so come one and all;
> Quit Books, and quit Business, your Cure and your Care,
> For a long winding Walk, and a short Bill of Fare.
> I've Mutton for you, Sir; and as for the Ladies,
> As Friend Virgil has it, I've Aliud Mercedes;
> For Letty, one Filbert, whereon to regale,
> And a Peach for pale Constance, to make a full Meal ...
>
> We obeyed the Summons, and had a very elegant Entertainment; and afterwards proceeded to our Business, which we completed, to the Satisfaction of all Parties.[61]

This poem is interesting within the context of the *Memoirs* because it simultaneously lauds Laetitia—Wit should flow "to her Honour" and "Wine to her Health"—while Barber or "Saphira" is the one whose poetry must be improved. That Grierson and Pilkington figure as invitees to the Senatus Consultum not only places them on a par with each other (and the men in the group), but also completely excludes Barber.

Barber remains unredeemable for Pilkington throughout the *Memoirs*, evidence of what Elias describes as her "power to repay old injuries through the *Memoirs*."[62] By the time Pilkington published her *Memoirs*, Barber, like Pilkington, had also experienced what Adam Budd characterizes as "financial collapse and social regression."[63] In 1737, Barber's patron Lord Orrery expressed concern that "melancholy and languor" had "got possession" of her "heart and head." He described her as a "drooping Muse," lamenting that "her illness is even beyond the Power of Apollo."[64] Yet the intensity of Pilkington's description of Barber suggests that she still harbored some competitive feelings (or memories) toward Barber, despite the latter's relative obscurity. Pilkington questions the marketability of Barber's "Volume of Poems, some of which I fancy might, at this Day, be seen in the Cheesemongers, Chandlers, Pastry-cooks, and Second-hand Booksellers Shops."

The tributes among Barber, Grierson, and Pilkington reveal their complicated relationship and make visible their feminocentric network of poetic exchange. They seriously engaged each other's work as evidenced by narrative and poetic commentary. The alternately collaborative and competitive exchanges clearly fueled their compositions even as the material reality of their lived existence might have limited the movement from manuscript to print. An unpublished tribute poem of Grierson's found in her manuscript book most powerfully captures the intense passions of these relationships. A fragment addressed to an unnamed female recipient, "Illustrious Fair," anticipates a work "designd / To free you from the Oppression of mankind." The Muses, "ye harmonious Nine," inspire "mortal breasts with Godlike thoughts" specifically "To show th extensive powrs of Womans Mind." For Grierson, women's poetry, by her or her peers, begets more insight into women's condition, potentially "freeing" them from their oppressive state. More importantly, she engages the Muses as sisters, friends, members of a widening circle of women "Whom are Learning Wit and Arts assignd." In her construction, the "power of a woman's Mind" has no limits. Thus, she "who praises Women does the Muse praise," for women ultimately act as each other's inspiration.[65]

Notes

1. Mary Barber, *Poems on Several Occasions* (London, 1734), xlvi. The volume is dated 1734, but as A.C. Elias makes clear it did not appear until 1735. "Editing Minor Writers: The Case of Laetitia Pilkington and Mary Barber," *1650–1850: Ideas, Aesthetics, and Inquires in the Early Modern Era*, vol. 3, ed. Kevin Cope (New York: AMS, 1997), 129–47.

2. Laetitia Pilkington, *Memoirs of Laetitia Pilkington*, ed. A. C. Elias, Jr. (Athens: The University of Georgia Press, 1997), 19.

3. The group has often been considered primarily in relation with Jonathan Swift. The women were variously characterized as Swift's "original seraglio" by Lord Orrery (John Boyle, fifth Earl of Cork and Orrery, *Remarks on the Life and Writings of Dr. Jonathan Swift*, ed. João Fróes [Newark: University of Delaware Press, 2000], 168) or as a "female triumfeminate" by Swift himself. However, as Pilkington's biographer A. C. Elias notes, "not everything in their circle centred around Swift and his known preoccupations," as these poems make clear ("A Manuscript Book of Constantia Grierson's," *Swift Studies* 2 [1987]: 51). For a discussion of this group, see Paula Backscheider, "Inverting the Image of Swift's 'Triumfeminate,'" *Journal for Early Modern Cultural Studies* (2004): 37–71.

4. Five of Grierson's poems appear in Barber's 1734 *Poems on Various Subjects* and two appear in Pilkington's *Memoirs* (1747).

5. Swift to Pope, May 2, 1730, *The Correspondence of Alexander Pope*, ed. George Sherburn, Vol. III: 1729–1735 (Oxford: Clarendon Press, 1956), 107.

6. Swift to Alexander Pope, February 6, 1729, *The Correspondence of Jonathan Swift, Volume III 1724–1731*, ed. Harold Williams (Oxford: Clarendon Press, 1963), 369.

7. A. C. Elias, "A Manuscript Book of Constantia Grierson's," 54.

8. Ibid.

9. Ibid., 40.

10. *Journals*, House of Commons, Kingdom of Ireland, III, quoted in A. C. Elias, "A Manuscript Book of Constantia Grierson's," 40, n. 15.

11. Barber, *Poems*, xxviii.

12. Jonathan Swift to Alexander Pope, July 20, 1731, *The Correspondence of Alexander Pope*, III.208.

13. Swift to Pope, May 2, 1730. Ibid., III.107.

14. Dr. Patrick Delany to Mrs. Clayton, February 27 [1731?], in Mary Delany, *The Autobiography and Correspondence of Mary Granville, Mrs. Delany*, Vol. 1 (London: Richard Bentley, 1861), 321.

15. Barber, "Occasioned by Reading Memoirs of Anne of Austria," *Poems*, 75.

16. Mrs. Pendarves to Mrs. Ann Granville, October 9, 1731, in Mary Delany, *The Autobiography and Correspondence*, 301.

17. Swift to Lord Bathurst, October 1730, *The Correspondence of Jonathan Swift*, 411–12.

18. Pilkington, *Memoirs*, 18.

19. John Carteret Pilkington, *The real story of John Carteret Pilkington, Written by Himself* (London: 1760), 5–6.

20. Elias, "A Manuscript Book of Constantia Grierson's," 51.

21. Backscheider, "Triumfeminate," 44, 38.

22. Pilkington, *Memoirs*, 393.

23. Myra Reynolds, *The Learned Lady in England 1650–1760* (New York: Houghton Mifflin Co, 1920), 321.

24. Pilkington, *Memoirs*, 699.

25. Ibid., 26.

26. Ibid, 282.

27. Swift, *Correspondence*, 3.457

28. Adam Budd, "'Merit in Distress': The Troubled Success of Mary Barber," *Review of English Studies* 53, no. 210 (2002), 205. Budd's fine article details Barber's publication history and the implications of her subscription list. Also useful is Christopher Fanning, "The Voices of the Dependent Poet: The Case of Mary Barber," *Women's Writing* 8, no. 1 (2001): 81–97.

29. Pilkington, *Memoirs*, 13, 56.

30. Pilkington supported herself within London's active print culture variously running a book shop and writing poems for other people to present as their own, before publishing her *Memoirs*. "I was now full of Poetical Business," writes Pilkington, "by which my Poverty was relieved, and my Mind amused" (101).

31. Prior to publishing her *Memoirs*, Pilkington initially circulated a proposal to publish a volume of her own poetry. Her volume of poems was never published due to under-subscription and, perhaps, the carelessness of her daughter. Pilkington laments losing half of her poems in manuscript due to "the Ignorance of [her] Daughter," who took "a whole Bundle . . . to enliven" the fire and thus burned "half of [her] Writings" (225).

32. Colley Cibber to Laetitia Pilkington, January 29, 1747, *The Orrery Papers*, vol. 1, ed. the Countess of Cork and Orrery (London, Duckworth and Company, 1903), 316.

33. Barber, *Poems*, xxv.

34. Pilkington, *Memoirs*, 441.

35. Budd details the situation surrounding this arrest in "Merit in Distress."

36. Pilkington, *Memoirs*, 674.

37. Barber, *Poems*, xxvi–xxvii.

38. Ibid., xxvi.

39. Ibid.

40. Ibid., xxviii. *Orlando: Women's Writing in the British Isles from the Beginnings to the Present* (Cambridge: Cambridge University Press Online, 2006) notes that "Barber originates the belief" that Grierson "valued her English poems so little that she did not preserve them," http://orlando.cambridge.org/, accessed December 18, 2015.

41. Barber, *Poems*, xxvii, xxviii.

42. Ibid., xxix.

43. Ibid.

44. Ibid., xxx.

45. Ibid.

46. The poem was subsequently published in the *Gentleman's Magazine* after Barber's volume appeared. The title in the *Gentleman's Magazine* adds "which are now printed" to the end of the title. *Gentleman's Magazine* Vol. 5, August 1735, 492.

47. Elias, "A Manuscript Book of Constantia Grierson's," 44.

48. Barber, *Poems*, xiv.

49. Ibid., xlvii.

50. Backscheider, "Triufeminate," 43.

51. The entry in *Orlando* reads: "The boy in the poem is named Con (as was the one of Barber's sons who figures most frequently in her poetry), and the praise of Grierson is not such as she could have written herself." Susan Brown, Patricia Clements, and Isobel Grundy, eds., Constantia Grierson: Writing entry within *Orlando: Women's Writing in the British Isles from the Beginnings to the Present*, http://orlando.cambridge.org.

52. Bernard Tucker, *The Poetry of Mary Barber* (Lewiston, NY: Edwin Mellen Press, 1992).

53. Barber, *Poems*, 90.

54. Pilkington, *Memoirs*, 18.

55. Ibid., 17–18.

56. Ibid., 18.

57. The other, untitled poem that immediately follows, serves to praise not only Pilkington but also the charms of Matthew. The final stanza speaks directly of Matthew "the lovely *Damon*" who "languishes and dies" for Laetitia. Yet, as Paula Backscheider notes, "the real rivalry" the poem describes is between suitors and Grierson. The poem focuses "attention on lively, social life, thereby obscuring the intimacy lying just beneath the surface." Paula R. Backscheider, *Eighteenth-Century Women Poets and their Poetry: Inventing Agency, Inventing Genre* (Baltimore: Johns Hopkins University Press, 2005), 189. For a fuller discussion of the friendship poem and women writers, see chapter 5.

58. Pilkington, *Memoirs*, 674.

59. Barber, *Poems*, vii.

60. Elias reminds us that, "considering the deference which Matthew shows Mrs. Barber in his book, it is at least as likely that she helped to lick the Pilkingtons' verse into shape as the other way around" (Pilkington, *Memoirs*, 674), something Pilkington elides.

61. Pilkington, *Memoirs*, 283. For a fuller discussion of this group, see A. C. Elias, "Senatus Consultum: Revising Verse in Swift's Dublin Circle, 1729–1735," in *Reading*

Swift: Papers from the Third Münster Symposium on Jonathan Swift, eds. Hermann J. Real and Helgard Stover-Leidig (Munich: Wilhelm Fink Verlag, 1998): 250–67.

62. Pilkington, *Memoirs*, xxx.
63. Budd, "Merit in Distress," 209.
64. Lord Orrery to Ann Donallan, May 7, 1737, *Orrery Papers*, 223.
65. Elias, "A Manuscript Book of Constantia Grierson's," 48.

"Friendship, Better than a Muse, Inspires"

Anna Letitia Barbauld Claims the Sister Arts for Female Friendship

LAURA TALLON

In her verse epistle "To Mrs. P[riestley], with some Drawings of Birds and Insects" (written c. 1767, published in 1773), the poet Anna Letitia Barbauld (1743–1825) announces her participation in two related traditions: the competition between the sister arts and the discourse of same-sex friendship. Founded in sociability, these two discourses informed each other: eighteenth-century poets imagined poetry and painting as "sisters" and often staged friendly contests between the arts through the amicable genre of the verse epistle.[1] John Dryden's "To Sir Godfrey Kneller" (1694) and Alexander Pope's "Epistle to Mr. Jervas with *Dryden*'s Translation of *Fresnoy*'s *Art of Painting*" (1716) established a rhetorical pattern that was imitated by a range of poets from William Collins and Thomas Gray to Anna Barbauld and Anna Seward.[2]

In "To Sir Godfrey Kneller," Dryden's attitude toward painting is colored by professional jealousy. During his time as Poet Laureate, Dryden witnessed court painters attaining greater commercial success and he therefore asserts poetry's superiority throughout the poem.[3] According to James Winn, Dryden's works of the 1690s, including this poem to Kneller, "display considerable practical and theoretical knowledge about the visual arts, but betray his fear that the increasing prestige of painting might diminish the importance of his own art."[4] One of the primary ways that Dryden registers his disapproval of visual art encroaching professionally on poetry is by feminizing painting. From presenting painting as a beautiful but silent woman (1–6) and mocking the postlapsarian cosmetic activity of Eve (91–92) to complaining that "the Painter Muse; though last in place / Has seiz'd the Blessing first, like Jacob's Race" (95–96), Dryden repeatedly suggests the "sense of painting as female, illegitimate, and unjustly profitable."[5]

Although Alexander Pope's portrayal of painting is less critical, his "Epistle to Mr. Jervas, With *Dryden*'s Translation of *Fresnoy*'s *Art of Painting*" also relies on gendered divisions to depict the sister arts. Pope uses the sister arts as a way of linking himself and Jervas to the prestigious reputations of their male predecessors, Dryden and Fresnoy. Pope hopes that in reading Fresnoy's *Art of Painting*, translated by Dryden, Jervas will "wish" his and Pope's "fate and fame" to "shine thro' long succeeding age" (8–11). The muses of the sister arts act as a conduit between the poet and painter, affirming their friendship:

> Smit with the love of Sister-arts we came,
> And met congenial, mingling flame with flame;
> Like friendly colours found them both unite,
> And each from each contract new strength and light. (13–16)

By portraying himself and Jervas as "Smit with the love of Sister-arts," Pope depicts a sexualized dynamic between male artists and female arts. For poets in the period, as Winn has shown, "references to the 'sister arts', a metaphor derived from the nine muses of ancient lore, were commonplace: male artists often described themselves as courting the muses, though at other times, especially in dramatic prologues, they used 'the muse' or 'my muse' as a fairly straightforward form of self-reference, thus temporarily imagining some part of their creativity as female."[6] Through this shared creativity, figured as their shared love of personified "Sister-arts," the two male figures connect more powerfully, Pope imagines. In other words, Pope posits a heterosexual relationship between artist and muse that reinforces the homosocial bond between the male poet and male painter.

The model established by Dryden and Pope presents a particular challenge to female poets because it constructs an aesthetic hierarchy for the arts in which poetry is masculinized and painting feminized, and assumes that the poets and artists are male while the muses and objects of representation are female. By consciously adapting some of the language from Pope's epistle, Barbauld signals her revision of the gendered dynamics of this tradition. At the same time, she also borrows language and imagery from her female poetic predecessors: specifically, drawing on Katherine Philips's declarations of female friendship, Anne Killigrew's practice of writing ekphrastic poetry about her own artwork, and Anne Finch's imagery of dark retreats that foster female creativity. With these echoes of other pictorial poets, Barbauld situates her own exploration of the arts within a rich intertextual poetic tradition that includes both male and female poets. Scholarship on the sister arts has not yet fully explored the contributions of eighteenth-century female poets; by attending to Barbauld's poem, we may gain a better understanding of the literary history of this tradition as well as its gendered conventions.[7]

In this essay, I argue that Barbauld calls upon the "kindred arts" in order to pay tribute to her friend, Mary Priestley, and that she responds to the male-oriented conventions of this tradition in three major ways. First, Barbauld recognizes that the integral artistic process in Pope's poem—that poets and painters achieve fame through their shared relationship with the muses—is unsuitable for her. She therefore replaces the sexualized dynamic between the male poet and female muse with the inspirational bond achieved through female friendship, proclaiming that "friendship, better than a Muse inspires." Second, Barbauld claims both arts for herself. Unlike Dryden and Pope, who join their poetic ability to a painter's visual artistry, Barbauld writes poetry about her own drawings, a practice that grounds her aesthetic evaluation of the relationship between literature and visual art in first-hand experience. Third, Barbauld's ekphrasis—her description of her drawings of birds, insects, and flowers—contains a subtext of protest against the conventions that relegate women to the position of objects rather than artists. With this gift to Mary Priestley that combines image and text, Barbauld seeks at once to privately affirm her social bonds with a particular female friend and to publicly demonstrate her participation within the artistic contest of the sister arts.

Barbauld addresses this tribute to her friend and fellow dissenter Mary Priestley, wife of Joseph Priestley, a famous theologian, political writer, and natural philosopher. Barbauld first encountered the Priestleys at Warrington Academy, where Barbauld's father John Aikin and Joseph Priestley both taught.[8] Barbauld respected the couple and drew inspiration from her relationship with them; she wrote over a dozen poems in response to this friendship.[9] Mary Priestley was one of Barbauld's first close female friends. According to Barbauld's biographer William McCarthy, she "came to venerate [Mary] and called her, poetically, 'Amanda' (from the Latin meaning 'beloved'); she inscribed a silhouette of Mary with the motto, 'Grace was in all her steps.'"[10] Barbauld composed one of her first poems for Priestley, "On Mrs. P[riestley]'s Leaving Warrington," and threw it into her departing carriage. Another poem dedicated to this friendship, "To Mrs. P[riestley], with some Drawings of Birds and Insects," simultaneously offers a personal tribute to a close friend and a public declaration of Barbauld's participation in the sister arts.

By presenting her poem and drawings to Priestley, Barbauld figures her artistic production as a gift, a common convention in the sister arts. Dryden's "To Sir Godfrey Kneller," for example, is as an extended thank-you note for Kneller's gift of a portrait of Shakespeare. In fact, critics have suggested that Barbauld considered her poetic practice in terms of gift-giving more generally.[11] Susan Rosenbaum argues that "Barbauld develops a lyric aesthetic based on the miniature object" and presents many of her poems as gifts. "In this manner," Rosenbaum explains, "Barbauld defines her poetic labor as the consolidation of private, moral community, exploiting the association of women's writing with feminine handicrafts to distinguish her works from those sold for profit."[12] Though Rosenbaum does not discuss "To Mrs. P[riestley]," we can see a similar strategy at work in it: Barbauld appends her verses to her own drawings, thus crafting a multimedia gift to honor her friendship and to foster a "private, moral community" that includes the Priestleys.

In her essay in this volume, Shelley King shows how Opie crafts "verses that focus on an object related to some aspect of female friendship and that function either as supplements to memories of friendship or as accompaniments to gifts designed to evoke a strengthened sense of memory and connection."[13] By analyzing Opie's poetic treatment of a range of material objects—from poems focused on portraits painted by her husband John Opie of her friend Frances Kemble Twiss to private birthday poems for Elizabeth Lemaistre that accompanied such gifts as a brooch, almanac, or ivory box—King demonstrates how Opie celebrated her close female friendships in both the public and private spheres. In a similar manner, Barbauld's poem, figured as a gift, both fostered a private social connection and, after its publication in her *Poems* of 1773, provided a powerful public testament to women's creative talent and friendship within the tradition of the sister arts.

Barbauld's combined approach—at once offering her poem as a private gift to Priestley and as a public announcement of her participation in the sister arts—is deftly captured by her epigraph, in which she adapts two lines from Pope's "Epistle to Mr. Jervas." His lines read, "The kindred arts shall in their praise conspire, / One dip the pencil, and one string the lyre" (with "their" referring to various female "graces").[14] Barbauld rewrites these lines as "The kindred arts *to please thee* shall conspire, / One dip the pencil, and one string the lyre."[15] From the very beginning, her revision personalizes the aim of the "kindred arts," and calls upon them in order to offer a tribute to a specific friend. As this epigraph indicates, Barbauld consciously revises the model established by Dryden and Pope in order to celebrate female artistic talent and friendship throughout her poem.

For Barbauld and other female poets, the convention of poets courting their muses presents a challenge: they must decide how to relate to this personification of inspiration that shares their gender. Jennifer Keith has shown how Katherine Philips addresses specific female friends as muses.[16] Employing a similar strategy, Barbauld replaces the sexualized dynamic between the male poet and female muse with the inspirational bond achieved through female friendship. Her verse epistle opens:

> Amanda bids; at her command again
> I seize the pencil, or resume the pen;
> No other call my willing hand requires,
> And friendship, better than a Muse inspires. (1–4)

When she proclaims that "friendship, better than a Muse inspires," Barbauld dismisses the abstract muse and elevates a specific female friend to occupy her place. Like Philips, Barbauld denounces the assumption that friendships between women are inferior to those between men: in a letter to "Miss E. Belsham, afterwards Mrs. Kenrick" (1771), she writes: "It is not true, what Dr. Fordyce insinuates, that women's friendships are not sincere; I am sure it is not: I remember when I read it I had a good mind to have burnt the book for that unkind passage."[17] As her desire to incinerate *Sermons for Young Women* humorously emphasizes, Barbauld objects to the trivializing and denigrating of women's friendships. More seriously, in her poetic practice, she celebrates female friendship as the highest source of poetic and artistic inspiration.

Barbauld also addresses the "fate and fame" that Pope hopes he and Jervas may achieve through their participation in a network of artistic exchanges. In the final verse paragraph, she distinguishes between the pursuit of fame by some poets and her own desire to honor female friendship:

> Thy friend thus strives to cheat the lonely hour,
> With song, or paint, an insect, or a flower:
> Yet if Amanda praise the flowing line,
> And bend delighted o'er the gay design,
> I envy not, nor emulate the fame
> Or of the painter's, or the poet's name:
> Could I to both with equal claim pretend,
> Yet far, far dearer were the name of FRIEND. (121–28)

"FRIENDSHIP, BETTER THAN A MUSE, INSPIRES"

In this verse (composed before her writing made her famous), Barbauld states that even though she may not achieve the "fame" of the poet and painter, she can still participate in the sister arts. In fact, by treating "friend" as a third but superior category to "painter" or "poet," she defies the limited terms of this contest. Since Philips, women poets had claimed the discourse of same-sex friendship; here, by placing the word "friend" in the climactic position of the poem, Barbauld uses her tribute simultaneously to affirm her friendship with Priestley and declare female friendship a worthy source of inspiration for the renowned sister arts.

The humble tone that closes the poem, with the speaker professing to be satisfied by Priestley's delight and friendship instead of desiring "fame," has led one critic to read the framing addresses to Priestley as examples of "feminine grace and sisterly amiability" that are at odds with "the masculine interest in politics and rivalry at the heart of the poem."[18] According to Michele Martinez, "in a form of *paragone*, Barbauld challenges her friend's pencil with a fanciful description of insect wings. Yet Barbauld's bold speaker retreats into feminine decorum at the poem's conclusion, disowning the name of poet and finding contentment in female friendship."[19] This portrayal of Barbauld's inhibition relies, however, on a misreading of artistic practice in the poem. As the final verse paragraph emphasizes, Barbauld presents herself as the wielder of *both* the pencil and the pen. She hopes that Priestley will be pleased by both her "flowing line" and her "gay design" (123–24). That she claims both visual art and poetry for herself is, in fact, integral to an understanding of her bold contribution to the tradition of the sister arts.

At the opening of the poem, Barbauld confidently demonstrates her equal claim to both arts with a caesura that represents the moment of choice in which she can take up either the paintbrush or the pen: "I seize the pencil, or resume the pen" (2). Unlike Dryden and Pope, who liken their verses to the paintings of Kneller and Jervas, Barbauld practices both arts herself. Rather than reading her interest in the "rivalry" between the arts as "masculine" and separate from her dedication to "feminine grace and sisterly amiability," then, I suggest that we examine how Barbauld weaves the two together. Practicing both arts, she proclaims female talent within the contest of the sister arts and simultaneously celebrates inspirational female friendship.

Barbauld's dual talent in poetry and drawing bolsters her aesthetic authority as she explores the boundaries between visual composition and verbal expression. As she offers her own sophisticated evaluation of the competing arts, her balanced syntax catalogues the qualities of each:

> Painting and poetry are near allied;
> The kindred arts two sister Muses guide;
> This charms the eye, that steals upon the ear;
> There sounds are tun'd; and colours blended here:
> This with a silent touch enchants our eyes,
> And bids a gayer brighter world arise:
> That, less allied to sense, with deeper art
> Can pierce the close recesses of the heart;
> By well set syllables, and potent sound,
> Can rouse, can chill the breast, can sooth, can wound;
> To life adds motion, and to beauty soul,
> And breathes a spirit through the finish'd whole:
> Each perfects each, in friendly union join'd;
> This gives Amanda form, and that her mind. (5–18)

While at first the treatment of painting and poetry appears to be equitable ("eye" is balanced by "ear," and "colours" matched by "sounds"), Barbauld ultimately presents poetry as the "deeper art" because it penetrates beyond sensory perception into the "close recesses of the heart." With her focus on how language and visual art affect consciousness, she may have been drawing on Locke's "location of selfhood in consciousness," as Kathryn Ready has shown.[20] In fact, many of her comments reveal her familiarity with the discourse of the competing arts: she reproduces the common characterization of painting as primarily spatial and poetry as primarily temporal.[21]

Though Barbauld reiterates some of the standard commentary, she also turns the traditional gendering of the arts as feminine into an advantage. After offering a fairly typical assessment of the competing arts, she then relates them directly to Priestley: "Each perfects each, in friendly union join'd; / This gives Amanda's form, and that her mind" (17–18). Here, Barbauld repeats the common claim that painting better represents physical appearance, while poetry better represents internal thought or character, but her description of the two arts "perfect[ing]" each other "in friendly union join'd" simultaneously compares the relationship between the arts to her own friendship with Priestley. By describing painting and poetry "in friendly union join'd," Barbauld evokes the diction of marriage, a convention frequently employed in the poetry of same-sex friendship and exemplified in the poetry of Katherine Philips.[22]

In these moments, Barbauld merges language from the discourse of same-sex friendship with her aesthetic evaluation of the arts. In another example, when she describes painting and poetry as "near allied," she alludes to Dryden's celebration of friendship in his poem on the death of Oldham: "For sure our Souls were near ally'd; and thine / Cast in the same Poetic mould with mine."[23] By evoking the language of same-sex friendship from Philips, Dryden, and Pope, Barbauld forges a connection between the imagined sister arts and the reality of sisterly friendships. In response to a tradition that presents the bond between male artists and female arts, Barbauld capitalizes on the feminization of the arts, likening her own relationship with Priestley to the ideal relationship between the metaphorical sister arts. In "Painting in Bright Characters: Helen Maria Williams's Poetic Tributes to Anna Seward, Elizabeth Montagu, and Marie-Jeanne Roland," in this volume, Natasha Duquette examines how "Williams boldly presents the enduring strength of female friendship as sublime and thus challenges Edmund Burke's relegation of sociability to the weakness of a feminine beauty subordinated to masculine sublimity."[24] In a similar way to how Williams seizes on the typically masculinized category of the sublime to celebrate female friendship, Barbauld too defies the typical gendering of aesthetic categories that masculinize the agency of artistic creation and feminize the passive objects of representation.

Framed by addresses to Priestley, the center of the verse epistle contains an elaborate description of the drawings of birds and insects that accompanied the poem.[25] This structure closely resembles another poem by Barbauld, "To a Lady, with some painted flowers," which Theresa Kelley suspects may also have been addressed to Priestley.[26] In these two gifts to Priestley that combine image and text, Barbauld draws on the conventions of natural history and botanic drawings in order to celebrate friendship. Charlotte Smith employs a similar strategy in sonnets such as "Sent to the Honorable Mrs. O'Neill, with painted flowers" and "To Dr. Parry of Bath, with some botanic drawings which had been made some years." Ann Bermingham has shown that many women, both amateurs and professionals, participated in flower drawing and painting during this period. "Because it was seen as an appropriate feminine pastime," Bermingham explains, "flower painting and drawing allowed women a certain liberty to pursue it with seriousness and something like real professionalism."[27]

Though many famous naturalists and botanists were men, eighteenth-century women like Barbauld, who practiced amateur flower painting, demonstrated a similar interest in the intersection between scientific and aesthetic representations of plants and flowers. With an impressive level of precision and artistic skill, Mary Delany created nearly a thousand "paper mosaics" of flowers and plants. In their analysis of Delany's work, the essays in *Mrs. Delany and Her Circle* "portray science and art as complementary forms of endeavor within the spectrum of female accomplishment."[28] In this way, Barbauld's practice resembles that in Delany's earlier work: both combine the role of natural historian and botanical artist, while also strongly supporting female sociability and friendship. Barbauld would also have been aware of well-known professional female flower painters, who exhibited and published their work. Mary Moser, for example, was admitted to the Royal Academy and "was eventually appointed Flower Painter to the Queen."[29] Bermingham suggests that "because it was so closely associated with women, flower painting legitimated women's artistic endeavors, and so gave women a kind of cultural agency and, finally, authority."[30] Barbauld may have drawn inspiration from an exhibition of the work of the flower and insect painter Maria Sibylla Merian, on display at the British Museum at the time.[31]

Because of the long tradition of women being represented or symbolized by flowers, female writers and amateur artists developed various methods for handling the commonly feminine connotation of floral imagery. In *Clandestine Marriage: Botany and Romantic Culture*, Theresa Kelley identifies Barbauld as one of several female figures who "sidestepped the iconographic tradition that rendered women as passive flowers in need of care" and "deflect[ed] normative accounts of how women could be identified with plants, in part by creating botanical figures instead of themselves becoming such figures."[32] In "To a Lady, with some painted flowers," Barbauld compares her friend to the drawn flowers, "Emblems of innocence, and beauty too" (4). In *A Vindication of the Rights of Woman*, Mary Wollstonecraft famously lambasted Barbauld's "To a Lady" for glorifying feminine weakness and the desire to please. Of Barbauld's comparison of women to flowers, Wollstonecraft writes, "This has ever been the language of men, and the fear of departing from a supposed sexual character, has made even women of superior sense adopt the same sentiments."[33]

In her "counterreading" of the poem, however, Theresa Kelley suggests that Wollstonecraft was missing the subtle subtext that Priestley would have picked up on in Barbauld's lines. With the poem, Barbauld includes an epigraph from Virgil's *Eclogue* that translates to "See, for you the Nymphs bring lilies in heaped-up baskets."[34] Kelley explains that Barbauld and Priestley would have recognized the significance of lilies: "in the Gospel of Matthew, it is of course the lilies of the field that neither reap nor sow," and in Rousseau's *Lettres élémentaires*, lilies are notably part of an "extended family" of related flowers and household plants.[35] When Barbauld figures the flowers in the poem as part of a "soft family" (13), then, she may be offering a "riddle" addressed specifically to Priestley that refers to the extended social network of dissenting academics and family members at Warrington Academy.[36] Read in this manner, with attention to the symbolic significance of botanical detail, Barbauld's poem subtly criticizes the masculinized imperialist impulse of the "sheltering oak" and the "yew" that "repels invading foes, / And the tall pine for future navies grows" (9–11), in order to instead offer a strong tribute to peaceful female friendship represented by the lilies.

In "To Mrs. P[riestley], with some Drawings of Birds and Insects," I suggest, Barbauld addresses another tribute to Priestley that challenges gendered aesthetic conventions with its encoded description of the depicted scene. Previous scholarship, particularly on "To a Mouse," provides a strong precedent for reading Barbauld's descriptions of animals as allegories for the human condition or as social critiques.[37] In this ekphrasis, I suggest, Barbauld differentiates between songbirds, which represent poetic or artistic creators, and insects, which stand for the objects of representation. Just as insects are literally the natural prey of birds who "cleave the crumbling bark for insect food" (23), insects as objects of representation are figuratively vulnerable to the artists that construct them. Through her use of a clever pun on nymphs as both insects and damsels, Barbauld critiques the typical dynamic in which women are relegated to the position of objects rather than agents of creativity and representation. As poet and artist, she associates herself with the "feather'd tribe" (20), and subtly criticizes the artistic conventions that portray femininity as beautiful, sensual, and aimless.

When she describes her own visual art in verse, Barbauld resembles Anne Killigrew, who wrote ekphrastic poetry about her own paintings almost a century earlier.[38] With her dual talent in poetry and painting, Killigrew would have offered a model for female achievement in the sister arts. Although Barbauld may not have read *Poems by Mrs Anne Killigrew* (1686), the volume of Killigrew's poetry published posthumously and never reprinted, she would have seen Killigrew's poems in the popular mid-century *Poems by Eminent Ladies* (1755).[39] In fact, Barbauld herself was included in the later edition of this collection, *Poems by the Most Eminent Ladies of Great-Britain and Ireland* (1780). Integral to Killigrew's legacy, John Dryden's elegy "To the Pious Memory of the Accomplisht Young LADY Mrs Anne Killigrew, Excellent in the two Sister-Arts of Poesie, and Painting" presents Killigrew as a talented practitioner of the sister arts, at one point representing her as a poetic conqueror invading the realm of painting.[40]

With a similar emphasis on martial metaphors, Barbauld first offers vaguely political descriptions of an eagle and pheasant in her ekphrasis. Resonating with Thomas Gray's "Theban eagle" "Sailing with supreme dominion / Through the azure deep of air,"[41] Barbauld's eagle is characterized primarily by his keen predatory visual power: "Thro' the wide waste of air he darts his sight" and "marks his destin'd victim" with a "cruel eye" (37–40). With a nod to Pope's pheasant in *Windsor-Forest,* Barbauld then describes a "silver" pheasant with "his purple crest" as a "beauteous captive . . . oppress'd by bondage, and our chilly spring" (47–54). By writing about the birds in this manner, Daniel Watkins explains, Barbauld "is able to think imaginatively about nations and violence and imperialism—about human experience—without becoming too weighed down by historical specificity, for which she would be obliged to account."[42] In her section on "the proud giant of the beetle race," who "O'er many an inch extends his wide domain" (113, 119), Barbauld "swerves into mock-heroic," according to Isobel Grundy, "combining the technique of Dryden's *MacFlecknoe* ('Through all the Realms of *Non-sense,* absolute') with an echo of Johnson's *Vanity of Human Wishes:* 'O'er love, o'er fear, extends his wide Domain.'"[43] From her explicit appropriation of an epigraph from Pope to her much more subtle echoes of the language and imagery of Dryden, Philips, Finch, Johnson, Gray, and others, Barbauld demonstrates her interaction with a rich Augustan tradition through her ekphrastic practice.

While the contrast between the eagle and the pheasant vaguely suggests a political focus, the contrast between the songbirds and the insects instead allegorizes the gendered conventions of artistic representation.[44] Unlike the eagle and the pheasant, which are referred to with male pronouns, the songbirds appear collectively without any explicit gender references.

> To claim the verse, unnumber'd tribes appear
> That swell the music of the vernal year
> Seiz'd with the spirit of the kindly May
> They sleek the glossy wing, and tune the lay. (55–58)

Claiming "the verse" and tuning "the lay" (a word that denotes both "a short lyric or narrative poem intended to be sung" and "the song of birds" in the eighteenth century[45]), the songbirds embody poetic qualities. When winter arrives, the songbirds "Pursue the circling sun's indulgent ray, / Course the swift seasons, and o'ertake the day" (71–72). Pursuing the sun, which is classically associated with Apollo, the god of poetry, "the songbirds take on the identity of poets following the prophetic spirit of the sun," as Watkins explains.[46]

Barbauld offers a rich sensory description of the poetic songbirds and a heightened sense of their natural freedom, as they fly off into the horizon.

Earlier, at the opening of the third verse paragraph, Barbauld reveals her own identification with the poetic "tribe" of songbirds. After her introduction to the competition between the arts, she writes, "But humbler themes my artless hand requires, / Nor higher than *the feather'd tribe* aspires" (19–20; emphasis mine). The first line of this couplet has led some critics to read Barbauld's speaker as self-effacing.[47] Barbauld's suggestion that the "unnumber'd tribes" of songbirds metaphorically represent poets in the ekphrastic section reveals a more sly and paradoxical construction at work within this couplet. Rather than voicing a sincere expression of Barbauld's diffidence, the first line can instead be read as a humility topos, which Barbauld immediately undercuts by linking her artistic ambition to the flight of (poetic) birds in the following line.

The transition from the poetic songbirds that chase the sun and "o'ertake the day" to "Not so the Insect race" immediately signals the contrast Barbauld intends to draw between the two groups. Her pictorial description of "the Insect race" does not easily align with one art over another. Instead, Barbauld's emphasis on the limitations placed on these insects, despite their creative aspirations, begins to sound eerily like a metaphor for women. Like the songbirds, the insects are described collectively, without any explicit gender identification at first:

> Not so the Insect race, ordain'd to keep
> The lazy sabbath of a half-year's sleep.
> Entomb'd, beneath the filmy web they lie,
> And wait the influence of a kinder sky;
> When vernal sun-beams pierce their dark retreat,
> The heaving tomb distends with vital heat;
> The full-form'd brood impatient of their cell
> Start from their trance, and burst their silken shell;
> Trembling a-while they stand, and scarcely dare
> To launch at once upon the untried air:
> At length assur'd, they catch the favouring gale,
> And leave their sordid spoils, and high in Ether sail. (73–84)

The "heaving tomb," though clearly enough a cocoon, takes on the sense of a womb, birthing this "brood" of creatures that have been forced to await their liberation in "silken shell[s]" in a conflation of imagery that begins to suggest the feminine nature of this condition. The insects collectively occupy a "dark retreat" that resembles the "sunless haunts" and "cool damp grotto" that foster female creativity in "A Summer Evening's Meditation" (18, 19), a poem in the tradition of Finch's "A Nocturnal Reverie."

Barbauld draws an explicit connection between the insects and women when she plays with the pun on "nymphs" as both insects and damsels.[48] She compares the insects bursting forth to nymphs emerging from trees in Torquato Tasso's *Jerusalem Delivered* (1581). She might also have been aware that Handel's opera *Rinaldo* (1711, revived in 1731) contained a similar scene.[49] An English translation of Tasso's poem published in London in 1764 describes this episode:

> While round the champion cast a doubtful view,
> A greater wonder his attention drew:
> A lab'ring oak a sudden cleft disclos'd,
> And from its bark a living birth expos'd;
> Whence (passing all belief!) in strange array,
> A lovely damsel issu'd to the day.
> A hundred diff'rent trees the knight beheld,
> Whose fertile wombs a hundred nymphs reveal'd.
> As oft in pictur'd scenes we see display'd
> Each graceful goddess of the sylvan shade;
> With arms expos'd, with vesture girt around,
> With purple buskins, and with hair unbound:
> Alike to view, before the hero stood
> These shadowy daughters of the wond'rous wood;
> Save that their hands nor bows nor quiver wield;
> But this a harp, and that a timbrel held.[50]

Even in Tasso's version, the nymphs are associated with the sister arts: they resemble painted figures and hold musical instruments. When Tasso compares Rinaldo's vision of the nymphs with "pictur'd scenes" featuring sensual "graceful goddess[es]," he expects his readers to easily imagine this common portrayal of female figures (such as in Botticelli's *La Primavera*). In eighteenth-century painting as well, nymphs appear pervasively as sexually objectified female figures.

When Barbauld compares her insects to the nymphs of Tasso's poem, she draws attention to the common representation of women within the sister arts as the sensually depicted female figures of paintings, composed for masculine viewing pleasure. She employs an epic simile to compare her insects to the nymphs of Tasso's poem, thus emphasizing their feminine association and elevating the episode to grander proportions:

> So when Rinaldo struck the conscious rind,
> He found a nymph in every trunk confin'd;
> The forest labours with convulsive throes,
> The bursting trees the lovely births disclose,
> And a gay troop of damsels round him stood,
> Where late was rugged bark and lifeless wood.
> Lo! the bright train their radiant wings unfold,
> With silver fring'd and freckl'd o'er with gold:
> On the gay bosom of some fragrant flower
> They idly fluttering live their little hour;
> Their life all pleasure, and their task all play,
> All spring their age, and sunshine all their day. (86–96)

Barbauld conflates Rinaldo's discovered nymphs with her own depicted insects. By shifting into the present tense at "Lo!" Barbauld moves seamlessly from the "gay troop of damsels" back to the insects with their "radiant wings" of "silver" and "gold." Her description of the insects as nymphs—with their dazzling wings and their carefree, pleasure-filled existence—encapsulates how women are traditionally depicted in art. Unlike the poetic songbirds, whose freedom is symbolized by their ability to fly to the horizon, the nymphs are beautiful but limited; their "radiant wings" are aesthetic rather than functional. Allotted only to "idly fluttering live their little hour," the nymphs live a brief, restricted, and frivolous existence.

By allying herself with the "feather'd tribe," and demonstrating her talent in both poetry and visual art, Barbauld shows that women need not be limited to acting as muses and objects of representation within the tradition of the sister arts, but instead can act as artistic creators. With her expansive vision, Barbauld's speaker combines the cataloguing impulse of the natural historian with the imaginative eye of the poet. When she describes the variety of insect life, for example, she seeks to record the colors of the creatures, while also adding the metaphorical embellishment of gems and jewels that emphasize her sense of aesthetic admiration:

> What atom forms of insect life appear!
> And who can follow nature's pencil here?
> Their wings with azure, green, and purple gloss'd,
> Studded with colour'd eyes, with gems emboss'd,
> Inlaid with pearl, and mark'd with various stains
> Of lively crimson thro' their dusky veins. (103–8)

When she asks, "who can follow nature's pencil here?" Barbauld evokes the standard Renaissance *paragone* between art and nature, but she enters this esteemed contest with the specific aim of pleasing her friend. By combining the strengths of poetry and visual art, outlined earlier in her aesthetic commentary, Barbauld creates a gift that she hopes will lead Priestley to "praise the flowing line / And bend delighted o'er the gay design" (123–24). She insists at the end of the poem that this affective aim—to delight and entertain the recipient, Priestley—surpasses any other measure of success, including fame.

The year after "To Mrs. P[riestley]" was published in Barbauld's *Poems* (1773), Mary Scott offered her own tribute to Barbauld in *The Female Advocate* (1774), a poetic encomium that features a range of female intellectuals. "With this pantheon of over sixty accomplished women from the sixteenth century to her own day," Moira Ferguson explains, "Scott displays the extent and development of female learning and culture and effectively sketches a highly concentrated (and versified) female literary history."[51] Scott presents Barbauld in the final position within this female literary history, a placement that emphasizes her esteem for the poet. In her own "joyful tribute" to Barbauld, Scott calls upon the language of the sister arts:

> Fir'd with the Music, Aikin, of thy lays,
> To thee the Muse a joyful tribute pays;
> Transported dwells on that harmonious line,
> Where taste, and spirit, wit, and learning shine;
> Where Fancy's hand her richest colourings lends,
> And ev'ry shade in just proportion blends.
> How fair, how beauteous to our gazing eyes
> Thy vivid intellectual paintings rise!
> We feel thy feelings, glow with all thy fires,
> Adopt thy thoughts, and pant with thy desires.[52]

Blending the language of music and visual art in her praise of Barbauld's poetry, Scott situates Barbauld's work in the realm of the sister arts. Scott refers to Barbauld's poems as "vivid intellectual paintings" that stun her readers' "gazing eyes." By figuring Barbauld's poems as paintings, Scott offers a testament to Barbauld's pictorial power and to her lasting legacy for the female poets following her.

Notes

1. The "sister arts" are considered to be poetry, painting, and music, but sometimes include categories (such as sculpture, architecture, or gardening). As Jean Hagstrum

explains in his foundational text on the subject, poetry and painting "are the two arts that have most commonly been called 'sisters'"; see *The Sister Arts: The Tradition of Literary Pictorialism and English Poetry from Dryden to Gray* (Chicago: The University of Chicago Press, 1958), xiii.

2. See William Collins's "Verses Humbly Address'd to Sir Thomas Hanmer" (1743), Thomas Gray's "Stanzas to Mr. Bentley" (1775), and Anna Seward's "Epistle to Mr. Romney, Being Presented by Him with a Picture of William Haylay, Esq." and "Verses to the Celebrated Painter, Mr. Wright, of Derby" (written in 1780s; published in 1810).

3. On the biographical context that informs Dryden's approach, see Cedric D. Reverand II, "Dryden on Dryden in 'To Sir Godfrey Kneller,'" *Papers on Language and Literature* 17, no. 2 (Spring 1981): 164–80; and James Winn, "When Beauty Fires the Blood": Love and the Arts in the Age of Dryden (Ann Arbor: The University of Michigan Press, 1992), 346–64.

4. James Winn, *"When Beauty Fires the Blood,"* 29–30.

5. Ibid., 362.

6. Ibid., 21.

7. Jean Hagstrum's *The Sister Arts* offers a literary history of how many canonical male poets participated in the sister arts. Scholarship has generally continued to focus on male poets; see *Articulate Images: The Sister Arts from Hogarth to Tennyson*, ed. Richard Wendorf (Minneapolis: University of Minnesota Press, 1983) and *So Rich a Tapestry: The Sister Arts and Cultural Studies*, eds. Ann Hurley and Kate Greenspan (Lewisburg, PA: Bucknell University Press, 1995). For scholarship that has helped to establish that female poets participated in this tradition, see: Jacqueline Labbe, "Every Poet Her Own Drawing Master: Charlotte Smith, Anna Seward and *ut pictura poesis*" in *Early Romantics: Perspectives in British Poetry from Pope to Wordsworth*, ed. Thomas Woodman (New York: St. Martin's Press, 1998); Kathryn Ready, "Mind Versus Matter: Anna Barbauld and the 'Kindred Arts' of Painting and Poetry," *Eighteenth-Century Women: Studies in Their Lives, Work, and Culture* 6 (2011): 229–52; Lisa L. Moore, *Sister Arts: The Erotics of Lesbian Landscapes* (Minneapolis: University of Minnesota Press, 2011); and Shelley King, "Portrait of a Marriage: John and Amelia Opie and the Sister Arts," *Studies in Eighteenth-Century Culture* 40 (2011): 27–62.

8. For an account of the Aikin-Barbauld family and their Dissenting community, see *Religious Dissent and the Aikin-Barbauld Circle, 1740–1860*, ed. Felicity James and Ian Inkster (New York: Cambridge University Press, 2012).

9. See Deirdre Coleman, "Firebrands, Letters and Flowers: Mrs. Barbauld and the Priestleys" in *Romantic Sociability: Social Networks and Literary Culture in Britain, 1770–1840*, ed. Gillian Russell and Clara Tuite (New York: Cambridge University Press, 2002), 88.

10. William McCarthy, *Anna Letitia Barbauld: Voice of the Enlightenment* (Baltimore: The Johns Hopkins University Press, 2008), 69.

11. Angela Keane, in "The Market, The Public, and the Female Author: Anna Laetitia Barbauld's Gift Economy," *Romanticism: The Journal of Romantic Culture and Criticism* 8, no. 2 (2002): 161–78, argues that "Barbauld effaces her individual body and figures herself and her texts as part of a gift economy, not only in exchange or circulation but *in relation* . . . She thus presents her work not only as a commodity with the freedoms and

pleasures of consumption that implies, but also as a 'gift,' with attendant obligations on the recipient and the giver" (163).

12. Susan Rosenbaum, "'A Thing Unknown, without a Name': Anna Laetitia Barbauld and the Illegible Signature," *Studies in Romanticism* 40, no. 3 (Fall 2011): 369–99; quotations are on 372 and 389.

13. Shelley King, "Lyric Sociability: Object Lessons in Female Friendship in Amelia Opie's Occasional Verses," in this volume.

14. Alexander Pope, "Epistle to Mr. Jervas, With *Dryden*'s Translation of *Fresnoy*'s Art of Painting" (1716), *The Twickenham Edition of the Poems of Alexander Pope, Vol. 6: Minor Poems*, ed. Norman Ault (New Haven, CT: Yale University Press, 1954), lines 69–70.

15. Anna Barbauld, *The Poems of Anna Letitia Barbauld*, ed. William McCarthy and Elizabeth Kraft (Athens: The University of Georgia Press, 1994). All quotations from Barbauld's poetry are from this edition and line numbers are cited parenthetically.

16. Jennifer Keith, *Poetry and the Feminine from Behn to Cowper* (Newark: University of Delaware Press, 2005), 54.

17. *The Works of Anna Lætitia Barbauld*, ed. Lucy Aikin, 2 vols. (London: Longman, Hurst, Rees, Orme, Brown, and Green, Paternoster-Row, 1825), 2:59.

18. Michele Martinez, "Women Poets and the Sister Arts in Nineteenth-Century England," *Victorian Poetry* 41, no. 4 (Winter 2003): 623.

19. Ibid., 623.

20. Ready, "Mind versus Matter: Anna Barbauld and the 'Kindred Arts,'" 241.

21. Ibid, 237.

22. Harriette Andreadis argues that Katherine "Philips's use of the discourse of 'union' both to affirm her passion for her female friends in her poems and to create a sociofamilial network of intimate relations exemplifies female appropriation of masculine—and masculinist—ideology" (525) in "Re-Configuring Early Modern Friendship: Katherine Philips and Homoerotic Desire," *Studies in English Literature, 1500–1900* 46, no. 3 (Summer 2006): 523–42. Here I am not suggesting that Barbauld's address to Priestley expresses same-sex desire, but I would argue that Barbauld consciously applies the "discourse of 'union'" dominant in the tradition of poetry about same-sex male friendships to poetry about female friendship.

23. John Dryden, "To the Memory of Mr. Oldham" (1684), in *The Works of John Dryden, Vol. 2: Poems 1681–1684*, ed. H. T. Swedenberg (Berkeley: University of California Press, 1972), lines 3–4.

24. Natasha Duquette, "Painting in Bright Characters: Helen Maria Williams's Poetic Tributes to Anna Seward, Elizabeth Montagu, and Marie-Jeanne Roland," in this volume.

25. Unfortunately, no manuscript version of the poem survives today, and we have no copy of the drawings; most of Barbauld's papers have been destroyed or lost. An album that Mary Priestley kept of Barbauld's poetry was also destroyed in the Birmingham Riots, or Priestly Riots, of 1791 when the mob attacked Joseph Priestley's house; see McCarthy, *Anna Letitia Barbauld*, xviii.

26. See Theresa M. Kelley, *Clandestine Marriage: Botany and Romantic Culture* (Baltimore: Johns Hopkins University Press, 2012), 101.

27. Ann Bermingham, *Learning to Draw: Studies in the Cultural History of a Polite and Useful Art* (New Haven, CT: Yale University Press, 2000), 215.

28. Mark Laird, "Introduction," *Mrs. Delany and Her Circle*, eds. Mark Laird and Alicia Weisberg-Roberts (New Haven, CT: Yale University Press, 2009), 35. See also Ruth Hayden, *Mrs Delany: Her Life and Her Flowers* (New York: New Amsterdam Books, 1992).

29. Bermingham, *Learning to Draw*, 205.

30. Ibid., 202.

31. See McCarthy, *Anna Letitia Barbauld*, 97. McCarthy speculates that Barbauld describes the drawings of birds and insects by Maria Sibylla Merian on display at the British Museum. In the text of the poem, however, Barbauld repeatedly presents both the poem and drawings as the products of her own hand. During the eighteenth century, it was common practice to copy the work of famous artists, and it is possible that Barbauld may have based her drawings on Merian's work. Daniel P. Watkins, in *Anna Letitia Barbauld and Eighteenth-Century Visionary Poetics* (Baltimore: John Hopkins University Press, 2012), also argues that Barbauld refers to her own drawings (213n5).

32. Kelley, *Clandestine Marriage*, 93.

33. Mary Wollstonecraft, "Chapter 4: Observations on The State of Degradation to Which Woman is Reduced by Various Causes," *A Vindication of the Rights of Woman*, ed. Sylvana Tomaselli (New York: Cambridge University Press, 1995), 128.

34. *The Poems of Anna Letitia Barbauld*, 267.

35. Kelley, *Clandestine Marriage*, 101.

36. Ibid.

37. For an overview of recent trends in the scholarship of "To a Mouse" as "a musine allegory of human rights," a commentary on "eighteenth-century women's increasing participation in scientific culture," or as questioning "the potentially damaging nature of the scientific mindset," see Olivia Murphy, "Riddling Sibyl, Uncanny Cassandra: Barbauld's Recent Critical Reception," in William McCarthy and Olivia Murphy, eds., *Anna Letitia Barbauld: New Perspectives* (Lewisburg, PA: Bucknell University Press, 2013), 277–98; quotations are on 280–83.

38. See "St. John Baptist Painted by her self in the Wilder-ness, with Angels appearing to him, and with a Lamb by him," "Herodias Daughter presenting to her Mother St. John's Head in a Charger, also Painted by her self," and "On a Picture Painted by her self, representing two Nimphs of Diana's, one in a posture to Hunt, the other Batheing," in *Poems by Mrs Anne Killigrew* (1686).

39. *Poems by Eminent Ladies* (London: R. Baldwin, 1755) was reprinted many times and was reissued as *Poems by the Most Eminent Ladies of Great-Britain and Ireland*.

40. John Dryden, "To the Pious Memory of the Accomplisht Young LADY Mrs Anne Killigrew, Excellent in the two Sister-Arts of Poesie, and Painting. An Ode," in *The Works of John Dryden, Vol. 3: Poems, 1685–1692*, eds. Earl Miner and Vinton A. Dearing (Berkeley: University of California Press, 1969), lines 89–105.

41. Thomas Gray, *The Progress of Poesy. A Pindaric Ode*, *The Poems of Thomas Gray, William Collins, and Oliver Goldsmith*, ed. Roger Lonsdale (New York: W. W. Norton, 1969), lines 115–17.

42. Watkins, *Anna Letitia Barbauld and Eighteenth-Century Visionary Poetics*, 99.

43. Isobel Grundy, "'Slip-Shod Measure' and 'Language of Gods': Barbauld's Stylistic Range," in *Anna Letitia Barbauld: New Perspectives*, 37–58 (32).

44. Adelaide Morris has argued that all of Barbauld's birds "symbolize" "literary women" of various "genres and types": she sees the eagle as the poet "marking a satiric target," the pheasant as "the *parvenu* novelists, whose flight is confined by a patriarchal 'wiry net' which denies women's autonomy and contains their writing in the cult of sensibility," and the songbirds as a "self-fashioning middle class" of female poets marked by their "lack of seriousness" in "Woman Speaking to Women: Retracing the Feminine in Anna Laetitia Barbauld," *Women's Writing* 10, no. 1 (2003): 47–72; see especially 56–61. Because Barbauld refers to both the eagle and the pheasant with male pronouns, I find it difficult to read them as representative of women writers. Instead, I argue that the songbirds represent poets generally (both male and female).

45. *Oxford English Dictionary Online*, s.v. "lay, n.4," www.oed.com, accessed July 24, 2015.

46. Watkins, *Anna Letitia Barbauld and Eighteenth-Century Visionary Poetics*, 101.

47. Michelle Levy, for example, explicates this line as a sign that "Barbauld retreats from her evaluation of the respective merits of the 'kindred arts' . . . thus denigrating both her chosen subject matter and her poetic ability"; see "Barbauld's Poetic Career in Script and Print" in *Anna Letitia Barbauld: New Perspectives*, 37–58 (50). Similarly, on Barbauld's relationship to the sister arts more generally, Michele Martinez argues that "Anna Barbauld feminized the male writer's approach to art, representing the decorum and limits of the lady writer," in "Women Poets and the Sister Arts in Nineteenth-Century England," 623.

48. *Oxford English Dictionary Online*, s.v. "nymph, n. 2b and 3," www.oed.com, accessed July 24, 2015.

49. Dryden imitates this scene in *King Arthur* (1691; Act IV), and Handel's opera *Rinaldo* (1711) was loosely based on Tasso's *Jerusalem Delivered*.

50. Torquato Tasso, *Jerusalem delivered; an heroic poem: translated from the Italian of Torquato Tasso, by John Hoole*, vol. 2, second ed. (London: printed for R. and J. Dodsley, P. Valliant [sic], T. Davies, J. Newbery and Z. Stuart, 1764), XVIII, lines 169–84; accessible on Gale database *Eighteenth Century Collections Online*.

51. Moira Ferguson, "'The Cause of My Sex': Mary Scott and the Female Literary Tradition," *Huntington Library Quarterly* 50, no. 4 (Autumn 1987): 370.

52. Mary Scott, *The Female Advocate* (London: Joseph Johnson, 1774), accessible through *Women Writers Online*, Northeastern University, https://wwp.northeastern.edu/wwo/.

Painting in Bright Characters

Helen Maria Williams's Poetic Tributes to Anna Seward, Elizabeth Montagu, and Marie-Jeanne Roland

NATASHA DUQUETTE

The history of friendship has been an obscure one in every dimension, but most of all, for women.
—Joan Chittister, *The Friendship of Women: A Spiritual Tradition*

I blend the feelings of private friendship with my sympathy in public blessings.
—Helen Maria Williams, *Letters Written in France*

Helen Maria Williams blended tributes to female mentors and friends with political and philosophical analysis throughout her poetry of the 1780s and '90s. Critics have tended to separate Williams's early British verse of sensibility from the political prose she wrote after her permanent move to Revolutionary France in 1790, but Williams's laudatory portrayal of women's sympathetic, intellectual, and artistic connections is a constant thread throughout her writing, tying her narrative verse written in London to the sonnets she composed in Paris. Throughout her texts, Williams represents women's friendship in a variety of metaphors. In her early poems, she compares female friendships to shrines or temples, suggestive of spiritual sustenance and protection. Within her poems of the 1780s, which commemorate major events on the global stage, such as the American Revolution and the Túpac Amura uprising in Peru, she pauses to pay tribute to specific female intellectuals and friends. In her *Ode on the Peace* (1783), she praises Anna Seward's political verse, within which Seward lamented the loss of human life in war, and Elizabeth Montagu's Bluestocking gatherings, which functioned as artistic and literary salons in eighteenth-century London. In 1784, Williams re-emphasized her indebtedness to the Queen of the Bluestockings by prefacing her six-canto epyllion *Peru* with a poem titled "To

Mrs. Montagu." In Williams's *Julia, a novel interspersed with poetical pieces* (1790) and in her translation of Jacques-Henri Bernardin de Saint-Pierre's novel *Paul et Virginie* (1787) as *Paul and Virginia* (1795), she provided more detailed accounts of the everyday realities present in relationships between women.

The representation of female friendship amidst adversity in *Paul and Virginia* is especially poignant given Williams's context in the mid-1790s. She began work on her translation of Saint-Pierre's story when she herself was confined with her sisters and mother in Paris's Luxembourg prison during the Reign of Terror. She had lost several female friends, who were executed by guillotine, including philosopher Marie-Jeanne Roland. By 1795, in her depiction of female friendship within *Paul and Virginia*, Williams no longer represented women's companionship as an idealized, abstract temple but instead symbolized its life-giving sustenance in a concrete, everyday, *and sublime* organic form with real physical, as well as emotional, intellectual, and spiritual benefits.

Williams boldly presents the enduring strength of female friendship as sublime and thus challenges Edmund Burke's relegation of sociability to the weakness of a feminine beauty subordinated to masculine sublimity in his *Philosophical Enquiry into the Origin of Our Ideas of the Sublime and the Beautiful* (1757, 1759). For Williams, the affective bonds of female friendship are a source of powerful social, economic, and political transformation, and so she does not limit her poetic imagery to Burke's condescending diminishment of "the endearments of friendship."[1] As Paula Backscheider observes, by the 1780s, "friendship poems had become important places for personal expression, places where subjectivity and agency developed, and upon that foundation women poets increasingly exercised a social and ethical awareness. . . . The poets of Anna Seward's generation took assertive steps into the public sphere and provided support for one another."[2] Backscheider cites Williams's tributes to Montagu as one example of such mutual support. Angela Keane argues that Williams, in particular, depicts "the power of femininity (but not necessarily maternity), and of national affection to effect a transformation in the institutions of the state."[3] Keane's phrase "national affection" suggests that Williams was a British nationalist. Even more explicitly, Rebecca Heinwitz Cole presents Williams as engaging in a "patriotic poetics of sensibility."[4] However, Williams's writing, from the very beginning, actively constructs friendship as a dynamic that crosses boundaries of national, racial, and socio-economic difference. In *Peru*, for example, Williams presents intercultural friendships, such as those she envisions between indigenous Peruvians and the Spanish Dominican Bishop Bartolomé de Las Casas, as a model for bridging boundaries of national difference. By the mid-1790s, the transformative capacity and enduring stability of Williams's own cross-cultural connections to French women writers led her to explicitly present female friendship as sublime.

In her early work *An Ode on the Peace*, Williams was already foregrounding public women intellectuals as both wise and sympathetic, just and supportive, through her poetic tributes. In this poem, she first takes a pacifist position and critiques the violence of the American Revolution. She then commends her friend Anna Seward's poetic public response to that violence, personifies the Treaty of Paris ending the American Revolution (signed on September 3, 1783) as a gentle but transformative female figure, and finally pays tribute to Elizabeth Montagu's social and intellectual circles in London as a similar source of transformation. In her *Ode*, Williams repeatedly laments the extinguishing of love in "streams of blood" during times of war.[5] The "soul of war" for Williams is a hellish figure that "burns" with a desire for violence.[6] She presents the battles of the American Revolution taking place not under an honorable national flag, but under a "bloody banner," representing the grotesque physiological trauma on both sides.[7] Her male personification of battle wields not an idealized sword of chivalry but a "reeking blade" of oppression that contributes to a "purple flood" of suffering.[8]

In answer to the severity and destruction of military strife, Williams refers to Seward as an indignant yet compassionate elegist who sympathetically tempers the grief caused by war. Within her *Ode*, Williams praises Seward's "Monody on Major André" (1781) as a gracefully elegiac response to British officer John André's hanging, for the crime of espionage, by the Americans. Seward was outraged by this execution and critiqued it via an allusion to the Hebrew story of the first murder in Genesis, when Cain "rose up against his brother Abel, and slew him" (Genesis 4.8, King James Version). Seward wrote of John André's corpse, "its dust, like Abel's blood, shall rise, / And call for justice from the angry skies!,"[9] clearly situating the American Revolutionaries in the place of the murderer Cain. Reflecting on the cultural impact of Seward's "Monody," literary historian Harriet Devine notes, "the poem's attack on 'remorseless Washington' caused the American president to send a defensive message to Seward a few years later."[10] Seward's ability to provoke a response from President Washington motivated other women poets, including Helen Maria Williams, in their own representations of women bringing about justice and peace within their poems and novels.[11]

Harriet Guest notes Williams's admiration of Seward's political influence, arguing, "The *Ode* asserts that it is because the British nation is capable of participating in the grief of individuals, and the pleasures of Seward's poetry, that peace finally comes about."[12] In her biography of Anna Seward, Teresa Barnard includes Williams within Seward's "circle of friends."[13] Barnard highlights Seward's praise of Williams's poetic "Genius" in 1784 but does not note this praise was in fact a reciprocation of Williams's own tribute to Seward in 1783.[14]

Helen Maria Williams's admiration of Anna Seward is easily discernable in her tribute to a fellow woman poet's talent for lyrical, politicized consolation. Williams imagines Seward throwing a mantle of light over the executed André's memory through her elegiac verse. She paints Seward in the politically charged role of national bard playing on her harp.

> While Seward sweeps her plaintive strings,
> While pensive round his sable shrine
> A radiant zone she graceful flings,
> Where full emblaz'd his virtues shine,
> The mournful Loves that tremble nigh
> Shall catch her warm melodious sigh,
> And drink the precious thrilling drops that flow
> From Pity's hov'ring soul, that pants dissolv'd in woe.[15]

Seward's lament—both for the multitudes who died in the American Revolution and for André's hanging, specifically—is represented by Williams literally, as the playing of a plaint on a harp or lyre, and symbolically, as the casting of a radiant zone over the darkness of his death. By depicting Seward's ability to portray André's virtues as transcending the horror of his execution, Williams imparts hope to the reader. Williams's section on Seward's "Monody" is the turning point of her own *Ode on the Peace*, where it shifts from exposé of the grotesque violence of war to celebration of the societal regeneration enabled by peace.

Williams follows her tribute to Seward's poetic strength with a female personification of Peace, which leads into her portrayal of Elizabeth Montagu as peaceable literary *salonnière*. In Williams's poem, the female figure Peace brings the generation to Britain of new life, new communities, and new developments in art, poetics, and science. Echoing her imagery surrounding the effect of Seward's verse, Williams describes a "lucid stream of light" surrounding "mild benignant Peace," descending from heaven, with an almost Marian quality, and she "gilds the black Abyss" of war.[16]

Williams does not stop at this personification of Peace but spends the second half of her poem describing the social, textual, and cultural expansion that peacetime enables, including the fostering of intellectual and artistic networks. She pictures "bright Painting's living forms" receiving greater attention after the conclusion of war, citing works by British painters Joshua Reynolds and George Romney as particularly worthy of study.[17] She then moves on to praise the expansion of scientific enquiry and literary production in the social context of the Bluestocking gatherings at Elizabeth Montagu's home:

> Ah! still diffuse thy mental ray,
> Fair Science, on my Albion's plain!
> While oft' thy step delights to stray
> Where Montagu has rear'd her Fane;
> Where Eloquence shall still entwine
> Rich attic flowers around the shrine.[18]

It is striking that Williams associates the "mental ray" of expanding scientific knowledge with gatherings facilitated by Montagu, a female intellectual, hostess, and Shakespearean scholar.

Williams emphasized Montagu's brilliance in various print forms from 1783 to 1790. She alluded to Montagu's *Essay on the Writings and Genius of Shakespear, compared with the Greek and French Dramatic Poets* (1769) in her *Ode on the Peace, Peru* (1784), and *Julia* (1790), as it set a precedent for women writers to venture further into the field of literary criticism. Williams painted a cumulative poetic portrait of Montagu as a creator of spiritual sanctuary and an intellectual leader, as well as a personal mentor and friend. As early as January 1783, Williams was visiting Montagu's London home on Hill Street, Mayfair, where she actively sought out critical advice on her own poetry. Montagu's Bluestocking gatherings included socially conscious male and female writers, such as Anglicans Hannah More and Elizabeth Carter, as well as dissenting Presbyterians Williams and James Beattie, the latter for whom Montagu was an important patron.

Williams continued to express her admiration for the female leader of the Bluestockings in 1784 by dedicating her six-canto epyllion *Peru* to Elizabeth Montagu.[19] In her prefatory poem "To Mrs. Montagu," she again praises Montagu's "Fane," now as a nurturing shelter to which "deserted

Genius" can lead "his drooping spirit."[20] It is a place of intellectual community "where attic joy the social Circle warms."[21] Williams's tribute "To Mrs. Montagu" concludes:

> . . . while Fame thro' each successive Age
> On her exulting lip thy name shall breathe;
> While Woman, pointing to thy finish'd Page,
> Claims from imperious Man the Critic Wreathe;
> Truth on her spotless Record shall enroll
> Each moral Beauty to her Spirit dear;
> Paint in bright Characters each Grace of Soul—
> While Admiration pours a gen'rous tear.[22]

In the above lines, Williams celebrates Montagu's polished and professional prose, protests controlling masculine reign over critical discourse, and expresses her hope that women writers will venture more and more frequently into the domains of literary criticism and moral philosophy, where they may perhaps begin to lead the way. Two years later, Montagu would reciprocate Williams's tribute by adding her name to the list of subscribers supporting Williams's *Poems in Two Volumes* (1786), within which *Peru* was reprinted, complete with the dedication "To Mrs. Montagu."[23]

Later, it was through her gracious extension of intellectual hospitality and loyal friendship to other women writers that Williams continued to honor the memory of Montagu's role in fostering her own early development as a writer and thinker. Williams herself hosted literary gatherings in her Hampstead home from 1787 onwards, to which she invited Scottish writers such as novelist Henry Mackenzie and poet Joanna Baillie.[24] In 1790, Williams paid further tribute to Montagu in her novel *Julia*, which contains strong allusions to Montagu's *Essay on the Writing and Genius of Shakespear* embedded in its heroine's verse. A pattern of influence *and* differentiation is especially evident in "An Address to Poetry," within which Williams responds to Montagu's interpretation of *Macbeth*.[25] The narrative prose of *Julia* itself celebrates the lasting quality of fictional female friendships in relationships between two cousins and between the heroine and an impoverished friend. Through her metaphors for friendship in *Julia*'s poetic prose, Williams continues to present the bonds formed between women in terms of the sacred. Just as she compared the Bluestocking community generated by Montagu's intellectual mentorship to a "Fane" or "shrine,"[26] Williams extends this metaphor in *Julia* to compare female friendship to a "holy temple" with "sainted shrines."[27] Williams's repeated representation of friendship as spiritual may have inspired Anna Seward's 1796 tribute to Eleanor Butler and Sarah Ponsonby's "sacred Friendship," explored by Susan Lanser in her contribution to this book. After *Julia*'s publication, the spiritual and emotional refuge of steady friendship took on crucial significance for Williams biographically during her permanent transition to the Continent and Revolutionary Paris.

From her earliest prose descriptions of the French Revolution, Williams intentionally tied social justice to the enduring bonds of friendship. She was initially drawn to France by an invitation from her friends Thomas and Monique Du Fossé, who had been teaching her to read and speak French in London. The Du Fossés' own return back to France, from exile in England, was enabled by revolutionary legal reforms.[28] From the onset of the French Revolution, Williams's feelings of friendship and sympathy for those oppressed by unjust regimes continued to prompt her mixing of politics with the discourse of sublimity.[29] In her *Letters,* Williams explains how her friendship with the Du Fossés, and the justice of their dignified re-entry to their homeland, drew her into the "sublime spectacle" of the French Revolution.[30] She would later expand upon the connection between sociability and justice through her defense of French men and women's "sublime public virtues" exhibited during the Revolutionary era.[31] In her prose and poetry written during the 1790s, Williams focused on the forms such sublime public virtues can take within the networks of women's friendships. Mary Wollstonecraft, in 1792,[32] the same year she visited Williams in Paris, argued in her *Vindication of the Rights of Woman* that "Friendship is a serious affection: the most sublime of all affections, because it is founded on principle, and cemented by time. The very reverse may be said of love."[33] Both Williams and Wollstonecraft represent friendship as sublimely constant and thus connected to the eternal. Williams's role as a *salonnière* in Paris, hosting gatherings of male and female writers, followed the pattern first modeled by her mentor Montagu and then by French women such as Marie-Jeanne Roland. Williams's mixing of French and expatriate British citizens in her home suggests a reciprocity to what Elizabeth Eger has identified as "the bluestockings' contribution and response to the major literary and intellectual developments taking place, particularly in France."[34]

Williams herself exhibited steadfast female friendship in 1793, during the Reign of Terror in France, by visiting moderate Girondist philosopher Roland in a Parisian prison. Roland was imprisoned for questioning the more extremist Jacobins led by Maximilien Robespierre, and she would die for her convictions. Williams would later memorialize her, writing, "Madame

Roland was indeed possessed of the most distinguished talents, and a mind highly cultivated by the study of literature. I had been acquainted with her since I first came to France, and had always observed in her conversation the most ardent attachment to liberty, and the most enlarged sentiments of philanthropy, sentiments which she developed with an eloquence peculiar to herself, with a flow and power of expression."[35] Here, Williams alludes to her earlier personification of Freedom, in the 1780s, as a woman who "eloquently pours her potent strain," by repeating similar imagery in her eulogy for Roland.[36] Williams continues painting her portrait of Roland by remembering, "She was tall and well shaped; her air was dignified, and although more than thirty-five years of age she was still handsome. Her countenance had an expression of uncommon sweetness, and her full dark eyes beamed with the brightest rays of intelligence. I visited her in the prison of St. Pelagie, where her soul, superior to circumstances, retained its accustomed serenity."[37] Steven Blakemore notes that Williams "demonstrated courage by twice visiting Madame Roland, who had been imprisoned since 31 May 1793—when any association with Girodins was dangerously compromising."[38]

Later the same year, Williams was herself imprisoned in Paris's Luxembourg prison, along with her two sisters and mother.[39] Robespierre shortly thereafter had Roland executed.[40] According to Williams, when Roland was tied to "the fatal plank, she lifted her eyes to the statue of liberty, near which the guillotine was placed, and exclaimed 'Oh, Liberty! How men have made sport of thee!'"[41] An idealist like Williams, Roland died for holding to her high philosophical and political ideals. Grief at losing friends like Roland no doubt motivated Williams to valorize the sublimity of female friendship in her translation of Bernardin Saint-Pierre's novel *Paul et Virginie*, as *Paul and Virginia*, begun when she was imprisoned by Robespierre in October 1793, and published in England in 1795.

The exhibition of sublime public virtues within Parisian networks of heroic Girondist women gave birth to Williams's own poetic representation of female friendship's sublimity in her "Sonnet: To the Calbassia Tree," one of the eight sonnets she inserted in *Paul and Virginia*. She wrote these sonnets while enduring suspicion, surveillance, and persecution as a Girondist and British citizen living in Paris during Robespierre's Reign of Terror. She explains in her preface to *Paul and Virginia*, "Society had vanished, and amidst the minute vexations of Jacobinical despotism, which, while it murdered in *mass*, persecuted in detail, the resources of writing, and even reading, were encompassed with danger."[42] Angela Wright suggests that in constructing her preface, Williams was keenly aware of her anti-Jacobin detractors in

England and so negotiated her translation "with care and subterfuge."[43] Williams bravely continued to write, nevertheless, no doubt inspired by Roland's example. After Williams had actively participated in courageous networks of women in Paris, she explicitly lauded the healing and sustaining power of female friendship in her writing for print. Williams's own work testifies to how participation in and observation of female literary, artistic, and philosophical networks can give fresh vigor to a woman's poetic voice. She presents the generation of her sonnets, while translating Saint-Pierre's novel, as an act of poetic political defiance, recounting how "writing was a forbidden employment: even reading had its perils; for books had sometimes aristocratical insignia, and sometimes counter-revolutionary allusions."[44] By writing her sonnets, Williams imaginatively burst the bounds of state control and of Robespierre's silencing laws. Despite the threat of the guillotine, she devoted "a few hours every day" to the translation and poetic elaboration of *Paul et Virginie*.[45]

Williams found aesthetic and spiritual consolation in her time of trauma and grief through reading Saint-Pierre's story and by composing the sonnets she added to it. She reflects autobiographically: "I found the most soothing relief in wandering from my own gloomy reflections to those enchanting scenes of the Mauritius [the setting of *Paul and Virginia*] . . . I also composed a few sonnets adapted to the peculiar productions of that part of the globe, which are interspersed in the work."[46] Williams requests her readers' patience with her sonnets, as they were composed "amidst the turbulence of the most cruel sensations, and in order to escape awhile from overwhelming misery."[47]

After her firsthand experiences of Girondist community and subsequent political imprisonment, Williams expresses gratitude for concrete, tangible, and steadfast female friendship in *Paul and Virginia*. She presents the eight sonnets interspersed throughout its narrative as the productions of a female character of Saint-Pierre's whom Williams translates into a poet-prophet leader, Madame de la Tour. By adding her own sonnets to Saint-Pierre's original text and presenting Virginia's mother Madame de la Tour as their composer, Williams interjects a clearly female, poetic voice into the male narrator's account of events. This has irked some critics. Phillip Robinson labels her translation a "trahision" or betrayal and condemns it as "infidel."[48] Robinson reads Williams's addition of the sonnets as evidence of feminine "vanité" and demands to know, "Est-il possible de justifier leur presence?" (Is it possible to justify their presence?).[49] Robinson's very vehemence testifies to the power of Williams's poetic voice. Her explicit display of women's creativity in verse, through de la Tour, outrages Robinson, but this is also what makes her translation so appealing, unique, and empowering. More promising than Robinson's dismissal of the sonnets is Louise Joy's argument that they situate "Madame de la Tour as a doubling of Williams herself."[50] Joy continues, "Her expressive writing thus opens up a new channel of communication about the emotions that transcends gendered boundaries."[51] It is in the second-to-last poem of de la Tour's sonnet series, "Sonnet: To the Calbassia Tree," that the term "sublime" first appears in her verse. She uses "sublime" as an adjective for constant, healing, and revitalizing friendship. David Sigler rightly views Williams's act of translating Saint-Pierre's *Paul et Virginie* as "a record of friendship finding stability in the intimacy of translation and agitation of geopolitics,"[52] yet he does not mention Williams's powerful symbolization of friendship as both female and sublime in "Sonnet: To the Calbassia Tree."

Saint-Pierre's narrative already celebrates a friendship between two single women—the widowed Madame de la Tour, mother of Virginia, and the abandoned Margaret, mother of Paul—in the French colony of Mauritius, or as the French rulers termed it, *l'Île de France*. In Saint-Pierre's original text, de la Tour is a spiritual leader but has no literary aspirations. In Williams's translation, she is also a woman poet who conceptualizes a female sublime of community, friendship, and light in her verse, and actualizes such community through her just and merciful actions in aid of others. In her translation *Paul and Virginia*, Williams envisions a feminist version of active social virtue in the small group of people led by the poet de la Tour. Margaret and Madame de la Tour, together with their children, and the two Africans Domingo and Mary, form what post-colonial critic Anna Neill refers to as a "little community ... consolidated by a sense of itself as non-European."[53] It is also decidedly matriarchal rather than patriarchal.

Williams's narrator portrays the affection between Margaret and de la Tour as a vehicle of divine grace and connects their friendship to the eternal, stating, "Providence which lends its support when we ask but the supply of our necessary wants, had a blessing in store for Madame de la Tour, which neither riches nor greatness can purchase, that blessing was a friend."[54] The second edition of Williams's translation *Paul and Virginia* (1796) illustrates the close, supportive friendship between the two women with an engraving. Williams's earlier, more allegorical representation of friendship—in female personifications like Peace and Freedom, and in symbolic representations of the hospitable sympathy extended by Seward and Montagu as temples or shrines—is fleshed out in this visual image of physically sheltering maternal intimacy. Madame de la Tour and Margaret together shelter their children as they take refuge in each other's friendship and find protection from the tropical sun under a tree's branches. The healing affective force of de la Tour and Margaret's friendship extends out toward others, including their children, Paul and Virginia, to form an organic and flexible community. Margaret and de la Tour share the history of their afflictions, provide consolation for one another, and form, with their children, a community bonded through mutual vulnerability and struggle. Nevertheless, it is a community still dependent on the indentured labor of Africans. Domingo and Mary are legally slaves. Mary's African origins are made explicit when the narrator refers to a Calabash tree planted by Domingo and Mary in a spot named "Foullepointe" after Mary's birthplace "in Africa."[55] Foullepointe is a city in Madagascar, an island nation off the Southeast Coast of Africa, in between the continent and the smaller island of Mauritius.

In his narrative, Saint-Pierre attempts to depict the situation of the Africans Mary and Domingo in this little community as somewhat egalitarian. All the members of the community share in the labor of tilling the soil, and Margaret and Madame de la Tour begin to wear "the coarse blue linen of Bengal, which is usually worn by slaves."[56] Mary and Domingo eventually marry and form their own household. As Paul grows into a robust child, he digs alongside Domingo in the garden and carries his small hatchet into the woods in order to gather fruit on his walks with Domingo. It is clear in the novel that Domingo fills the role of father figure for the fatherless Paul. Reflecting the eighteenth-century interest in the art of tableau, the children also learn the craft of pantomime from Domingo and Mary, and together they perform biblical scenes from the Hebrew Scripture, such as the story of Ruth. Within these small scriptural dramas Paul, Virginia, Domingo, and Mary all have roles. However, quite disappointingly for the modern reader, the white characters Paul and Virginia tend to act in the more central roles, such as Boaz and Ruth, and Domingo and Mary play more peripheral characters, such as the harvesters in Boaz's fields.

As Paul and Virginia grow into teenagers, the members of de la Tour and Margaret's little society—young and old, black and white, male and female—gather each evening on a rugged cliff to look over the Indian Ocean. These meetings by the seaside, atop a bold prospect, lift all of the members of the little community together into a sublime space. Their act of reverential gathering and the name of the rugged cliff upon which it takes place—"*The Discovery of Friendship*"[57]—challenge Burkean separations of beautiful friendship, feminine smoothness, and light from sublime solitude, masculine ruggedness, and darkness. In Williams's translation, the narrator notes: "on this rock the two families assembled in the evening, and enjoyed in silence the freshness of the air, the fragrance of the flowers, the murmurs of the fountains, and the last blended harmonies of night and shade."[58] The *chiaroscuro* effect of smooth tonal variegation in the liminal time of dusk suggests the future potential for harmony within the multiracial population of Mauritius. The naming of the rock *The Discovery of Friendship* symbolizes the strength, stability, and endurance of the interracial and intergenerational affection in their little community, despite the ever-present and troubling realities of slavery in Mauritius.

Though Saint-Pierre was not an explicit abolitionist, there are nascent anti-slavery sympathies in his novel, as he attempts to portray an almost familial, or at least companionate, adaptation of slavery. He contrasts the situation of Mary and Domingo with that of an escaped slave with whom Paul and Virginia interact under the shade of their family's plantain trees. In Williams's translation, the narrator describes the female fugitive thus:

> She appeared almost wasted to a skeleton, and had no other garment than a shred of course cloth thrown across her loins. She flung herself at Virginia's feet, who was preparing the family breakfast, and cried, "My good young lady, have pity on a poor slave: for a whole month I have wandered amongst these mountains, half dead with hunger, and often pursued by the hunters and their dogs. I fled from my master, a rich planter of the Black River, who has used me as you see"—and she shewed her body marked by deep scars from the lashes she had received.[59]

Saint-Pierre witnessed the abusive violence of slavery up close, first traveling with his uncle to the West Indies as a twelve-year-old, and then spending time engaged in botanical studies on Mauritius in 1768. The result of this second experience was his travel narrative *Voyage à l'Île de France*, published in 1773, within which he exposed the inhumanities of slavery on the island. The philosopher Condorcet admired Saint-Pierre's travel narrative, claiming it depicted slavery with uncensored truth, and Saint-Pierre's documentation of exploitation did indeed provoke hostile defensiveness from the wealthy white landowners of Mauritius.

In Saint-Pierre's novel, Paul and Virginia provide the female fugitive with food, promise her they will persuade her cruel owner to "forgive" her for running away, and then take her back to his plantation. When they see how truly domineering the slave owner is, Virginia makes a quick speech on the

African woman's behalf, and then they leave her. This conclusion to the episode may dissatisfy modern readers, especially considering Saint-Pierre's critique of French colonial cruelty in *Voyage à l'Île de France*. However, Christopher Mitchell argues that to eighteenth-century readers this story of an escaped female slave would have constituted "a daring exposé of the cruelty of slavery,"[60] and he continues, "It was reported that this brief episode in *Paul et Virginie* was powerful enough to cause reforms on l'Île de France, improving the lives of slaves" and this "sympathy that initially produced reforms likely contributed to abolition."[61] This sympathy arose from a moment in the narrative within which suffering triggers compassionate friendship under the shade of plantain trees.

Williams symbolizes friendship's ameliorative potential through the refuge of a tree's shade in de la Tour's mature sonnet "To the Calbassia Tree,"[62] which appears toward the end of *Paul and Virginia*. The very fact that this sonnet issues from de la Tour, a woman who speaks with "such sublime confidence of the Divinity, that the sick, while listening to her, believed that he was present,"[63] marks it as an expression of feminine fortitude and faith. The tree itself, as portrayed within the poem, is literally and physically a source of healing. The medicinal balm extracted from the tree is a life-sustaining, rather than life-threatening, sublime force. "To the Calbassia Tree" blends two trees found in the garden of the little society: "an old tree beneath the shade of which Madame de la Tour and Margaret used to relate their misfortunes called *The Tears Wiped Away*" and the actual "calbassia" planted by Domingo and Mary. What Williams translates into "Calbassia" is most likely a Calabash, or *Crescentia Cujete*, a tree brought to Mauritius by botanists in the eighteenth century. Medicinally, the balsam of the Calabash may be applied to ruptures in the skin, used as a poultice for bruises and burns, or turned into a cough syrup. De la Tour displays her medical knowledge of the tree's healing physical properties in her sonnet.

De la Tour presents the bright foliage, floral generation, and abundant vitality of her poetic Calbassia as sublime. The Calbassia tree, as described in her Petrarchan sonnet, is remarkable for its lush and verdant qualities amidst the general aridity of Mauritius. The speaker exclaims,

> Sublime Calbassia! Luxuriant tree
> How soft the gloom thy bright-hu'd foliage throws,
> While from thy pulp a healing balsam flows,
> Whose power the suffering wretch from pain can free.
> My pensive footsteps ever turn to thee!

> Since oft, while musing on my lasting woes
> Beneath thy flowery white-bells I repose.[64]

Though the shade cast by this tree is referred to as a "gloom," carrying connotations of terrifying Burkean obscurity, this is a soft, or feminine gloom. It recalls Williams's earlier imagery, in her *Ode on the Peace*, where she depicts the silent presence of wisdom, grace, and invention "Beneath thy olive's grateful shade."[65] Now, in *Paul and Virginia,* the heroine de la Tour is drawn to the comfort of a tree addressed as "thee." The source of the Calbassia's soft gloom lies in the tangible, empirically verifiable combination of tropical sunlight and "bright-hu'd foliage." The matter of the Calbassia tree itself emits a sublimity that depends not on "the ability to hurt,"[66] but conversely on the ability to lessen bodily suffering and pain. It is at the sonnet's *volta* or turning point, marked by the dash at the end of line eight, that de la Tour begins to compare such physiological healing to the emotional benefits of friendship.

Through her "Sonnet: To The Calbassia Tree," de la Tour offers thanks for the saving grace of friendship discovered in the midst of grief and loneliness. At the *volta*, the tree's representation of friendship becomes explicit:

> Symbol of friendship, dost thou seem to me;—
> For thus has friendship cast *her* soothing shade
> O'er my unsheltr'd bosom's keen distress;
> Thus sought to heal the wounds that love has made,
> And temper bleeding sorrow's sharp excess!
> Ah! Not in vain she lends her balmy aid—
> The agonies she cannot cure, are less![67]

The centrality of friendship in de la Tour's life is emphasized through her placement of the word "friendship" at the midpoint of her sonnet and repetition of the word again in the following line, directly beneath its first occurrence, where it is explicitly gendered female through the phrase "*her* soothing shade." Just as the Calbassia provides shelter from the tropical sun, Margaret's empathy soothes de la Tour's "unsheltr'd bosom's keen distress." Just as the balsam from the Calbassia heals ruptures in the skin, Margaret's friendship seeks to "heal the wounds that love has made." De la Tour suggests that the *agape* of sublimely enduring female friendship transcends the pain of such wounds. Friendship casts its compassionate sorrow over de la Tour's "sharp excess." Female friendship both soothes de la Tour and brings her balance by smoothing the sharp edges of her grief. "To the Calbassia Tree" concludes by giving thanks for female friendship's "balmy aid."

This balm can stay the bleeding of wounds left by love and loss. It lessens agony but does not repress or eradicate the memory of wounding.

Williams's sonnet parallels the reflections on friendship of another woman writer who was a mentor for her from as early as 1790, Anna Barbauld.[68] In her essay "On Friendship," Barbauld writes of those for "whom, in the mature season of life, there remains one tried and constant friend: their affection, mellowed by the hand of time, endeared by the recollection of enjoyments, toils, and even sufferings shared together, becomes the balm, the consolation, and the treasure of life."[69] As Laura Tallon has illustrated in her contribution to this book, Barbauld's early verse celebrated female friendship as a source of artistic inspiration. For Williams, especially in the tumultuous 1790s, such friendship between women was also an important source of comfort.

From her early verse onward, Williams expressed gratitude to female mentors and friends for their roles as sympathetic listeners, astute critics, hospitable facilitators, and strengthening consolers. Williams consistently portrayed women's friendship as a source of solace and refuge, but sadly, by 1795, she had lost multiple mentors and friends due to political disagreements, international relocation, and in the case of Marie-Jeanne Roland, death. Williams's praise of female mentors and friends, so prominent in her early tributes to role models such as poet Anna Seward and literary critic Elizabeth Montagu, was never sycophantic or naïve. Seward's determination to cross into the realm of political elegy with her "Monody on Major André" opened up a space for Williams's own early political verse on revolutions in the Americas, within which she also acknowledged her indebtedness to Montagu. Williams commended Montagu, in particular, for providing encouragement to writers via the intellectual, physical, and emotional support she offered them within the Bluestocking circles. Williams attempted to replicate Montagu's generous creation of space for writerly exchange by hosting similar gatherings, first in Hampstead, England, and then in Paris, France, providing intellectually generative spaces for women writers such as Joanna Baillie and Mary Wollstonecraft.

Williams's extension of Bluestocking-style sociability into Paris was shattered, however, by Robespierre's silencing and oppressive reign, which led first to Roland's imprisonment and then to her own. However, while imprisoned, Williams continued to take the risks associated with her politically charged connections to other writers by celebrating cross-cultural and interracial friendships in her translation *Paul and Virginia*. Her "Sonnet: To the Calbassia Tree," in particular, invites interpretation as a veiled tribute to Roland and the other French women Williams lost to the guillotine. The memory of their companionship, even after their executions, obviously sustained Williams through her own time of imprisonment and beyond.

Notes

1. Edmund Burke, *Philosophical Enquiry into the Origin of Our Ideas of the Sublime and the Beautiful* (London: Routledge, 1958), 43.

2. Paula Backscheider, *Eighteenth-Century Women Poets* (Baltimore: John Hopkins University Press, 2005), 228.

3. Angela Keane, *Women Writers and the English Nation in the 1790s* (Cambridge: Cambridge University Press, 2000), 3.

4. Rebecca Heinwitz Cole, *Spanish America and British Romanticism* (Edinburgh: Edinburgh University Press, 2010), 49.

5. Helen Maria Williams, *An Ode on the Peace* (London: T. Cadell), 24, 31.

6. Ibid., 25.

7. Ibid., 28.

8. Ibid., 31, 32.

9. Anna Seward, *Monody on Major André* (London: J. Jackson, 1781), 437–38. Interestingly, Jane E. Kim suggests another woman poet closely connected to Helen Maria Williams, Joanna Baillie, also draws on the biblical account of Cain and Abel in Genesis 4. See Kim's article "My Brother's Keeper: The Striving of Siblings in Joanna Baillie's *De Monfort*," *European Romantic Review* 23, no. 6 (December 2012): 711–13.

10. Harriet Devine, "Anna Seward," in *The Literary Encyclopedia, English Writing and Culture of the Romantic Period*, ed. Daniel Robinson, first published November 27, 2002, http://www.litencyc.com/php/speople.php?rec=true&UID=4027.

11. The public profile of Seward's monody bolstered eighteenth- and early nineteenth-century women poets and theorists. Ann Radcliffe, for example, uses a line from Seward's *Monody*, "And venom'd with disgrace the dart of death," as an epigraph for chapter twenty of her 1791 novel *Romance of the Forest*, ed. Chloe Chard (Oxford: Oxford University Press, 1986), 307. In her *Theory on the Classification of Beauty and Deformity* (London: John and Arthur Arch, 1815), the philosopher Mary Anne Schimmelpenninck praises Seward for writing "the memorials of those she shortly followed to the tomb" (132).

12. Harriet Guest, *Small Change: Women, Learning, Patriotism* (Chicago: University of Chicago Press, 2000), 266.

13. Teresa Barnard, *Anna Seward: A Constructed Life* (Aldershot, Hampshire, UK: Ashgate, 2009), 1.

14. Ibid., 73.

15. Helen Maria Williams, *An Ode on the Peace*, 65–72.

16. Ibid., 97, 103, 104.

17. Ibid., 185, 187, 188.

18. Ibid., 233–38.

19. Helen Maria Williams, "To Mrs. Montagu," dedication prefatory to *Peru, a Poem in Six Cantos* (London: T. Cadell, 1784), iii-vi.

20. Ibid., 16–17.

21. Ibid., 18.

22. Ibid., 35–42.

23. Though, in the "Note on the Texts" accompanying her edition of *Peru* and "Peruvian Tales" (Guelph, ON: Broadview Press, 2014), Paula Feldman observes, "'To Mrs. Montagu,' which appeared in 1784 . . . was only printed in some copies of *Poems* (1786)" (41).

24. Peter Clayden notes in *The Early Life of Samuel Rogers* that Williams "was a woman of much conversational power, and had the charm of sympathy and the art of bringing people together" (London: Smith, Elder & Co., 1887), 77. In his diary entry "April 21, 1791.—At Miss Williams's" (qtd. in Clayden, 165–74), Samuel Rogers records meeting Henry Mackenzie, Joanna Baillie, and publisher Thomas Cadell at Williams's home.

25. For more detail on Helen Maria Williams's poetic response to Elizabeth Montagu's interpretation of the witches in *Macbeth*, see Natasha Duquette's "Julie and Julia: Tracing Intertextuality in Helen Maria Williams's Novel," in *Editing Women's Writing*, eds. Amy Culley and Anna Fitzer (London: Routledge, 2017), 76–95.

26. Williams, *Ode on the Peace*, 236.

27. Helen Maria Williams, *Julia*, ed. Natasha Duquette (London: Pickering and Chatto, 2009), vol. 2, 123.

28. The Du Fossés were French political refugees living in London when Williams met them. Williams began taking French lessons from Madame Du Fossé in London in 1785 (Williams, *Letters*, 194). She soon learnt the story of the Du Fossés: they were forced to leave France because Monsieur Du Fossé's father, the Baron Du Fossé, had issued a *lettre de cachet* against their marriage across class boundaries. Williams notes that the "new constitution" (72) created by the National Assembly rendered such *lettres de cachet* defunct and thus enabled the Du Fossés' "return to prosperity, honours, and happiness" (ibid). Williams does not give the first names of the Du Fossés in her 1790 *Letters*, but Deborah Kennedy cites "Monique Coquerel" as Madame Du Fossé's maiden name. See Kennedy's *Helen Maria Williams and the Age of Revolution* (Lewisburg, PA: Bucknell University Press, 2002), 69.

29. For example, see the discussion of her poem "The Bastille: A Vision," inserted toward the end of *Julia*, as engaging the "interface between poetic prophecy and political justice" in Natasha Duquette's introduction to *Julia, a novel interspersed with poetical pieces*, xxi. See also Orianne Smith's discussion of the poem in *Romantic Women Writers, Revolution, and Prophecy: Rebellious Daughters, 1786–1826* (Cambridge: Cambridge University Press, 2013), 111–12.

30. Earlier in her 1790 *Letters*, Williams refers to the "Festival of Federation" in celebration of the first anniversary of the fall of the Bastille as "the most sublime spectacle which, perhaps, was ever presented on the theatre of this earth" (2).

31. Helen Maria Williams, "Introductory Remarks on the Present State of Science and Literature in France," in *Poems on Various Subjects* (London: Whittaker, 1823), xix.

32. Mary Wollstonecraft first mentions meeting Williams in a 1792 letter to Everina Wollstonecraft now published in *Collected Letters of Mary Wollstonecraft*, ed. Janet Todd (New York: Columbia University Press, 2003), 215.

33. Mary Wollstonecraft, *Works of Mary Wollstonecraft*, eds. Janet Todd and Marilyn Butler (London: William Pickering, 1989), vol. 5, 142.

34. Elizabeth Eger, "The Bluestocking Circle: Friendships, Patronage and Learning," in *Brilliant Women: 18th-Century Bluestockings*, eds. Elizabeth Eger and Lucy Peltz (London: National Portrait Gallery, 2008), 47.

35. Helen Maria Williams, *Memoirs of the Reign of Robespierre* (London: John Hamilton Ltd., 1929), 96.

36. Williams, *Peru*, Canto 3, 336.

37. Williams, *Memoirs*, 96.

38. Steven Blakemore, *Crisis in Representation* (Madison, NJ: Fairleigh Dickinson Press, 1997), 160.

39. See the facsimile of the "Order for imprisonment of H.M. Williams, her mother and Two Sisters, in the Maison D'Arrêt of the Luxembourg, October 11, 1793 (20 Vendémiaire, Year II)," taken from the Archives of the Prefecture of Police in Paris, and inserted between pages 58 and 59 of Williams's *Memoirs*. While describing her removal from Luxembourg to the prison at the "Convent des Anglaises," Williams writes of the guards, "the common principles of justice taught these unlettered patriots to lament the severity of our fate, which they endeavoured to soften by every mark of honest kindness" (*Memoirs*, 92).

40. Her execution took place on November 9, 1793 (Williams, *Memoirs*, 95).

41. Ibid., 99.

42. Helen Maria Williams, "Preface" to *Paul and Virginia* (Oxford: Woodstock, 1989), iii.

43. Angela Wright, *Britain, France, and the Gothic, 1764–1829, The Import of Terror*, (Cambridge: Cambridge University Press, 2013), 89.

44. Ibid., iv-v.

45. Ibid., v.

46. Ibid. Saint-Pierre's original narrative is set on the French island colony of Mauritius, in the Indian Ocean.

47. Ibid., viii-ix.

48. Philip Robinson, "Traduction ou Trahison de *Paul et Virginie?*," *Revue d'histoire littéraire de la France* 89 (1989): 843, 846. Nevertheless, Robinson records that it was published in at least fifteen distinct editions between 1795 and 1850. For more details, see Robinson's comprehensive list of the editions of Williams's text published up to the year 1850 in his footnotes 1–15 (843–50). According to Gary Kelly, writers Maria Edgeworth, Charles Dickens, and Thomas Hardy each refer to Williams's translation. See Kelly, *Women, Writing, and Revolution* (Oxford: Clarendon Press, 1993), 56.

49. Robinson, "Traduction ou Trahison de *Paul et Virginie?*," 852.

50. Louise Joy, "Emotions in Translation: Helen Maria Williams and the 'Beauties Peculiar to the English Language,'" *Studies in Romanticism* 50, no. 1 (2011): 167.

51. Ibid.

52. David Sigler, "'The Ocean of Futurity, Which Has No Boundaries': The Deconstructive Politics of Helen Maria Williams's Translation of *Paul and Virginia*," *European Romantic Review* 23, no. 5 (October 2012): 590.

53. Anna Neill, "The Sentimental Novel and the Republican Imaginary," *Diacritics* 23 (1993): 44.

54. Williams, trans., *Paul and Virginia*, 8.

55. Ibid., 76.

56. Ibid., 17.

57. Ibid., 62.

58. Ibid., 61.

59. Ibid., 37.

60. Christopher Mitchell, *The French Atlantic Triangle: Literature and the Culture of the Slave Trade* (Durham, NC: Duke University Press, 2008), 106.

61. Ibid., 107. By at least the 1780s, Williams herself was publically taking an abolitionist stance in works such as her *Poem on the Bill Lately Passed for Regulating the Slave Trade* (1788). For more on this poem, see Natasha Duquette's *Veiled Intent: Dissenting Women's Aesthetic Approach to Biblical Interpretation* (Eugene, OR: Pickwick, 2016), 22, 157–63.

62. There are eight sonnets in total in Williams's translation, *Paul and Virginia*, which she presents in the following order: "To Love" (20), "To Disappointment" (36), "To Simplicity" (56), "To the Strawberry" (67), "To the Curlew" (79), "To the Torrid Zone" (86), "To the Calbassia Tree" (156), and "To the White Bird of the Tropic" (158). The sonnet series as a whole moves through passionate tumult, cold despair, content acceptance, consolation in friendship, and finally, tension between individual freedom in exile and the social connections of "home" ("To the White Bird," 14). Sigler considers only "To the Strawberry," "To Love," and "To the White Bird," separately and out of their textual order, in his argument in "'The Ocean of Futurity.'"

63. Williams, *Paul and Virginia*, 76.

64. Williams, "Sonnet: To the Calbassia Tree," 1–7.

65. Williams, *Ode on the Peace*, 246.

66. Frances Ferguson, *Solitude and the Sublime* (London: Routledge, 1993), 46.

67. Williams, "Sonnet: To the Calbassia Tree," 8–14, my italics.

68. On February 27, 1790, Williams wrote to Hester Thrale Piozzi, "Mr. & Mrs. Barbauld will drink tea with me, & I hope you are not engaged" (unpublished letter, qtd. in Kennedy, *Helen Maria Williams*, 54).

69. Anna Barbauld, "On Friendship" in *The Works of Anna Barbauld with a Memoir by Lucy Aikin, Vol. II* (New York: G & C Carvill, et al., 1826), 354.

Sapphic Circuitry

Anna Seward's Equivocal Tribute to "Llangollen's Vanished Pair"

SUSAN S. LANSER

In 1778, two wellborn Anglo-Irish women, Lady Eleanor Butler and Sarah Ponsonby, escaped their homes in Ireland and settled in the village of Llangollen, Wales. For the next half-century they lived as a public couple, sharing bed, board, and belongings, signing their correspondence jointly, calling each other "my Beloved" and "my Better half." Although there was private speculation about their relationship, the metonymically named "Ladies of Llangollen" succeeded in cultivating a politically conservative, upper-class, literary and pastoral self-presentation that made Plas Newydd, their cottage with its renowned gardens, a site of pilgrimage. They were "sought by the first characters of the age, both as to rank and talents"[1]; invitations to visit them were selective and allegedly coveted, and several renowned guests left verbal traces of these encounters. Hester Thrale Piozzi became a frequent and enthusiastic friend to "the Hermitesses" during the last years of the eighteenth century and gave them a prominent place in her diaries. Anne Lister movingly evoked her longing for a woman life partner after meeting Ponsonby at Plas Newydd in 1822.[2] Walter Scott found them at once amiable, romantic, and amusing when he finally visited in 1824, and in that same year, William Wordsworth offered a panegyrical sonnet after his own pilgrimage.

But it was an earlier encounter with Plas Newydd and its tenants, by a poet at the height of her fame, that occasioned the long and complex public tribute that helped to spread Butler and Ponsonby's fame to these later visitors. In September 1795, Anna Seward met the "Ladies" while she was staying with her friends the Robertses in nearby Dinbren. After returning home to Lichfield, Seward began a "fervent, equal, and unalterable" attachment to Butler and Ponsonby that lasted until Seward's death in 1809.[3] In the wake of that inaugural visit, she also composed "Llangollen Vale," which she published together with a few shorter poems in 1796. *Llangollen Vale, with Other Poems,* with a frontispiece sketch by Sarah Ponsonby of the Plas Newydd cottage and a prefatory sonnet by Henry Cary that celebrates this "simple shrine" that the "fair Wanderers from Ierne's coast" have erected to "fond Friendship's gentle power," went through three editions in that single year. It received enthusiastic reviews from the *Gentleman's Magazine,* the *European Magazine,* the *New Annual Register,* the *Analytical Review,* and the *Monthly Magazine,* though these commentaries were often tinged, as Paula Backscheider observes, with discomfort and suspicion about the Ladies themselves.[4]

On its surface and as treated by most critics past and present, "Llangollen Vale" is sheer encomium. Fiona Brideoake sees it as a "romantic celebration" of both the couple and the Welsh landscape.[5] Paula Backscheider similarly hails it as "a portrait of the women's lives and devotion to each other."[6] Claudia Kairoff recognizes it not only as a celebration of two women "who have redeemed" the "barbarous past" of valley, but also as the poet's commitment to "a political model based on 'domestic affections' in place of the twisted patriarchal paradigm that was wreaking havoc in Europe."[7] JoEllen DeLucia puts it most enthusiastically when she sees "Llangollen Vale" as an "experiment in historical methodology" aimed "to reconcile Welsh and British history," offering an "alternative account of national and imperial development" that both queers and feminizes the idea of progress.[8]

I will not focus here on the transformative historical project embedded in "Llangollen Vale" that DeLucia and Kairoff have richly analyzed, but I do want to complicate readings of the poem in relation to the "Ladies" by arguing that Seward's naturalizing tribute to Butler and Ponsonby's "sacred Friendship" is effected at a certain price. Especially when seen within the panoply of women's tributes to women that are the focus of this book, "Llangollen Vale" gives us the "Circuit of Apollo" with a queer and ultimately fatal twist, evacuating the material underpinnings of literary encomium and turning praise of the living into elegy for the dead. In so doing, "Llangollen Vale" calls into question the material future of same-sex intimate relationships.

It could not have been easy to find a public form for honoring a relationship forged against both family wishes and heteronormative expectations. The idea of a praise poem to Butler and Ponsonby would not have conformed to the prevailing panegyrical norms, even the prevailing norms of this volume in which individual women praise other individual women mostly for literary, artistic, or intellectual accomplishments in the public sphere. Nor was there much eighteenth-century precedent for praise poems to couples, whether same-sex or cross-sex, other than, say, a king and queen. Moreover, as far as grounds for praise are concerned, Butler and Ponsonby accomplished nothing public and nothing in print; they played no visible role in the "Republic of Letters" nor inflected the London scene. Their accomplishment is precisely their "retirement," as it is called, from "the world." They must be recognized, therefore, not for what they did, exactly, but for what they refused to do, for how they lived. And how *did* they live? In an odd, curious, irregular union—as words applied to them suggest—that should (and in some quarters did) make them as much suspect as praised.

In short, public tribute to a female couple who have done nothing but reject marriage to men in favor of a commitment to each other, set up household in the Welsh countryside, and invested their homestead and its gardens with their Gothic tastes, surely placed burdens on the poetic text. I will argue that in "Llangollen Vale," the burden of tribute led to an erasure of the very couple who are the objects of praise, who become defined by and absorbed into the land like another pair of fallen warriors. Seward's solution for honoring a female couple, I will also suggest, becomes a primary solution of the Romantic age: to render Butler and Ponsonby metonymic and thus dissolvable into transcendence of their own material existence. Ultimately, then, Seward's poem functions as elegy and eulogy to two women who are very much alive, and in so doing inscribes the problem of publicly acknowledging what is in effect a same-sex marriage.

In both public and private ways, if not in their political alignment, Seward was ideally positioned to pay homage to the "Ladies of Llangollen." Dubbed the "Swan of Lichfield" for her lifelong adherence to the Midlands town that was also the birthplace of Samuel Johnson and David Garrick and for many years the home of Erasmus Darwin, Seward was already a strong advocate of provincial life and had proved through her own poetic celebrity that provincial women could be significant players in the public sphere. That she also came to be called "Queen Muse of Britain" suggests the degree to which provincial intellectuals and artists like Seward had already succeeded in promoting the aesthetic and moral values that would underlie the English cultural imaginary even as urbanization grew. Her own home was a site of visitation by admirers and intellectual associates both from London and from the extensive Whig intelligentsia in the Midlands, and she was no stranger to controversy especially in her public excoriation of Samuel Johnson's conservative political opinions and urban(e) literary practices. Butler and Ponsonby's political leanings aligned them much more closely with Johnson than with Seward; the "Ladies" were ardent Tory royalists while Seward adhered to what she called "whig principles." Had Seward met the couple five years sooner, they might well have tangled over the French Revolution and would certainly have taken different sides in the "pamphlet wars" spurred by Edmund Burke's *Reflections on the Revolution in France*.[9] Seward's disillusionment with Republican France brought her closer to the views of the "Ladies"; she also opposed Britain's war with France, and that opposition probably motivated her poetic attention to the costs of war in "Llangollen Vale."

Even in the absence of political alignment, though, Seward's aesthetic and emotional propensities would have drawn her to both the "Ladies" and the Vale. As John Brewer notes, Seward was given to a metaphoric investment in landscape and particularly to scenes that "embodied history as well as nature," scenes in which "sinuous variety and romantic setting engaged the eye," and sublime views "provoked a frisson of combined awe and fear" rather than the "tame" and "orderly."[10] This natural interest in the Llangollen landscape would have aligned with Seward's personal interest in the life partnership of Butler and Ponsonby. Seward never married, though she doubtless had passionate attachments to some men, not only to mentors like Darwin and friends like William Hayley but, closer to home, to John Saville, vicar choral at Lichfield who was separated from his wife and whose closeness to Seward occasioned both gossip and efforts by Seward's father, Bishop of Lichfield, to banish him from his daughter's company. But although Seward spoke of Saville as "scarcely less dear" to her than her beloved foster sister Honora Sneyd,[11] her poetic imagination had been long and longingly captured by Honora. Sneyd, several years younger than Seward (as Sarah Ponsonby was younger than Eleanor Butler), came to live with the Sewards as a child and became Anna's personal project of devotion and tutelage. In 1773, Honora became the second wife of Richard Lovell Edgeworth, much to Seward's sorrow and concern, and departed with Edgeworth for Ireland. Honora apparently broke with Seward for unknown reasons, and she died in 1780. Fiona Brideoake is surely right to see in Seward's fascination with Butler and Ponsonby the melancholy longing for the kind of lifelong intimacy she would have wished to share with the "lost Honora" and her wistful sorrow over the impossibility of that imagined life.

Sneyd was not the only female friend who engaged Seward's affections. She allegedly had intense relationships with at least three other women, especially Elizabeth Cornwallis, whom Seward named "Clarissa" and called the "unpartaken and secret treasure of my soul." The sublime natural setting for a same-sex marriage thus readily became Seward's passionate cause.

Seward began "Llangollen Vale" almost immediately after first meeting Butler and Ponsonby. In Brewer's words, "Plas Newydd and its surroundings" became "the perfect inspiration for Anna Seward's literary imagination. Its history, ruins, and scenery offered an ideal environment for tranquil reflection, and the love between the two women represented an ideal of romantic female friendship to which Anna Seward, with her memories of Honora Sneyd, had always been attached."[12]

It is this melding of place and person that underwrites Seward's tribute. Aside from its dedication "To the Right Honorable Lady Eleanor Butler, and Miss Ponsonby," "Llangollen Vale" does not mention its honorees until after its midpoint.[13] The protagonists of the first fourteen of its twenty-nine stanzas are Welsh princes and warriors and its motif the heroism of the Welsh against the British.[14] In this way, the poem is able to place the couple in a lineage of resistant and independent personalities from the colonized margins of Britain.[15] The defiance begins with setting the entire first half of the poem in times that precede the 1536 act by which Henry VIII annexed Wales to England. The text opens by rehearsing the violent "unequal fray" enacted on the River Deva's banks when Owain Glyndŵr (d. 1415), the "irregular and wild," "gallant," and "virtuous, tho' gay" last Welsh Prince of Wales, who led the heroic and futile Last Welsh War of Independence against the "imperious" Henry IV, determined to subdue Cambria until the river itself was "stained with warrior-blood."[16] The poem then turns, with an achronicity that is itself a rejection of linear progress, to the twelfth-century Welsh-Irish warrior poet and prince Hywel ab Owain Gwynedd (d. 1170). On the basis of Hywel's love for Lady Mifanwy Vechan, who lived at Castel Dinas-Bràn, Seward claims a hero who died in battle and who has turned Llangollen into a "love-devoted Vale." In this way, with a rather queer atemporality and something of a sleight of hand—since Hywel himself did not come from Llangollen and since his love for the Llangollen lady was "unrequited"—the poem deftly builds the hinge that turns the Vale from a site of bloodshed to a site "consecrate to LOVE" (6). Seward is also, through this move, able to praise the poetic arts that Butler and Ponsonby could not themselves represent and that she herself signifies as a national figure.

With this transition, the exact middle stanza of "Llangollen Vale" enters the "Circuit of Apollo" by showing how "Eleanora and her Zara," as Butler and Ponsonby are here romantically named, follow in the spirit of the high-minded rebellions of Glyndŵr and Hywel by completing the transformation of the vale of war into a vale of "sacred Friendship." The "peerless Twain" are heroized for the "sacred" "permanent" and "pure" friendship that has resisted both "the stern Authorities" and the "silken lure" of "Persuasion" to live amongst "Nature's charms" (6–7). Perhaps evoking Butler's Catholic parentage and convent youth, the poem also contrasts the chosen fealty of the now-Protestant couple to the "rash irrevocable vow" that Catholic "Superstition" demands (10). Seward praises Butler and Ponsonby not for literary achievement but, in effect, for rejecting achievement and for "scorning" the "Pride, Pomp, and Love" that could so easily have been their lot given their early "genius, taste, and fancy" and given the "graceful Arts" that flow through them as the river Deva flows through the Vale (6–7). They are praised not for their labors but for their "letter'd ease" and for their "Friendship's blest repose," not for worldly engagement but for their retreat from it, and especially for the inner sanctum of their library, "the dear, minute Lyceum of the Dome" (7–8). They are praised too for adhering to a code of femininity, standing in their "own soft sex" as a model of "pure Friendship" and "Virtue" to "the prouder sex" (9). The pair who were in reality heir to the strongest prejudices of their class are presented as without any "withering influence" of envy or bigotry and as paragons of "endowment" and "Charity" (11).[17] And while buzzwords of artistic accomplishment are tapped in a kind of word-cloud fashion—"Graceful arts," "genius, taste, and fancy," "energy and taste," and "whate'er the Pencil sheds in vivid hues" (7)—the fact that these words and phrases are not syntactically attached to any concrete achievements renders them curiously void, a sleight of hand. There is thus already a project of negation working here.

If there is a work of art to be lauded by "Llangollen Vale," it is surely the estate of Plas Newydd itself, acquired despite Butler and Ponsonby's financial strains,[18] and rendered here as the "Fairy Palace of the Vale" with its "Arcadian bowers" and "lawny crescent," images that again unite them with the land. Yet if we read "Llangollen Vale" as a country house poem,[19] we then encounter a continued syntactic detachment that yields rather attenuated praise. "Llangollen Vale" evokes the country house as utopian retreat in ways that reference both the mainstream tradition inaugurated by Ben Jonson's "Penshurst" and the female-centered idyll pioneered by Aemelia Lanyer ("Description of Cooke-ham") and Anne Finch ("Petition for an Absolute Retreat"). Seward's relationship to Butler and Ponsonby does not fit the conventional basis for country house praise; if she was grateful for the welcome at Plas Newydd that others may have coveted, Seward was not in need of patronage nor would Butler and Ponsonby have been positioned to provide it. Strikingly, "Llangollen Vale" gives fleeting attention to the house and gardens of which Butler and Ponsonby were so proud, collapsing their creation into a single stanza. Their enormous aesthetic labor is rendered in passive voice: "Then rose the Fairy Palace of the Vale, / Then bloom'd around it the Arcadian bowers." To be sure, their work is work "of Energy, and Taste," but its "plastic hand" (7) is barely visible.

Indeed, this brief tribute to the creation of Plas Newydd effects the poem's turn toward intimations of mortality, for in the verses that follow, the "Ladies" become textually enshrouded in images of gloom, dusk, and darkness. Although they "shine" in that darkness, the buildup is ominous. It begins in the library, the center of their "letter'd ease," now set as a scene of "gathering gloom" and "twilight gray," with lamps diffusing "a pale, green light" of the kind that barely illuminates a "starless night." The women are, to be sure, a "bright Pair" among the "rising gales"; the "lustre" of their Virtue glows, but the discourse piles on the images of "deep'ning veils," "shadowy elegance," "dark woods," and "dusk expanse" (8–10). By the time the text reaches its final stanzas (9–10), the images of gloom and darkness have slid into images of death, as the text itself drops a "dark cowl on each devoted head" and spreads a pall "o'er the breathing Corse." And although at the time of the poem's composition Butler and Ponsonby were only fifty-six and forty years of age respectively and were to live for three more decades, the last verses of "Llangollen Vale" imagine them already in the grave. The speaker hopes that "ne'er may Pain, or Sorrow's cruel blight, / Breathe the dark mildew thro' these lovely bowers. / But lengthen'd Life subside in soft decay," and in a final act of romantic fancy, the poem envisions the women being killed together by "one kind ice-bolt" rather than condemned to a "sad course of desolated hours." The poem's last image is that "all who honor Virtue" will "gently mourn / LLANGOLLEN'S VANISH'D PAIR, and wreath their sacred urn" (10). In short, in paying tribute, Seward makes them disappear. Poetically speaking, "Llangollen Vale" preserves the idea of the couple at the expense of the couple's life.

Why this elegaic tone for a pair of women in the prime of life? One could argue that Seward's ongoing grief at the loss of Honora Sneyd turned all thought of intimacy between women toward death. Certainly Seward is known for the elegaic quality of her poetry, and so one could claim that *Llangollen Vale* simply follows in that mode. Or one might recall that panegyric, as a poetic practice, encourages eulogy as well. Arguably too the gloom fits the mood of the vale itself, making friendship in a sense a kind of heroic battle, rather than only the antithesis of such a battle, by enmeshing both love and war with death. Certainly the trajectory of "Llangollen Vale" differs dramatically from Seward's representation of Butler and Ponsonby in her private correspondence from the same period. Her first letter about the couple describes the two "enchantresses" as pictures of vibrancy. Lady Eleanor is "somewhat beyond the *embonpoint* as to plumpness; her face round and fair, with the glow of luxuriant health." There is "enthusiasm in her eye, hilarity and benevolence in her smile" and she is deeply engaged in the events and culture of her times: "Exhaustless is her fund of historic and traditionary knowledge, and of every thing passing in the present eventful period. She has uncommon strength and fidelity of memory; and her taste for works of imagination, particularly for poetry, is very awakened, and she expresses all she feels with an ingenuous ardour, at which the cold-spirited beings stare."[20] Sarah is "very graceful. Easy, elegant, yet pensive, is her address and manner," and she is "charming," "sweet and feminine" of feature and equally talented and accomplished of mind.[21] And they are as much the survivors of their natural surroundings as they are its adherents: "they have not once forsaken their vale, for thirty hours successively, since they entered it seventeen years ago; yet neither the long summer's day, nor winter's night, nor weeks of imprisoning snows, ever inspired one weary sensation, one wish of returning to that world, first abandoned in the bloom of youth, and which they are yet so perfectly qualified to adorn."[22] The architecture of Plas Newydd likewise receives more detailed attention in Seward's letters than in her poem.

Strikingly, however, the poetic "solution" of "Llangollen Vale" turns out to be a more widespread practice: other poems about Butler and Ponsonby, and other late eighteenth- and early nineteenth-century poems about sapphic couples, likewise see them to their deaths. As I discuss more fully elsewhere,[23] female couples figure idyllic harmony in a significant number of European works of the same period, including Elizabeth Post's *Het Land* and Bernardin de Saint-Pierre's *Paul et Virginie* (both 1788) and, a bit later, Percy Shelley's "Rosalind and Helen" (1818), Therese Huber's pastiche novel *Die Ehelosen* (1829), as well as in the sonnet "To the Lady E.B. and the Hon. Miss P." that Wordsworth composed in 1824. In each of these instances, female coupling is figured both as idyllic and as a kind of death knell, with the sapphic ushering, as it were, a harmony in which it has no future. Together, these texts create elegaic contours that enable a certain instrumentality of signification for same-sex intimacies at a cost to those intimacies themselves. More informal tributes like Walter Scott's find the "romantic spinsters" at once amusing and melancholy throwbacks to a bygone age.[24]

Wordsworth's sonnet, to take the most relevant instance, reads Butler and Ponsonby in a tone similar to Seward's and is worth quoting in full for its echoes of "Llangollen Vale":

> A Stream, to mingle with your favourite Dee,
> Along the Vale of Meditation flows;
> So styled by those fierce Britons, pleased to see
> In Nature's face the expression of repose;
> Or haply there some pious hermit chose
> To live and die, the peace of heaven his aim;
> To whom the wild sequestered region owes,
> At this late day, its sanctifying name.
> Glyn Cafaillgaroch, in the Cambrian tongue,
> In ours, the Vale of Friendship, let this spot
> Be named; where, faithful to a low-roofed Cot,
> On Deva's banks, ye have abode so long;
> Sisters in love, a love allowed to climb,
> Even on this earth, above the reach of Time![25]

Here, as in "Llangollen Vale," Butler and Ponsonby are subordinated to the landscape, as an elaborate set of synecdoches substitutes the place for the persons rather than evoking the persons through the place. The Vale is here peopled only by the "fierce Britons" and "pious hermit"—rather less heroic images of the Welsh than Seward offers—and the "Ladies" do not appear until the final couplet, when they become chaste "sisters in love." Instead of the "mingling" of the women, we get the "mingling" of stream and river. The women "favour" the river rather than one another; they "have abode so long" not with each other but "on Deva's banks." These images both naturalize and neutralize the marital relationship, and when the women's love is finally proclaimed twice over in the closing couplet, it arrives in the safe trope of a sisterhood that transcends time and thus also corporeal existence.

Wordsworth's romantic tribute, like Seward's, praises the same-sex couple at their own expense. Together, the poems and the examples I have mentioned here suggest that tributes to women who might be read as lesbians walk a fine line just as do those sapphic women themselves, and that some kind of swerve in the "Circuit of Apollo" might have helped to wrest these women from a sense of their earthly—and corporeal—subjectivity to a transcendence that also required imagining away their bodies and enshrining them in immortality.

Seward herself may have had second thoughts about the tribute so widely circulated in *Llangollen Vale,* for there is a sequel to the poem. In 1802, she wrote a blank-verse poem of some one-hundred lines entitled "A Farewell to the Seat of Lady Eleanor Butler, and Miss Ponsonby, in Llangollen Vale, Denbighshire: September, 1802."[26] The poem was apparently not published until after Seward's death, when Walter Scott included it in a three-volume edition of her poetic works. "A Farewell" also carries a slight sense of epitaph, but in this case the departing one is Seward herself rather than the "peerless mistresses" who are the Vale's "guardians." Here, it is her own mortality of which the poet is conscious ("Time, that for me hath pass's full many a year / On broad and withering pinion"), and what she grieves are her own "exhausted powers," and her loss "of the skill to please, varied praise, the taste made coy by riot of encomium."[27] The "Farewell" sees the "Bless'd pair" into a future as she offers them a "benediction of increasing love." Llangollen is here an "Eden," a place of eternal happiness, and the poet implies regret for her inability to do the couple justice during "Friendship's primal hours"—the very hours when she composed "Llangollen Vale." There follows a long description of the varied, rugged, and sublime landscape of Llangollen Vale, but the poem's short closing stanza, which I quote here in full, affirms the triumph of life, not the memory of a "vanish'd pair":

> Haste to the scene, benignant powers of life,
> Mild Lachesis, and gay Hygeia, haste
> From day to day propitious!—on that bank
> Mossy and canopied with gadding boughs,
> Spin from the vital thread! And brim the cup
> With juice salubrious! Breathing soft, the while,
> Dear Eleanora, and her Zara's name.[28]

Here, in imagery that is also arguably erotically suggestive, the land is verdant and the cup overflows. As Stuart Curran notes, the apostrophe asks "that the Ladies continue to live their happy and healthy lives,"[29] a closing image quite distant from the final tenor of "Llangollen Vale."

If the 1795 poem with its death knell remains the popular tribute, it is a tribute doubtless overdetermined by the convergence of Seward's melancholy poetic imagination with the circumstantial challenges of sapphic circuitry. From this vantage point, it is the later, posthumously published, and lesser-known poem that stands out for its affirmation of "dear Eleanora, and her Zara's name." And if "Llangollen Vale" itself creates a "vanish'd" couple, Anna Seward—bold and independent like the characters she honors—has given Eleanor Butler and Sarah Ponsonby a place in the poetic firmament.

Notes

1. Anna Seward to the Reverend Henry White, September 7, 1795 (Letter XX), in *Letters of Anna Seward: Written Between the Years 1784 and 1807* (Edinburgh: George Ramsay, 1811), IV: 104.

2. See Anne Lister, *I Know My Own Heart: The Diaries of Anne Lister 1791–1840*, ed. Helena Whitbread (London: Virago, 1988), 209–10.

3. Seward to Lady Eleanor Butler, May 22, 1797 (Letter LXIX) in *Letters*, IV: 347.

4. For accounts of the reviews, see Paula Backscheider, *Eighteenth-Century Women Poets and Their Poetry: Inventing Agency, Inventing Genre* (Baltimore: Johns Hopkins University Press, 2005), 305, 309–10.

5. Fiona Brideoake, "'Extraordinary Female Affection': The Ladies of Llangollen and the Endurance of Queer Community," *Romanticism on the Net*, no. 36–37 (2004–5): 11.

6. Backscheider, *Eighteenth-Century Women Poets*, 307.

7. Claudia Kairoff, *Anna Seward and the End of the Eighteenth Century* (Baltimore: Johns Hopkins, 2012), 114–15.

8. JoEllen DeLucia, *A Feminine Enlightenment: British Women Writers and the Philosophy of Progress 1759–1820* (Edinburgh: Edinburgh University Press, 2015), 90–91, 114. I find DeLucia's arguments mostly persuasive, but as my own analysis suggests, I'm not sure British and Welsh history are so much reconciled here as reversed: "Llangollen Vale," I submit, offers history from the perspective of the losing side.

9. Butler and Ponsonby were friends of their Anglo-Irish compatriot Edmund Burke; Seward remained critical of Burke's defense of a monarchy that she considered "oppressive and barbarous" (quoted in Kairoff, *Anna Seward*, 102). Writing to Butler on December 9, 1795, after reading the just-published memoirs of Madame Roland, executed by the Jacobins in 1793, Seward suggests that had the Rolands lived to see "as we have seen, the miseries resulting from an overturned empire, and from democratic sway, their virtue would have prevented their disseminating those ideas and principles, to which such numbers of wretched people have, with themselves, been sacrificed." But she adds that reading Mme Roland "has taught me to believe the murdered king more blameable than I supposed;—that if he had acted sincerely, he might yet have been a monarch, with limited powers, and saved his people from the miseries of lawless disorganization, under the idiot name of equality" (letter to Lady Eleanor Butler, December 9, 1795, in *Letters*, IV:136–37). For a fuller sense of Seward's politics vis-à-vis the Revolution, see Kairoff, *Anna Seward*, 99–104.

10. John Brewer, *The Pleasures of the Imagination: English Culture in the Eighteenth Century* (New York: Farrar Straus Giroux, 1997), 582.

11. Seward to Mrs T—— (Letter XLIV), June 19, 1796, in *Letters* IV: 218.

12. Brewer, *Pleasures of the Imagination*, 606.

13. "Llangollen Vale" deploys a six-line verse form, with a rhyme scheme of ababcc, the first five lines in iambic pentameter and the sixth an alexandrine, lending weight and French formality. It is thus close, though shorter by two lines, to Spenserian stanza (the form of *The Faerie Queene*), which will be taken up by Romantic poets who postdate Seward. Many of the stanzas, especially those in the first half, are annotated with information about people, places, and the author's personal encounters with both.

14. Claudia Kairoff is surely right to see the poem's urgent engagement with the conversation from savagery to peace as a protest against the Revolutionary Wars in which England was already embroiled. See Kairoff, *Anna Seward*, 114–16.

15. In elevating Welsh and Irish figures and in heroizing their struggles against the English, "Llangollen Vale" reverses English superiority, speaking from the margins of a still new "Great Britain" that has struggled with—and often against—its proclaimed mission to unite in spirit the kingdoms brought together by its several Acts of Union of which the last, with Ireland, was not executed until 1800. On representations of English superiority over British outsiders see, for example, Michael Ragussis, *Theatrical Nation: Jews and Other Outlandish Englishmen in Georgian Britain* (Philadelphia: University of Pennsylvania Press, 2010); and Franco Moretti, *Atlas of the European Novel 1800–1900* (New York: Verso, 1998), especially chapter 1.

16. Anna Seward, *Llangollen Vale, with Other Poems* (London: G. Sael, 1796), 2–4. Further references to the poem will appear in parentheses within the body of the text.

17. On what I call the "compensatory conservatism" of Butler and Ponsonby, see Susan Lanser, "Befriending the Body: Female Intimacies as Class Acts," *Eighteenth-Century Studies* 32, no. 2 (1998–99): 179–98.

18. For details about Butler and Ponsonby's financial situation, and a rich sense of both of their lives together and the responses to them over time, see Fiona Brideoake's deeply informed new study, *The Ladies of Llangollen: Desire, Indeterminacy, and the Legacies of Criticism* (Lewisburg, PA: Bucknell University Press, 2017). As Brideoake notes, Butler and Ponsonby "struggled to live on less than three hundred pounds a year" until 1787, when the campaign of a high-placed friend succeeded in placing Butler on the Irish Civil List for an additional one hundred pounds per year (11).

19. I am grateful to Susan Staves for recognizing "Llangollen Vale" as a country house poem.

20. Seward to the Reverend Henry White (Letter XX), September 7, 1795, in *Letters*, IV: 103.

21. Ibid., 103–4.

22. Ibid., 104.

23. See Susan Lanser, *The Sexuality of History: Modernity and the Sapphic, 1565–1830* (Chicago: University of Chicago Press, 2014), chapter 7.

24. Scott's remarks are quoted in JoEllen DeLucia, *A Feminine Enlightenment: British Women Writers and the Philosophy of Progress 1759–1820* (Edinburgh: Edinburgh University Press, 2015), 108.

25. Wordsworth wrote about his first glimpse of Butler and Ponsonby that "so curious was the appearance of these ladies, so elaborately sentimental about themselves and their 'Caro Albergo,' as they named it in an inscription on a tree that stood opposite," and "so oddly was one of these ladies attired that we took her, at a little distance, for a

roman Catholic priest.... They were without caps, their hair bushy and white as snow, which contributed to the mistake." See William Wordsworth, *The Complete Poetical Works* (Boston: Houghton Mifflin, 1904), 640.

26. Anna Seward, "A Farewell to the Seat of Lady Eleanor Butler and Miss Ponsonby, in Llangollen Vale, Denbighshire: September, 1802," in *The Poetical Works of Anna Seward; with Extracts from her Literary Correspondence*, edited by Walter Scott, Esq., 3 vols. (Edinburgh: James Ballantyne, 1810), 345–50. I am indebted for knowledge of this poem to Stuart Curran's essay, "Anna Seward and the Dynamics of Female Friendship," in *Romantic Women Poets: Genre and Gender* (Amsterdam: Rodopi, 2007), 11–21; it is also mentioned briefly in Backscheider, *Eighteenth-Century Women Poets*, 311.

27. Seward, "Farewell to the Seat of Lady Eleanor Butler and Miss Ponsonby," passim.

28. Ibid., 350.

29. Curran, "Anna Seward and the Dynamics of Female Friendship," 13.

"I Delight in the Success of Your Literary Labours"

Friendship as Platform for Reinvention

KATHARINE KITTREDGE

The socialite and the quakeress made a strange pair of friends: one rarely left her modest home in the tiny Irish town of Ballitore, and the other was rarely found in either her fashionable London digs or her palatial estate in the Hampshire countryside. Melesina Trench traveled the continent as a young widow, had an intimate relationship with George III's seventh son, and was at the center of a scandal thirty years after her death when her letters were published.[1] Mary Leadbeater kept bees, tended to the ills of the local peasants, and wrote didactic works that, according to Niall 'O Ciosáin, ushered in a "new stage in literature for the peasantry by elite reformers."[2] Leadbeater wrote poetry, biography, fiction and instructive prose that won critical approval and respectable sales; Trench's books of poetry were printed rather than published, and it was not until her posthumous work, *Thoughts of a Parent on Education*, was published that she had any literary success. In spite of their differences, the two shared some of their most intimate thoughts and feelings: maternal guilt, professional aspirations, recipes for soup and pickled cabbage, and instructions for home remedies. The tributes that they wrote for each other serve as bookends of their relationship: Leadbeater's poem of praise signaled the start of their relationship, and Trench's eulogizing letter to Leadbeater's daughter looked back on her friend after her death. In the first, Leadbeater subtly describes the person she hopes her friend will be; in the second, Trench describes the nature of her friend as it was revealed over the decades of their correspondence.

Most of what we know about this friendship comes from the correspondence between the two women. For the last twenty years of their lives, they wrote to each other on a weekly (and sometimes daily) basis. Each woman cherished the relationship and her friend's letters, but their different personalities, lifestyles, and domestic situations have produced a definite inequality in the archival materials. Trench, who spent her final years still caught up in parenting young children, seems to have lived in a state of disarray; she apologizes for her writing, noting that "I generally write with a lively child at each elbow . . . and you know how [unseas]onable this must be to the exactness or propriety of my style."[3] It was also not unusual for her to lose letters—both ones she received and those she was writing. In March 1824, she enclosed an additional scrap of paper that reads: "Dear friend, I wrote a letter to Ballitore—lost it—re-wrote it, & having been called away hastily—doubt whether I sent either copy—I now rather risk sending this, which I have found on my table, then expose myself to having forgotten both—If you receive duplicates excuse your faithful (in all that does not concern the head) tho' forgetful."[4] Trench referred to her writing space as "The Chaos" and when Leadbeater sympathetically indicated that her own correspondence was also disorganized, Trench jovially corrected her: "You talk of a *chaos*, and your verse and prose are separate, and your papers *of the same size* are sewed *together*—& your letters form a class apart—My dear Mrs. Leadbeater, you know not what a Chaos is."[5] History has proven Trench correct, for the letters that she sent to Leadbeater are preserved in the Beinecke Library in two massive volumes; each letter is placed in chronological order, reinforced with tape, and hand-sewn into place. In contrast, the preservation of Leadbeater's letters to Melesina seems to have been more a matter of chance. There were sufficient examples for Leadbeater's daughter, Lydia Jane Fisher, to feature them in *The Leadbeater Papers*, published in 1862, but the examples we have in the Hampshire Record Office and in the Beinecke Library are incomplete and unbound. After their mother's deaths, each family recognized its matriarch as a person of significance and sought to preserve her writing—Richard Chenevix Trench published excerpts from his mother's papers as *The Remains of the Late Mrs. Richard Trench* in 1862—but it may be that Melesina's descendants were more daunted by the expanse of "The Chaos," or that Melesina's son was less handy with a needle than Leadbeater's daughter, resulting in a less orderly and complete archive. As a result of this disparity, we know considerably more about Melesina's side of the friendship than Leadbeater's.

The original letters allow us to gain important insights into the two women's friendship. Although over a hundred of their letters were published in the 1862 collections, the editorial choices made by their offspring were greatly influenced by the time of publication. Richard Chenevix Trench's excerpts focus on literary and political commentary and on his mother's domestic concerns. In contrast, Leadbeater's daughter included more information about the women's own literary projects. This disparity may be due to the difference in the reception of their writing—by most measures, Trench must be considered a "failed" poet, and her continued insistence on writing and printing her verses may have been an embarrassment to her son, who was himself a respected man of letters.[6] In contrast, Leadbeater's writing was both critically acclaimed and commercially successful, so it is natural that her daughter would have wanted to highlight that aspect of her life. However, both offspring-editors found the women's intermingling of domestic and professional concerns daunting. For example, Fisher printed the first part of a letter in which Trench describes the effect of the recent death of her youngest child ("do not be surprised at my not writing . . . I am not at present fitted for common subjects . . ."),[7] but she deleted the latter part of the missive in which Melesina describes her work on the "final" copies of her most recent book: "I shall correct one Campaspe & one Moonlander exactly. . . . one more evening will do it—I have sent two Moonlanders—present one in my name to Mr. Shakleton—whose corrections I shall gratefully acknowledge."[8] This intermingling of the profoundly personal with the literary is one of the hallmarks of the women's epistolary relationship. Both offspring-editors also took care to delete the references to Trench's role as an absentee landowner, and to Leadbeater's acting as her unofficial agent, although a predominant topic in the original letters was the well-being of the tenants and the progress of a variety of reforms and strategies for their relief. These two efforts—the direct relief of local poor, and serious literary endeavors encompassing both works of social activism and personal expression—were the primary concerns in the later years of both women, and although their immediate heirs did not see these aspects of their lives as ones to be celebrated, they are the roles that resonate most with women in the twenty-first century.

A Shared Literary Life

Trench and Leadbeater met for the first time in April of 1802. Following the 1798 Irish Rebellion,[9] Trench was determined to take personal control over the properties she had inherited from her grandfather, the Bishop of Waterford. When she went to visit her property in County Kildare, about thirty miles outside of Dublin, she was unable to find housing at the inn in nearby Ballitore, and instead stayed as a houseguest of the local hotel owners, the Quaker family, the Leadbeaters. Trench felt an immediate connection with Mary Leadbeater, and remained a houseguest for two weeks.

Both women combined a keen interest in literary matters, and a devotion to social causes with a daily immersion in homely arts like gardening, cooking, and family medicine. These myriad points of connection created a bond that belied their late meeting and infrequent personal encounters. As Leadbeater writes, at the end of that first visit, "our friendship became confirmed in strong and enduring bonds, and we constantly corresponded."[10]

Early in the friendship the two also exchanged samples of their literary productions, with Leadbeater sending Trench her long prose work "Ballitore." Trench is extravagant in her praise of Leadbeater's description of her village, saying that it "resembles a highly finished Dutch painting, in which one of the best artists has represented village scenery and manner, and where one is not only struck by the general effect, but amused and interested in the details"[11]; she goes on to say that the details conveyed by the work will "increase in value as they increase in years," becoming most significant in the time of "our great grandchildren" who will have no better source for the description of that time. Trench's wholehearted support was important to Leadbeater, since she was discouraged from spending time writing (let alone publishing her work) by her influential mother[12] and her diary records her own reservations about "the business of my publications," which she felt were "thus exposing myself."[13] Thus, it was crucial to her to have a trusted friend who could offset the discouragement that she received within her own community, encouraging her to publish and write: "The press gives one a firm property in the mental exertions of those we love."[14]

Leadbeater responded with a letter thanking Trench for a copy of Trench's poems, *Mary Queen of Scots*, praising their "irresistible" "simplicity clothed in elegance."[15] The letter concludes with a six-stanza tribute poem, "When Melesina wakes the living lyre," in which Leadbeater celebrates her new friend's literary achievement. The opening stanza contains an excessively panegyrical response to Trench's historical poem:

> While Melesina wakes the living lyre,
> And Truth and History guide the moral Song,
> The raptured heart is kindled at her fire.
> And quaffs the harmonious tide which rolls along.[16]

The refrain of the poem: "Wealth, Beauty, Genius, all combine to pour / Their brilliant gifts upon their favourite fair" is found at the beginning of the second and the end of the sixth stanzas, and summarizes the status that Trench held in Leadbeater's eyes. The first two aspects were undisputed (and unearned), but the third attribute, "Genius" represented a stature that

Trench strove for her whole life, and for which she never achieved recognition. Leadbeater's valedictory poem, while somewhat overblown in its literary response to Trench's mediocre verse, certainly fulfilled its primary role of reassuring Trench that she need not fear any harsh critiques from her new friend and reader. For the next twenty-four years, Leadbeater would perfectly play the role of the "gentle reader" and fan of Trench's work, rather than that of the Critic. Both women had been raised in environments that discouraged their writing, and both had considerable insecurities around both their own abilities and the way that a wife and mother's writing would be viewed. Thus, the reciprocal acclimation expressed by each in these early days of their friendship created a powerful bond that not only allowed them to be supportive of each other's work, but also encouraged them to view themselves as authors of accomplishment and power.

Leadbeater's ability to produce well-received publications while continuing to tend to her family and maintain her role as a respected member of her community no doubt encouraged Melesina to think more seriously about her own work. Although she had had some contact with published female authors in the past, specifically, Anna Seward and Hester Thrale Piozzi, neither of them presented the kind of role model that would encourage a late-life entry into a literary career by a woman who was still devoting most of her time to raising her children. In the short essay "A Memoir of Mary Leadbeater," which precedes her posthumously published *The Annals of Ballitore* (1862), Leadbeater's daughter describes her mother's work habits: "Her power of turning in a moment from one occupation to another was amazing . . . Exposed to continual interruptions from friends . . . from visitors . . . from the poor, who daily came to her for advice and help; she never seemed in a hurry, and with perfect regularity carried on her various occupations . . . She wrote a good deal while her friends were conversing around her, and sometimes joined in the conversation."[17] As their friendship via correspondence grew, Trench and Leadbeater also came to supply an important function as the primary readers of each other's work. As Barbara Hughes states, "As the 'representative reader' to whom Leadbeater's texts are primarily addressed, her [Melesina's] comments and tactfully phrased advice are especially valued. While she invariably praises Leadbeater's works, she also indicates where changes should be made in any further editions, or, if she receives the text at draft stage, how the finished work should appear."[18]

Leadbeater's first publication had been a collection of essays and poems titled *Extracts and Original Anecdotes for the Improvement of Youth*, whose entries bore titles like "Daniel in the Lions' Den," "Extract of a Letter to

R.S. [Richard Shackleton]," "Concerning Slavery," and "The Punishment of Covetousness." Although she had been composing poetry since childhood, it was not until 1808, at the age of fifty, that Leadbeater ventured to publish a book of her own verse. She wrote to Trench that even though she had previously declared that "nothing could induce me to print by subscription . . . that I have adopted this mode in compliance with the advice of several intelligent friends."[19] It seems that the most difficult aspect of this for Leadbeater was asking her friends to support the book, as she wrote to Trench, "thy assistance is most valuable, and that we should never blush to receive the favours we solicit."[20] Trench responded by immediately reassuring her friend that publishing by subscription was the correct path, saying "be assured I think that as a wife and mother, it was your duty to publish in such a way as left no possibility of your family's suffering any pecuniary loss by the bad taste of the public,"[21] and she went on to declare, "I am a little affronted at your not having employed me in the same way as your other friends, and beg you will now do so."[22] Trench subsequently put in for six volumes for herself, for another three in her son Charles's name, and for an assortment of orders from her other friends, including Viscount Clifden. The first edition contained more than five hundred subscribers, with Trench's order representing the largest number of copies assigned to any single subscriber, although two booksellers were down for multiple copies: "Darton and Harvey, London, 25," and thirty copies for "Benjamin Wells, Esq. Dublin." For the most part, the subscribers were Irish, with some subscribers from York (a Quaker enclave), and a few from London.

In 1808, *Poems by Mary Leadbeater (Late Shackleton) To which is prefixed Her Translation of the Thirteenth Book of the Aeneid* was published in both Dublin and London. It included over four hundred pages of original poetry dealing with nature, personal events, and national news stories, some dating as far back as 1776. In addition to domestic poems such as "Inscription on a Bee-House," Leadbeater included poems on the impact of the 1798 rebellion: "Summer-morning's Destruction" and "The Beggar," about an old man whose sons rose up and were killed in the rebellion. The valedictory poem that she had written for Trench six years earlier appears on pages 397–98 under the title "On Reading Poems by a Lady." The only way in which it differs from the original is in its inclusion of an additional stanza:

> And whilst the tear of sweet benevolence
> Adds tenfold lustre to the radiant eye,

> Th'admiring pupil steals the side-long glance,
> And grateful feelings prompt th'unconcious sigh.

This direct reference to Trench's beauty (in her youth she was bombarded with poems and other written effusions addressed to her "fine eyes") and to a young peasant's admiration of it may originally have seemed too personal a point to raise in a poem addressed to a newly acquired friend.

Trench's response came some months later, and contains high praise for the work's delightful "softness and refinement, both of ideas and language" and thanks for "the address you have honoured me with": "so gratifying to my feelings, that all vanity at being over-praised is lost in more pleasurable sensations."[23] She also urged her friend to ignore the negative reviews she had received for her book: "I am sorry to hear your feelings have been hurt by criticisms. Remember to consider them only as burrs thrown on us in the way of holiday foolery," and also that "if we walk not in the trodden path, our very petticoats will catch them" (quoting from Shakespeare's *Midsummer Night's Dream*, act 1, scene 3). "Is not this overbalanced by having stepped into an untrodden path of greater beauty and fragrance, and collected in it a very delightful choice of sweets?"[24] During this time, Leadbeater was certainly working on the manuscript that would become *The Cottage Dialogues*, and she was also shepherding a family project, a "manuscript magazine" "to which most of the young, and occasionally some of the old contributed, and several extracts were made from this compilation for the *Belfast Magazine*."[25] She would eventually send copies of "The Hinter" to Trench, who shared them with her children and eventually contributed a few pieces of her own to the magazine.

Following the publication of her poems, Leadbeater was emboldened to seek support from others for her work. Throughout 1810 she was sending Trench drafts of her book-length didactic work "Rose and Nancy," and the two had engaged in discussion of the topics covered therein, and of the extent to which religion should be explicitly featured in the book. Buoyed by Trench's approval, in the Spring of 1810, Leadbeater sent a manuscript copy to her friend the Bishop of Meath, with a note requesting that he pass it along to Maria Edgeworth.[26] In a few months she received a response from Richard Lovell Edgeworth, indicating that Maria would be writing an advertisement for the volume and notes for an English edition. He offered to shepherd the volume through its British publication using the Edgeworth's own bookseller, and, finally, he arranged subscriptions for five hundred copies—three hundred for the Edgeworth family, and another two hundred among their friends. Upon hearing this, Trench, in turn, rose to the occasion, subscribing for a dozen copies for herself, and 150 for Charles. The publication was met with very favorable reviews, and organizations such as the Society for Bettering the Condition and Increasing the Comforts of the Poor purchased copies to distribute to all of their members.[27]

Although Trench continued to offer (sometimes intrusive) commentary on *The Cottage Dialogues* and unhelpful advice—she insisted that it should be called *The Cabin Dialogues*, and wanted her son Charles to be hired to make illustrations for the next edition—Trench's support of her friend's successful publication was unstinting, and she triumphantly reported every favorable review or significant extract of it that she encountered. Perhaps it was the commercial success of her friend that encouraged Trench to raise her sights toward more visible forms of publication. In all of her new ventures, Leadbeater not only acted as a trusted advisor, but also frequently served as a conduit to publication by finding venues for Trench's work, and acting as an (unpaid) literary agent for her. The *Farmer's Journal* was a periodical edited by Leadbeater's friend William P. LaFanu and we know that she sent some of her own pieces, predominantly about social issues or rural husbandry, to him.[28] Leadbeater seems to have taken on the task of recruiting writers for him; we also have a note of her transmitting the work of another friend, "an elderly friend in an obscure station."[29] Around 1812, we find a flurry of notes in the correspondence indicating that Trench was having Mary pass on pieces of her work to LaFanu. Leadbeater also had a relationship with the *Belfast Magazine* (the first publication to laud *The Cottage Dialogues*), and Trench used her as a conduit for submitting material to that publication. As the years passed, Trench grew bolder, establishing a direct correspondence with LaFanu, and submitting directly to British-based publications like the *Hampshire Chronicle* and the *Weekly Intelligencer*.

In the next few years, Leadbeater devoted herself to writing a sequel to the *Cottage Dialogues* (Trench contributed an unsolicited additional dialogue for the volume, a denunciation of working-class whining, which Leadbeater graciously declined), and Trench turned her attention to authoring a variety of pamphlets on a number of social issues: chimney sweeps, servants' charitable giving, slavery, and the salt tax. Trench also threw herself into producing volumes of her original verse. The first of these, *Ellen: A Ballad: Founded on a Recent Fact. And Other Poems*, she had printed in Bath with the intention of selling the book "For the Benefit of the House of Protection."[30] She wrote of it to Leadbeater: "You attribute a better motive than I deserve to my having marked the price on Ellen—I do it, in the hope my friends may recommend it to their friends, or to Booksellers and thus cooperate with my attempts to be useful to an excellent charity."[31]

By using her book to raise money for a worthy cause, Trench was walking a careful line between appropriate and inappropriate behavior for an aristocratic woman. Doing so allowed her to print volumes of her verse in a way that freed her from accusations that she was attempting to be a "professional" author, but also allowed her to fulfill the admirable role of "lady bountiful" coming to the relief of the poor. We do not know how many copies of *Ellen* were printed, nor how much money it succeeded in raising for charity, but we do know that Trench took another route toward making her authorship gender-appropriate with her next two publications: *Campaspe, an Historical Tale; and Other Poems* (Southampton: T. Baker, 1815) and *Laura's Dream, or the Moonlanders* (London: J. Hatchard, 1816).[32] With both of these texts, she sent copies of her books to Leadbeater so that she could sell them to raise money for a variety of charitable causes. Trench wrote to her in 1816, "I have printed a large Edition for Charitable purposes—whatever number not exceeding 50 you think may be sold at three shillings each for your school—I am ready to give to it."[33] In a later letter, she further suggested that Leadbeater actively promote the volume, "When you have leisure and inclination, perhaps you will send an extract or two from it to the *Farmers Journal*—I should prefer a specimen of your selection to one of my own."[34] There is no record of Leadbeater's response to this, but Trench continued to send copies of her collections to Leadbeater for distribution and the next year also sent her leftover copies of the earlier collection, *Ellen*, to dispose of.

During all this time, the two women continued to read and critique each other's work, a practice that Leadbeater referred to as "these efforts of friendship." Leadbeater shared the burden of reading and correcting Trench's drafts and proofs with her relatives—her son-in-law Richard Shackleton was an especially respected critic—and she would sometimes give Trench's printed copy to her children so that they could correct the *errata*. Even though Leadbeater continued to ignore Trench's suggestions about new projects and marketing directions, she expressed great respect for Trench's textual analysis "the justness of thy criticism struck me so forcibly, that on reviewing the passages I wondered I had not written them exactly as thou pointed out; so convincing is truth."[35] There were also times when Trench's desire to be helpful led her to inadvertently wound her friend, and she would then apologize for the "eagerness and warmth that sometimes carries me beyond the limits I would on cool reflection wish to have observed,"[36] or a "carelessness of expression" that "has distressed me as often as I have recollected it."[37] Unfazed by Trench's lack of tact, Leadbeater continued to have Trench correct her proof sheets as late as 1822.[38]

Over time, as she watched Leadbeater's literary status rise, Trench felt empowered to move beyond the role of aristocratic "dabbler" in literary endeavors, and she began to seek more widespread literary recognition. After years of self-publishing for the benefit of charities, she wrote to Leadbeater in 1823 that her financial situation made it impossible for her to continue to "indulge" in privately printing her work: "it is an expensive amusement—I do not suppose I shall make up the deficiencies of rent by my performances—but if I can see them well printed—and have the pleasure of giving them to my friends without cost—it will be something."[39] She subsequently asked Leadbeater to negotiate with her own printers, Darton and Harvey, for the publication of *Thoughts of a Parent on Education*. Barbara Hughes remarks that Leadbeater was an unusual woman for her time because she negotiated her own publishing deals, controlling print size and quality and the prices charged for her works, in addition to negotiating to sell the copyright of her books at significantly more than the average price.[40] Leadbeater successfully negotiated with Darton and Harvey for the publication of Trench's work, and although the experience was not a wholly positive one (they failed to promote the book to Trench's satisfaction), placing her manuscript with publishers who had become the leaders in children's and nondenominational didactic works may have ultimately led to Trench's book eventually being published to some acclaim by the Society for the Promotion of Christian Knowledge. But that would take place long after both of the friends were dead.

Partners in Social Improvement

The other primary preoccupation reflected in the letters is the two women's shared concern for the cottagers who inhabited Ballybarney, the "townland" that Trench owned about four miles from Ballitore. Leadbeater writes in her *The Annals of Ballitore* about their first meeting, when she found her worldly, well-traveled guest "seated on one of the kitchen chairs in the scullery, for coolness, hearing a company of little children of her tenants sing out their lessons to her."[41] She makes this image the central conceit of her tribute poem, describing Trench[42] in the three middle stanzas:

> Not hers the joy to bask in Fortune's glow,
> Her simple taste from purer springs is fed;
> 'Tis hers to bid the golden current flow
> Where the bleak wilds of poverty are spread.
>
> Seek not in courts you shall not find her there,
> She proved the pomp of courts and found it vain—
> Behold her seated on the rustic chair
> Surrounded by the little lowly train!
>
> The uncouth accents strike her patient ear,
> Oft is the tedious task repeated o'er;
> Whilst winning smiles his wondering bosom cheer
> The little peasant learn the artless lore.[43]

These lines seem to be standard praise for a benevolent woman, and Trench's determination at that time to "take her tenants from under the 'middlemen' to her own protection"[44] is admirable. However, at the time they met, Trench had been the landlord over the Ballybarney lands for thirteen years and in all that time had failed to visit her Irish tenants or to ensure that they were being treated fairly by the agent. According to Leadbeater's own notes, Trench's neglect made "The place [Ballybarney] very bleak; the head tenants of that lovely lady having cut her timber and oppressed those under them."[45] And contrary to the depiction of Melesina in the poem, while the Ballybarneites were being reduced to misery by the rents, and the countryside despoiled by the rapacious agent, Trench *had* been enjoying "the pomp of courts," and when she did bid the gold to flow out of her purse it was to bring her all the trappings of the good and leisured life: the coach, the house in London, the best schools for her son, balls, theater, and continental travel. There had been no indication up until that time that Trench had any intention of ceasing to "bask in Fortune's glow."

This valedictory poem, written at the moment of mutual connection and vulnerability, is both a farewell and a hope for the future. As the years passed, both Trench and Leadbeater were able to devote more and more of their time to improving the lives of those around them, rather than solely devoting themselves to the needs of their own families. Although their backgrounds were very different, both women came from traditions of personal charity. Melesina was raised by her grandfather, Richard Chenevix, the Bishop of Waterford; in an unpublished autobiographical sketch, Trench reflected on his "unbounded Philanthropy" and describes how he "appropriate[d] a large part of his income to acts of Charity. He was sometimes thought to be too indiscriminate in his distributions, for his own candor prevented him from doubting the sincerity of others, and whoever excited his feelings, commanded his purse. . . . He was among the first promoters of many liberal establishments for the relief or prevention of distress."[46] In marrying into the Trench family, she became part of a network of landowners who worked actively to improve their lands and to support their tenantry. Her letters are filled with references to cottages and schools built by her husband's brothers, as well as notes about the charitable projects of other Irish Huguenot philanthropists, including her close friend Elizabeth LaTouche (who went so far as to construct a school and orphanage adjacent to her manor house).

Leadbeater's charitable activities reflected the values set forth by George Fox (founder of Quakerism), who encouraged members of the Society of Friends to engage within their local communities to improve the lives of all those in the community, regardless of religious affiliation.[47] In her book, *The Largest Amount of Good: Quaker Relief in Ireland, 1654–1921*, Elizabeth Hatton describes the emergence of "a position of humane practicality"[48] that was evident in the relief work of the Quakers in the eighteenth and nineteenth centuries. Quakers' humanitarian work was distinguished by their lack of proselytizing and their rejection of the dominant theoretical conceptualization of poverty as being derived from a fault or failing of the poor.[49] This philosophy facilitated cooperation with philanthropists from other religions, and made Quakers open to searching for new methods of relief that addressed the current needs of a particular group of people. A particularly intriguing aspect of the correspondence between Trench and Leadbeater is the expression of their willingness to experiment with different forms of relief and the extent to which they sought and trusted each other's judgment in the adoption (or modification) of creative solutions to the problems of the poor.

The year after Trench's initial visit to Ballitore, Leadbeater was writing with approval about the positive changes in the lives of the tenants: "She [Trench] put matters to rights. She took the poor out of the hands of their oppressors; they now derive immediately under her, and she refused the offers of those who would have rented the whole, which might have appeared a much readier method of getting her rent."[50] In the years that followed, Trench rarely returned to Ireland, turning the pragmatic aspects of overseeing her properties over to her husband Richard, who made extensive trips to Ireland on an annual basis. As a result, the primary source of Trench's knowledge of her tenants' daily needs was gained through Leadbeater's reports. She also depended on Leadbeater to carry out "the little commissions respecting thy [Trench's] tenants"[51] that she requested or authorized by post.

The intimacy of the relationship that both women had with the Ballybarney cottagers is reflected in one of the first notes in the first packet of Trench's materials at the Beinecke. It is a small scrap of paper that Trench gave to one of her tenants to present to Leadbeater: "Another patient—another intrusion on your universal goodness—The bearer's name is Flood, & she has a little girl very much afflicted with worms—I could not refuse her your advice, which I think I can insure her—She is not in a situation to *want* medicines, so I beg you will only prescribe."[52] This also shows that, although Leadbeater tended to give most of the credit to Trench as the "patroness," it was Leadbeater herself who carried the burden of assessing the situation of the tenants and working to make their lives better. Trench acknowledges this frequently, as in an 1815 letter when she requests that Leadbeater make a purchase that would supply "some assistance according to your judgment and knowledge of their wants and merits. At this distance, you know I am incompetent to decide."[53]

One of their earliest innovations was the establishment of a communal collection of childbed linen and infants' clothing, which rotated among the cottagers. At first, Trench supplied these items from refurbished articles from her own home: "Pray let me know what articles are wanting to complete the linen for the basket as I am now removing some trunks, & perhaps materials may be found amongst damaged House linen which you could find workwomen glad to make up in Ballitore."[54] Six years later, she wrote: "I am pleased to hear my childbed linen is nearly worn out, as it proves how extensively useful it has been and I wish it to be replenished as you propose."[55] When Leadbeater identified specific needs of individual cottagers, Trench authorized the purchase of more personal presents—"flannel waistcoats and warm stockings to Dillon's child,"[56] "any article of warm clothing you think proper for Nancy McCabe,"[57] and "a cloak for Biddy Ennis."[58]

She also enlisted Leadbeater to implement systems of relief that closely resemble what we now call "microlending": "I am glad the Widow Farrell accepts the offer of a loan payable by installments. I should be very glad to try how far five Guineas, always circulating in that way would be useful."[59] At other times, she requested that Leadbeater purchase an article, which the tenant would then pay for "by installments of sixpence a week."[60] We can see this as an attempt to empower her tenants so that they felt they were meeting their own needs rather than taking charity, though we should also note that she was setting up a system that would require Leadbeater to collect money from the tenants every single week.

Another way that the pair sought to improve the lives of the Ballybarney tenants was by rewarding positive behaviors like maintaining one's home or keeping a productive garden with annual monetary prizes. Leadbeater wrote in her *Annals of Ballitore* for the year 1808: "I was commissioned by Melesina Trench with the distribution of premiums to her poor tenantry in Ballybarney to encourage the cultivation of their gardens. The premiums were—one guinea and a half to the best, one guinea to the second, and a half guinea to the third. My husband and John Christy were the judges."[61] Over the years, these premiums would expand to those for "degree of cleanliness in habitation,"[62] diligence in schoolchildren,[63] and the preservation of trees. Trench and Leadbeater's discussions regarding these prizes reveal the hybrid sensibility that underscored their relief efforts—a philosophy also visible in Mary Leadbeater's *Cottage Dialogues*—whereby they sought to graft useful parts of Protestant Ascendancy innovations (e.g., gardening) with existing indigenous best practices in areas such as the care and maintenance of dirt floors and yards. Their letters show respect for the hard work and ingenuity of the Irish poor, and an awareness of the wide range of circumstances that contributed to their vulnerability.

It is not clear whether Trench fully appreciated how much time Leadbeater must have devoted to Ballybarney, or how much credit she gave her for the increased well-being of the cottagers. At one point, she refers to Leadbeater's "*motherly* care of Ballybarney" (emphasis Melesina's),[64] and later she thanks Leadbeater for "the kind, and efficient assistance you afforded me, without which nothing could have been done. Ballybarney is a child of your own."[65] In her final letter to Leadbeater's widower, Trench speaks of "the premiums and small charities" that Leadbeater was able to "render efficient by her zealous co-operation,"[66] which once again seems to assign Leadbeater a secondary role in the undertaking. This stance may have been merely a reflection of Trench's tendency toward egotism, or it may have been a reflection of Leadbeater being self-effacing by nature as well as by creed.

Another focal point of their collaboration was the desire to create economic opportunities for Trench's cottagers. For example, in 1809, Trench authorized the purchase of goods so that Derby Costello's wife could set up "a little shop and sell a few articles of the most daily necessity."[67] She authorized the purchase and installation of "a good, large shop window" and asked Leadbeater to "order and pay for articles to that amount [five pounds] as I am apprehensive of her laying in and selling spirits."[68] Trench was especially concerned that the women of Ballybarney have a means of supporting themselves and their families. At times, Trench questioned some of the traditional employment patterns of the Irish, as when she mused: "It appears extraordinary that in Ireland widows of middle age & without young children do not hire as servants as they do here [England]—but prefer living alone in cabins where apparently they cannot get an honest livelihood."[69] Yet, even though she was a strong advocate of going into service, she accepted her tenants' desire to live independently. She asks Leadbeater if there might be some way that Widow Farrell, could be "furnish[ed] with employment at home, as her son requires attendance,"[70] and suggests, "Can we not put the knitting needles into Farrell's hand? I will cheerfully supply materials and instruction, & Charles [Trench's eldest son] will buy her first half dozen petticoats."[71] Other strategies for supplying instruction, implements, materials, and creating a market for home-produced goods, especially those made by women, arise over and over again in Trench's correspondence. In many ways, Trench's view seems very similar to the dominant Quaker attitude of refusing to denigrate the poor for being ignorant or lazy, seeking instead to change the conditions that led to their distress.

Although we only have one side of the correspondence, there are many indications that Leadbeater's involvement with the Ballybarney peasants was a reflection of her activities on behalf of the poor in her own neighborhood. In 1810, in response to a falling linen market, Trench asked Leadbeater to arrange for "half a dozen Ballybarney girls to be taught to plat straw" at Trench's expense, hiring the same person to train them that Leadbeater's daughter had employed for a similar purpose.[72] When Trench decided to start a school for the Ballybarney children,[73] Leadbeater hired the schoolmaster, and then had him trained by the "Lancastrian" schoolmaster whom she had already installed in the local school in Ballitore. This exchange reveals Leadbeater's crucial involvement with the local children, and her expertise in the field of education (not surprising for a woman who was the daughter and granddaughter of famous schoolmasters).

It is important to put the work that Trench and Leadbeater did within the larger context of nineteenth-century Irish poor relief. Their tactics in Ballybarney—the provision of clothing, shelter, and medical supplies coupled with the promotion of alternative food sources and new forms of small-scale industry—were also those most usefully employed twenty years later by wealthy women and Quaker organizations for the relief of the victims of the Great Famine. Their cross-religious collaboration can be seen as a precursor to the much larger-scale and highly effective work done by women of different faiths twenty years later.[74] Their work also created a legacy that was at once more personal and far-reaching. Trench's work with Leadbeater both set the tone for and established the patterns of charitable giving that were subsequently adopted by her sons, whose greater wealth and larger sphere of influence allowed them to make an even more significant impact. Trench supplied medicines and childbed supplies to her tenants; her eldest son, Charles Manners St. George, provided the land and the funds to build a hospital in his largest holding of Carrick-on-Shannon. Her third surviving son, Richard Chenevix-Trench, was Protestant Archbishop of Dublin during the Irish Famine of 1879. He moved quickly to reject religious exclusivity in his work as one of the founding members of The Mansion House Committee, where he served alongside Mary Leadbeater's kinsman, Abraham Shackleton.[75]

Final Valediction

Just as the friendship opened with a valedictory moment, it closed with Trench's celebration of her friend in the letter she wrote to her daughter, Mrs. Shackleton, following Leadbeater's death in June 1826. Leadbeater had not been ailing long; Trench's previous letter was full of medical advice (she advised Leadbeater to stop taking Mercury). Trench's initial response to the loss of her friend was surprise and regret: "How little gratitude did I show for her unbounded kindness and partiality, not half so much as I felt! how many attentions to her were *to be* performed, how long were they deferred! How often totally forgotten. Alas! I thought I should have her always." She emphasizes that Leadbeater was vital and forward-looking right up to the end: "She was so serene, so happy, so active . . . she had so many benevolent and literary plans." Leadbeater's abrupt transition from full engagement in life to death was especially jarring for Trench, "Death how unexpected! I never thought of this word as connected to her!"[76]

It was not until two months later that Trench was able to come to terms with her friend's death enough to produce a more comprehensive tribute. Like Leadbeater's valedictory poem of so many years before, Trench's final tribute to her friend is short, and much of it uses predictable language in its praise. The letter starts out by discussing a "character" (tribute-portrait) that Leadbeater's daughter Mrs. Shackleton had passed along. This document has not been preserved, and there is no information about its length or authorship. Trench feels the essay does not "touch upon many points which deserved a place in her portrait," so she goes on to list them:

> ... her anxiety to improve herself and others; her delicate feelings, highly refined, yet never degenerating into susceptibility, or exacting from others those attentions she never failed to bestow herself; her taste for every thing that was admirable in nature and art; her polished mind and manner, which seemed instinctively to reject all that others are taught to avoid; her quick-sense of wit and humour, and her own unaffected pleasantry; her entire absence of all self-comparison with any human being, which left her capable of doing complete justice to the merits of all; her rare suavity, and her uncommon talents.[77]

Much of this seems to be an attempt to drive home the point that, although she lived in rural retirement, Leadbeater was not to be considered a rustic or uneducated person; rather she was "refined," "delicate," "polished," and suave. It was important to Trench that Leadbeater be recognized as the equal of any member of high society or the intellectual elite, individuals whom Trench had known in London and in the great capitals of Europe. Just as Leadbeater's tribute poem had optimistically (and somewhat inaccurately) depicted her as the kind of woman that Leadbeater wanted her to be, in this final piece of writing, Trench recasts her humble friend, with whom she had discussed peasants' internal parasites, and "homely" recipes for soups, as the kind of woman whom she felt the larger world would honor and respect.

Perhaps most significant, Trench uses the piece's closing lines to defend her friend's place in the special form of literature that she pioneered. Trench says, "The writer of this 'character' has also placed her 'second' in the delineation of Irish manners and language." Clearly, the portrait had made a disadvantageous comparison of Leadbeater to her more famous mentor, Maria Edgeworth. Trench would not allow this comparison to stand; she asserts: "She [Leadbeater] is second to none in this. Others have taken a wider range; others have permitted themselves the free indulgence of humour on a greater variety of topics; but, as far as she goes, she is second to none."[78] Trench makes two important distinctions here. First, she identifies the significant differences in the way that Leadbeater and Edgeworth used humor in their depiction of the Irish poor. Edgeworth's work features stereotypical names and behaviors and uses phonetic spellings to poke fun at the rustic Irish dialect. Leadbeater's work creates rounded characters whose amusing foibles arise out of their personalities rather than their national identity. Her writing captured the rhythms of Irish speech, but never stooped to comic mimicry. Secondly, unlike Edgeworth, who depicted Irish people of all classes and in a wide variety of settings, Leadbeater limited herself to those she knew best: the rural peasants in her neighborhood who were her special care and her frequent delight. The tribute that Trench wrote for her lost friend thus brings together the two elements that Leadbeater's valedictory poem had combined so many years before: the celebration of her subject's social worth and uncommon talent/genius with a description of this extraordinary person humbly placing herself among the common folk.

In between these two tributes, the correspondence of the two women documents how each woman reinvented herself at mid-life, moving beyond the daily tasks of child-rearing and household oversight to strive to make an impact in a wider arena. In their last decades, Leadbeater became a bestselling author, and Trench became a prolific poet and social activist. Although they rarely met, they used their letters to provide encouragement and practical advice to each other: Trench read and commented on drafts of Leadbeater's work, and Leadbeater helped Trench find a publisher and distribute her books. Most importantly, the recognition that they shared common interests, values, and ambitions enabled them to support each other during their unconventional mid-life transitions. This support was essential as each struggled to achieve her larger goals while continuing to embody appropriate femininity within her family and immediate community.

Notes

1. For a discussion of the response to this publication and its contents, see Katharine Kittredge, "Missing Immortality: The Case of Melesina Trench (A Neglected, Celebrated, Dismissed and Rediscovered Woman Poet of the Long Eighteenth Century)," *Aphra Behn Online: Interactive Journal for Women in the Arts 1640–1830* 1, no. 1 (Spring 2011).

2. Niall 'O Ciosáin, *Print and Popular Culture in Ireland 1750–1850* (New York: St. Martin's Press, 1997), 149.

3. Melesina Trench to Mary Leadbeater, 12/27/1811, Beinecke Library, OSB MSS 50.

4. Melesina Trench to Mary Leadbeater, 03/1824, Beinecke Library, OSB MSS 50.

5. Melesina Trench to Mary Leadbeater, 1/15/1811, Beinecke Library, OSB MSS 50.

6. See Katharine Kittredge, "The Poetry of Melesina Trench: A Growing Skill at Sorrow," *British Journal for Eighteenth Century Studies* 28, no. 2 (Fall 2005): 201–14.

7. Mary Leadbeater, *The Leadbeater Papers* (London: Bell and Daldy, 1862), 1: 283.

8. Melesina Trench to Mary Leadbeater, 11/22/1816, Beinecke Library, OSB MSS 50.

9. Mary Leadbeater was also profoundly affected by the Rebellion, and the detailed account that she gave in her *Annals of Ballitore* is frequently cited. See Susan Egenolf,

"'Our Fellow Creatures': Women Narrating Political Violence in the 1798 Irish Rebellion," *Eighteenth-Century Studies* 4, no. 2 (2009): 217–34.

10. Mary Leadbeater, *The Leadbeater Papers*, 2: 288.
11. Ibid., 1: 143.
12. Barbara Hughes, *Between Literature and History: The Diaries and Memoirs of Mary Leadbeater and Dorothea Herbert* (New York: Peter Lang, 2010), 154.
13. Mary Leadbeater, qtd. in ibid., 159.
14. Leadbeater, *Leadbeater Papers*, 2:176.
15. Ibid., 2: 144–45.
16. Ibid., 1:146.
17. Ibid. 1: 8–9.
18. Hughes, *Between Literature and History*, 171.
19. Leadbeater, *Leadbeater Papers*, 2: 152.
20. Ibid.
21. Melesina Trench to Mary Leadbeater, 10 /1807, Beinecke Library, OSB MSS 50.
22. Leadbeater, *Leadbeater Papers*, 2: 152–53.
23. Ibid., 1: 163.
24. Ibid.
25. Ibid., 1: 310.
26. In seeking (and receiving) help from the Bishop, Leadbeater was following in the footsteps of earlier didactic writers like Hannah More. For a full discussion of this trend, see Susan Staves, "Women and the Clergy of the Church of England," *Huntington Library Quarterly* 65, nos. 1 and 2 (2002): 81–103.
27. For a discussion of the impact of this text in the context of similar didactic works, see Katharine Kittredge, "'For the Benefit of Young Women Going into Service': Late Eighteenth-Century Proto-Young Adult Novels for Labouring Class Girls," *Women's Writing* 23, no. 1 (2016): 106–26.
28. Leadbeater, *Leadbeater Papers*, 1: 346.
29. Ibid., 2: 205.
30. According to www.british-history.ac.uk, there was "a house of protection for orphans and destitute females" located in Bath.
31. Melesina Trench to Mary Leadbeater, 8/24/1815, Beinecke Library, OSB MSS 50.
32. The *Moonlanders* was remarkable for its time since it was a work of science fiction published prior to Mary Shelley's *Frankenstein*. For a full discussion of its place in the context of imaginative fiction, see Katharine Kittredge, "Wingless Women Living Backward on the Moon: Melesina Trench's *The Moonlanders*, 1816" in *Science Fiction Studies* 101, no. 34 (March 2007): 19–41.
33. Melesina Trench to Mary Leadbeater, 8/3/1816, Beinecke Library, OSB MSS 50.
34. Melesina Trench to Mary Leadbeater, 8/29/1816, Beinecke Library, OSB MSS 50.
35. Leadbeater, *Leadbeater Papers*, 2: 203.
36. Melesina Trench to Mary Leadbeater, 2/04/1812, Beinecke Library, OSB MSS 50.
37. Melesina Trench to Mary Leadbeater, 12/27/1811.
38. Leadbeater, *Leadbeater Papers*, 2: 320.
39. Melesina Trench to Mary Leadbeater, 1/1823, Beinecke Library, OSB MSS 50.
40. Hughes, *Between Literature and History*, 158–59.

41. Leadbeater, *Leadbeater Papers*, 1: 287.

42. Although Melesina still went by the name "Melesina St. George" at this time, I am referring to her as "Trench" to avoid confusion.

43. Leadbeater, *Leadbeater Papers*, 2:144–47.

44. Ibid., 1: 287–88.

45. Mary Leadbeater, qtd. in Hughes, *Between Literature and History*, 155.

46. Melesina Trench, "The Recollections of Melesina Trench, with Extracts from her Diary and Correspondence," autograph draft, Hampshire Record Office, ref. 23M93/2/1, n.d.

47. Carlos Figueroa, Assistant Professor of Politics, author of the forthcoming book, *Quakers, Race and Empire*, conversation with author, Ithaca College, August 17, 2017.

48. Helen Elizabeth Hatton, *The Largest Amount of Good: Quaker Relief in Ireland, 1654–1921* (Kingston, ON: McGill-Queen's University Press, 1993), 28.

49. For a full discussion, see Hatton, *The Largest Amount of Good*, chapter 2: "Good to All and Harm to None: Early Years in Ireland," 34–44.

50. Mary Leadbeater, qtd in Hughes, *Between Literature and History*, 155.

51. Leadbeater, *Leadbeater Papers*, 2: 145.

52. Melesina Trench to Mary Leadbeater, n.d., beginning of first packet, Beinecke Library, OSB MSS 50.

53. Melesina Trench to Mary Leadbeater, 7/8/1815, Beinecke Library, OSB MSS 50.

54. Melesina Trench to Mary Leadbeater, 2/8/1810, Beinecke Library, OSB MSS 50.

55. Melesina Trench to Mary Leadbeater, 8/29/1816.

56. Melesina Trench to Mary Leadbeater, 8/16/1811, Beinecke Library, OSB MSS 50.

57. Melesina Trench to Mary Leadbeater, 12/25/1815, Beinecke Library, OSB MSS 50.

58. Melesina Trench to Mary Leadbeater, 11/22/1816, Beinecke Library, OSB MSS 50.

59. Melesina Trench to Mary Leadbeater, 12/22/1809, Beinecke Library, OSB MSS 50.

60. Melesina Trench to Mary Leadbeater, n.d. 1807, Beinecke Library, OSB MSS 50.

61. Leadbeater, *Leadbeater Papers*, 1: 310.

62. Melesina Trench to Mary Leadbeater, 9/28/1810, Beinecke Library, OSB MSS 50.

63. Melesina Trench to Mary Leadbeater, 12/22/1810, Beinecke Library, OSB MSS 50.

64. Melesina Trench to Mary Leadbeater, 9/28/1811, Beinecke Library, OSB MSS 50.

65. Melesina Trench to Mary Leadbeater, 10/15/1813, Beinecke Library, OSB MSS 50.

66. Leadbeater, *Leadbeater Papers*, 2: 332.

67. Melesina Trench to Mary Leadbeater, n.d. 1809, Beinecke Library, OSB MSS 50.

68. Melesina Trench to Mary Leadbeater, 1/22/1810, Beinecke Library, OSB MSS 50.

69. Melesina Trench to Mary Leadbeater, 12/22/1810.

70. Melesina Trench to Mary Leadbeater, 1/15/1811.

71. Melesina Trench to Mary Leadbeater, 12/22/1810.

72. Melesina Trench to Mary Leadbeater, 4/9/1810, Beinecke Library, OSB MSS 50.

73. This school was another example of Trench's ability to look beyond religion to assess the needs of her tenants. According to an e-mail sent to me by Irish historian Dr. Eilís O'Sullivan, "The school in Ballybarney *appears* to have been still going strong in 1824. According to [*Second Report of the Commissioners of Inquiry* . . . , 1826–27 (12). XII. 1.] Appendix 22, 616, 617, the teacher by 1824 was one Martin Walshe, Roman Catholic who earned about £6 or £7 per year. The thatched cabin he worked in had cost about £5 to build. There were between 16 and 26 Roman Catholic children attending the school

(figures varied in the returns from the clergy of the area)." Email to author, September 2013.

74. Christine Kinealy, "'The Widow's Mite': Private Relief During the Great Famine," *History Ireland Magazine,* March/April 2008, 40–45. See also Rob Goodbody, "Quakers and the Famine," *History Ireland Magazine* 6, no. 1 (Spring 1998).

75. Dublin Mansion House Committee for the Relief of Distress in Ireland, *The Irish Crisis of 1879–80: Proceedings of the Dublin Mansion House Relief Committee* (Dublin: Browne and Nolan, 1880).

76. Melesina Trench, *The Remains of Mrs. Richard Trench* (London: Parker, Son and Bourn, 1862), 516.

77. Ibid., 517.

78. Ibid.

Lyric Sociability

Object Lessons in Female Friendship in Amelia Opie's Occasional Verses

SHELLEY KING

Throughout her career, Amelia Opie (1769–1853) produced occasional verses celebrating her relationships with friends and acquaintances in all walks of life. From the early elegant and amusing "Accept these sheets with roses grac'd" (1807) accompanying a packet of notepaper[1] supplied to a friend, to the late sincere "To A Prism Sent from London to My Friend David" (1831), Opie frequently took some material object as the inspiration for her verses, relying on it to provide the focus for a reflection on the emotional connection a poem celebrated. The poetic apostrophe accompanying the prism sent to sculptor Pierre Jean David opens, "Go, fair dispenser of celestial light / And charm my distant friend's admiring sight!" as she imagines him sharing her pleasure in the scattered colors its facets will produce, replicating the rainbow effects of the screen hung with prisms in her own sitting room.[2] She concludes, however, with a more intensely and intimately imagined sharing of mutual creative inspiration among artist, writer, and object: "The breathing marble & the poet's lays / Have the same source as thy prismatic rays"—the single faceted piece of glass refracting God's light becomes the means of uniting the English Quaker woman, once a celebrated beauty and poet, with the renowned French sculptor.[3] The arc of thought in this late poem illuminates a pattern developed by Opie over the decades of her career, one in which a gift object is accompanied by a text that articulates a perceived or desired relationship with the recipient, and in which meditation on the object leads to a deeper understanding and appreciation of sociable ties. This essay examines an important subcategory of sociable lyric that emerges from the lengthy catalogue of Opie's poems: verses that focus on an object connected specifically to her relationships with women and that function as supplements to memories of friendship, as accompaniments to gifts designed to evoke a strengthened sense of memory and connection, and as celebrations of the bonds of female friendship.

Beginning from the premise that Opie's occasional gift poems form part of the wider network of Romantic sociability that has reimagined Romanticism as a site of communal creativity rather than individual genius, this essay examines such social connections in the context of the role played by material objects in mediating identity. In his analysis of the human/object relationship, Bill Brown points to "a more general dynamic by which human subjects depend on inanimate objects to establish their sense of identity, dynamics described not just by anthropologists but by philosophers."[4] As he goes on to explain,

> John Locke, among others, imagined that identity was an effect of remembering thoughts and actions, but Hannah Arendt came to argue that our sense of ourselves and what we call identity stabilize foremost in relation to concrete objects. "The things of the world have the function of stabilizing human life," she wrote, "and their objectivity lies in the fact that—in contradistinction to the Heraclitean saying that the same man can never enter the same stream—men, their ever-changing nature notwithstanding, can retrieve their sameness, that is, their identity, by being related to the same chair and the same table."[5]

Arendt locates identity in a relationship to a material object that remains stable across time—we know our sameness by our relationship to "the same chair and the same table." I argue that Opie participates in this construction of self-identity in relation to specific objects, but that in her gift poems she also works to develop a sense of shared sociable identity grounded in an object consciously placed at the center of shared experience. Giver and recipient know themselves and their relationship to each other through the same gift object. Further, the lyrics accompanying the gift serve to imbue the object newly introduced to the friendship with a shared personal history, by expressing both personal affection and the imagined role of the object in mediating and sustaining the friendship. In her introduction to *Evocative Objects: Things We Think With,* Sherry Turkle notes, "We find it familiar to consider objects as useful or aesthetic, as necessities or vain indulgences. We are on less familiar ground when we consider objects as companions to our emotional lives or as provocations to thought. The notion of evocative objects brings together these two less familiar ideas, underscoring the inseparability of thought and feeling in our relationship to things."[6] Amelia Opie's gift lyrics engage in precisely that process of "consider[ing] objects as companions" to her emotional life and "provocations to thought"; more, they participate in constructing objects as means of mediating thought and feeling between two women, reifying the sociability embodied by the object.

This essay examines two categories of poems with clear associations to female friendship that reflect Opie's sense of the construction of identity through concrete objects: the first consists of two published and very public reflections on a portrait of her friend Frances Kemble Twiss (1759–1822), sister of Sarah Siddons, painted by Regency portrait artist John Opie as a gift for his wife; the second is a series of private poems written to accompany the birthday gifts she sent to her close friend Elizabeth Vassall Lemaistre (1771–1857). The material things meditated upon in the poems considered are thus of two kinds: the first is the portrait or representation of a female friend given as a gift *to* Opie, prompting reflections on her own role as a public poet celebrating female friendship as inspiration; the second is formed of non-representational objects, designed for personal or domestic use, given as gifts *by* Opie as tokens of female friendship. Both types of object prompt meditation on intense relationships and both inspire poetic response.

There is, perhaps, no object more evocative than a portrait—the speaking likeness vividly recalls the physical being of the sitter, and as time passes increasingly serves as a reminder of past selves and the relationship between sitter and observer. It is the type of object Arendt would understand as allowing individuals, despite "their ever-changing nature," to "retrieve their sameness, that is, their identity" through their relationship to it. When the painting offers a representation of a dear friend and is itself the work of a beloved spouse, the affective force intensifies. Opie wrote two poems reflecting on her husband's portrait of her close friend Frances Kemble Twiss. These verses, in fact, frame her career: "Lines Addressed to Mr Opie on his having painted for me a picture of Mrs. Twiss" (1799) appears at its very beginning, and "On the Portraits of Deceased Relatives and Friends, Which Hang Around Me" (1834), one segment of which reflects on the same painting, is among the last of her published works.[7] The poems highlight both the complex interconnections of Romantic sociality and the importance of what Christopher Rovee calls "the social nature of portraiture itself."[8] The portrait of Twiss is social in that it registers the ties of friendship within the circle and emerges from John Opie's painterly ability to satisfy his wife's private discourse of affective aesthetic desire. Amelia Opie's lyrics unlock the multiple affects of sociability evoked within her by the painting.

It should be noted at the outset that one of the most frustrating aspects of working on Opie's "object poems" is the difficulty in tracking down the original gifts described. Analogous items abound, but the things themselves remain stubbornly elusive. A case in point is John Opie's 1798 portrait of Twiss, despite its public renown. Frances Twiss was born Frances Kemble in 1759, a daughter of famed actor Charles Kemble and the sister of actress Sarah Siddons. Amelia Opie was friends with both sisters, and retained the portrait of Twiss, who died in 1822, until her own death in 1853. The portrait was exhibited at the Royal Academy show in 1799, the year following John Opie's marriage to Amelia Alderson.[9] In fact, in this year, Opie exhibited three portraits that gained considerable notice at this exhibit. The *Whitehall Evening Post* of April 27, 1799 offers the following description: "Mr. Opie's portraits this year have such charms of grace and delicacy, added to their force and truth, as entitle him to new praise. Mrs. Twiss, in the ante-room, Mrs. Price and Mrs. Opie (who is painted in the same canvass in two points of view), are most highly finished portraits." The portrait of Frances Kemble Twiss assumed a multiple role in identity formation for Amelia Opie. It was at once the commemoration of one of her most enduring female friendships and a honeymoon gift that propelled her husband to new fame and greater reputation. It was also the occasion of her own entry into the public sphere as the lyric poet "Mrs. Opie." Although she had previously published anonymously a series of poems in the *Norwich Cabinet* and the novella *Dangers of Coquetry*, and had allowed her maiden name "Miss Alderson" to be attached to two popular song lyrics, it was as Mrs. Opie that she would rapidly rise to literary celebrity. Very soon after marriage, the incipient literary career of Miss Alderson was promoted by the practical John Opie, who, as she wrote in her memoir of her husband, "always encouraged, instead of checking, my ambition to become an acknowledged author. Our only quarrel on the subject was, not that I wrote so much, but that I did not write more and better. . . ."[10]

In rapid succession, her poetry and her novels gained public recognition: in 1799 and 1800, several of her poems appeared in Robert Southey's *Annual Anthology*, and the lyric that garnered the most praise was "Lines Addressed to Mr Opie on his having painted for me a picture of Mrs. Twiss."[11] It opens with praise of the ability of the portrait to evoke the presence of her female friend, commenting on how "well" the artist's "glowing pencil" or paintbrush "Has traced those features painted on my heart: / Now, though in distant scenes she soon will rove, / Still shall I here behold the friend I love."[12] The very publicly displayed art object is hailed as the material realization of the private figurative portrait of Twiss "painted on [the poet's] heart." The portrait thus reflects an intriguing duality: it is at once the skillfully limned "lov'd semblance" of a close female friend that leads Opie to "exult" in its beauty, and the prized "gift ... bestowed" as the evidence of both a husband's love and his consummate skill as an artist. The poem was published in early 1799, coinciding with the exhibition of the portrait at the Royal Academy show, potentially enhancing public interest in the painting. And this is the point that I want to make—lyric sociability for Opie was sometimes entirely private and personal as it was with most of the occasional object poems like those addressed to Elizabeth Lemaistre, but sometimes it was markedly public and complex as in these portrait poems.[13] The private friendship between two women becomes the occasion of public display in its objectification as portraiture made available for gallery viewers. Twiss's portrait is both a private token of intense affection and the public expression of friendship between two women; it is also a token of erotic love between husband and wife, and the public exhibition of the commercial talents of both poet and painter.

As Laura Tallon argues in "'Friendship better than a Muse, inspires': Anna Letitia Barbauld Claims the Sister Arts for Female Friendship," eighteenth-century women poets were familiar with the "two related traditions: the competition between the sister arts and the discourse of same-sex friendship."[14] Tallon describes a complex tradition of the gendering of creativity as masculine, and of inspiration, in the form of the Muses, as feminine, and argues that Barbauld places female friendship in the role of inspiration while claiming creative power for the female poet. If the usual gendered coding of the arts cast poetry as a masculine endeavour and painting as a feminine one, then as a couple the Opies invert these normative expectations, with John taking a complex inspiration for his painting not so much from the beauty of Twiss's form as from the force exercised by the friendship between his wife and his subject, and Amelia taking the role of ekphrastic poet giving voice to her husband's graphic art. She in turn was inspired both by feminine admiration of her husband's artistic prowess and by the affection she felt for her female friend.

It is to this public/private nexus of sociability associated with the painting of Twiss that Opie turned thirty-five years later in her elegiac meditation on the portraits that hung around her. No longer on display in a London public gallery, the painting of Twiss figured among the variety of portraits mounted on the walls of Opie's private sitting room in Norwich. The art object serves to prompt recollection of both the artist spouse who died in 1807 and the female friend who died in 1822:

> The gift of love
> That speaking picture was—of bridal love.
> Now, both the painter and his subject are
> Where pictures come not!—but the gift on earth
> Unchang'd remains with her that lonely one,
> Whose friendship ask'd it, and whose song repaid,
> If song so humble could such gift repay.
> Now, for the requiem I must change the song,
> And let it float upon the chilly damps
> Of the dark vault to ears that cannot hear![15]

Notice that the triple strands of sociality established in 1799 are still entwined: artist husband, female friend, and poetic self are inextricably associated with each other, and each merits remembrance and celebration.

But perhaps more importantly, this elegiac lyric also functions to reaffirm and extend female friendship beyond the bounds of death. In bequeathing the painting to Twiss's daughter, Opie describes the portrait as an object that is imbued with a particularly feminine social connection:

> —and there is one
> Who, when on me death sets his awful seal,
> Will love to commune with those eyes, which tell
> Of her lost home, and youthful happiness!
> While in her filial heart they will awake
> A strain of melody, though mournful, sweet;
> And while she feels the spell that picture wears
> Perchance she'll give one grateful sigh to her,
> Whose dying hand bestow'd the magic boon.[16]

The portrait has the paradoxical power of both restoring to a daughter communion with a mother painted long before the daughter's birth, long before time and adversity had dimmed her beauty, and cementing bonds that would preserve those female friendships—peer to peer, daughter to mother, friend to friend's daughter—celebrated in the memories evoked by the portrait-object.[17]

The portrait of Twiss was a gift given to Amelia Opie, and her reflections on both subject and giver constitute meditations on an object received, but throughout her life Opie delighted in penning verses to accompany the presents that she gave to her friends. In a poem accompanying a volume of William Cowper's poems sent in 1822 to an unidentified female friend, she articulates clearly the social burden assumed by the gift: "Accept these deathless lays! & when their powers / Impart new pleasures, to thy social hours / Oh may the gift the giver's form recal."[18] Presents evoke presence, and the verses included in the gift insist on the connection between friends affirmed through material objects. A sequence of private lyrics written to her friend Elizabeth Vassall Lemaistre (1771–1857) offers Opie's most sustained documentation of gift exchange and enables a more complex exploration of the social mediation provided by the gift object. Occasional poems written to commemorate events are usually thought of as unique texts documenting a single specific occasion, but this sequence of annual birthday poems marking a friendship that extended over four decades provides a rare opportunity to examine the sustained poetic tribute offered by one of the most popular women writers of the long eighteenth century to a female friend. Of the many birthday poems Opie mentions writing to Lemaistre, fourteen are still extant, and of these, five are connected with a birthday gift selected to highlight some aspect of their friendship: an acrostic brooch, an embroidered reticule, an almanac, an ivory box, and a three-sided seal engraved "T'Amo." These gifts are a clue to Opie's habit of taking an object and imbuing it through lyric with some strong link to the desired presence of the feminine other and, through pointing to future memories associated with the object, constructing an ongoing shared identity as friends.

In her diaries, Opie recorded the following entry on June 18, 1847: "In the year 1809 I began to write lines to Mrs. Lemaistre, on her birthday, and ever since, from 1809 to the fifth of this month, 1847, I have never omitted writing the accustomed verses. I wonder if any king's laureate ever wrote so many to one potentate; perhaps Colley Cibber did to George III."[19] Of those forty-odd birthday poems, only one was published; the rest exist in manuscript form. They thus primarily record the private relationship between the two women. Of the group, thirteen are held by the Pforzheimer Collection in the New York Public Library and one by the National Library of Scotland. Spanning the years 1813–1844, this series of poems constitutes an extended example of the way in which Opie placed her poetic talents in the service of female friendship throughout her career. The poems addressed to "Elizabeth Lemaistre on her Birthday, 5 June" fall into two distinct categories: in the first group, the poem itself constitutes the birthday gift—the "votive lay" offered over many years;[20] in the second, the poem becomes a supplement glossing the material object that constitutes the gift proper. The latter verses are of particular interest because they are written to articulate the significance or symbolic value of the object in connection with the social relationship. Three of the poems establish an explicit connection with language—ways in which the objects are made to speak—and are associated with periods when Opie and Lemaistre were separated by significant physical distance. The other two poems, tied to dates in which the women lived if not in the same city then at least in the same country, take objects not related in any way to language and use them to figure the closer connections afforded by proximity.

Not a great deal is known about the relationship between Opie and Lemaistre beyond what can be deduced from these poems. An avid correspondent, and the subject of a full memoir upon her death in 1853, Opie has left considerable materials for tracing her career. The same cannot be said for Lemaistre, the evidence for whose life is both sparse and contradictory. It seems to be quite certain that she died on July 27, 1856, not quite three years after her friend Amelia did, and that she is buried in Holy Trinity Church in Cheltenham, though the plaque there gives her date of death as the July 11. It also seems certain that she married John Gustavus Lemaistre, traveler and physician, on March 6, 1794, at Bath. Ironically enough, given the subject of this essay, her date of birth has been more challenging to determine. The date given in the *New England Historical and Genealogical Register* is May 5, 1771. Somewhere along the line it would seem that Elizabeth grew a month younger, since all of Opie's verses to her celebrate the fifth of June as her birthday. The historical records give Elizabeth's place of birth as Massachusetts, and her parents as John Vassall and Elizabeth Oliver, both with family connections to Jamaica plantations.

Though the entire sequence of Lemaistre poems is of interest in its documentation of the Opie friendship, those accompanying a specific gift whose qualities figure largely in the verses themselves form a special subset. Dating from 1815, 1816, 1817, 1819, and 1823, the poems were written over nine years at a time in Opie's life when she was financially comfortable. A widow since 1807, she lived with her father in Norwich but visited London regularly. During these years, her publishers Longman & Company regularly reprinted her earlier novels and poems, and she was still actively writing: *Tales of Real Life* had appeared in 1813, followed by *Valentine's Eve* (1816), *New Tales* (1818), *Tales of the Heart* (1820), and *Madeline: A Tale* (1822). The only hint that her popularity (and thus soon her income) might be waning came with her anonymous publication of *The Only Child; or, Portia Bellenden* (1821). Thus possessed of comfortable means and not yet having joined the Society of Friends, which took a somewhat censorious attitude toward luxuries, Opie was in an economic position to find elegant and meaningful gifts for her friend Lemaistre.

The first poem in this sequence opens "So oft my muse has hail'd this day," and indeed by 1815, Opie had already composed six earlier birthday offerings and had established a lyric tradition cementing the bands of friendship between the two women who were both close in age (at this time Opie was not quite forty-six and Lemaistre forty-three) and also linked by the fact that John Gustavus Lemaistre was at times Amelia's physician. The only prior extant poem makes no mention of a gift, and the internal language suggests that this is perhaps the first poem that accompanied a material object:

> But on this morn not *words* alone
> Should make glad friendship's feelings known,
> A *gift* should mark the welcome day,
> A *gift* should friendship's homage pay.[21]

The object in question was that extremely fashionable and sentimental Regency item, a piece of acrostic jewelry—in this case a gold basket set with four gems: lapis lazuli, opal, garnet (or vermiel as it was known in the period), and emerald, the first letters of each gem spelling out the message "L.O.V.E." In a witty extension of the poem as gift, words still forge the bond, because this "golden gift" is one "where gems their speaking colours blend" (11–12); more, it "names a magic word" and "that precious word is L.O.V.E." (14, 16). A pretty bauble to remind the wearer of the giver and her declaration of affection, this type of gift is both intimate and intensely personal, but it is the language of the poem that codes its importance as a mutually recognized declaration of affection: it is a gift that pays "friendship's homage" (10) and that makes "glad friendship's feelings known" (8), with gems whose colors "speak" the word of love. So these verses to accompany what would seem to be the first of Opie's birthday gifts emphasize that the present itself is designed to speak the same language of affection that the poetry sent to Lemaistre typically declared.

The following year, Opie's poem accompanied a gift that might be considered even more intimately personal than the acrostic brooch—the hand-worked fashionable accessory named in "To Mrs. Lemaistre at Paris on her Birthday—the 5th of June 1816 with a ridicule worked with the flower called 'Forget me not.'" The poem opens with an account of the physical distance between the friends, as Lemaistre joins her husband on his travels:

> Time was when on this welcome day
> My lip could friendship's greetings pay
> And by its kiss upon thy cheek
> Its tributary feelings speak.[22]

When we read of a lip paying greetings, we might expect that this refers to words, but instead Opie offers the physical intimacy, the closeness, of the speaking gesture of the kiss upon the cheek. This closeness is belied, of course, by the travels undertaken by the Lemaistres. John Gustavus was a travel writer, and in 1802 had published *A Rough Sketch of Modern Paris . . . Written During the Last Two Months of 1801 and the First Five of 1802* followed by *Travels After the Peace of Amiens Through France, Switzerland, Italy and Germany* (1806).

The couple frequently traveled to the Continent; in 1822, her birthday poem would open, "Welcome dear wanderer! back to Albion's shores!— / Though no volcano here sublimely roars, / No orange groves their golden treasures bear."[23] The 1816 poem exhorts Lemaistre to remember her distant friends:

> Yet still on England's distant isle
> With tearful eye, & saddened smile
> Thou oft wilt think when Memory's hand
> Shall back departed scenes command
> And absent friends to memory dear
> Before thy swimming sight draw near.[24]

But the poem asks her to remember one friend in particular, who describes herself as "a jealous elf, [who wishes to] / Bring foremost in that group, *myself* / And every day before thy sight / Appear in colours warm, & bright" (15–18).

The 1816 birthday gift is thus designed as a prompt to daily remembrance. The object announced in the title of the poem is a "ridicule" or reticule, a kind of pocket or purse fashionable in the period. In this case, it has been handworked by Opie herself:

> I've deck'd it with those speaking flowers,
> The soothers sweet of parting hours,
> And lo! it cries from each blue spot,
> 'Forget me not! Forget me not!'[25]

The forget-me-not was a popular motif in Regency culture, figuring frequently in jewelry and crafts, and even becoming a garden favorite at this time.

However, forget-me-nots seem to have been especially meaningful to Opie. The phrase "forget me not" had formed the refrain of one of her most popular early lyrics, "Go youth beloved," a poem that had circulated widely with no fewer than three different musical settings between 1802 and 1816, when it was taken up in Henry Rowley Bishop's popular play "Love in a Village." It is thus perhaps no coincidence that the flower was on Opie's mind this year. The enduring popularity of "Go youth beloved" was attested to by a further original setting as late as 1874. In the lyric, the phrase that names the flower is associated with supportive love and friendship:

> But, oh, if grief thy steps attend,
> If want, if sickness be thy lot,
> And thou require a soothing friend,
> Forget me not! forget me not![26]

In 1825, the flower itself was the subject of a short poem by Opie published in *Friendship's Offering*:

> Fond memory's flower, of azure dye,
>   Permit thy bard one boon to crave;
> When in death's narrow bed I lie,
>   Oh! Bloom around my humble grave.
> And if some tender faithful friend
>   Should, led by love, approach the spot,
> And o'er thy flowers admiring bend,
>   Then say for me, Forget me not!

All of which is to say that when Opie sent Lemaistre a reticule embroidered with flowers there is every possibility that each woman might have recognized that the choice of decorative motif expressed more about the relationship than simple fashionability. It served as a reminder of Opie's record as a poet of sentiment and friendship, and articulated a commitment to memory—to *not forgetting*—as the force that sustains a relationship.

The final gift recorded in this sequence is "a Three-sided Seal on Which is Engraved T'Amo," sent by Opie to her friend in 1823. Examples of Georgian and Regency seals show them to be highly decorative jewels, with a wide range of colors and designs. Like the acrostic brooch, seals functioned as intimate personal ornaments since they were often worn. The item was used for sealing the letters sent between corresponding friends, and thus the sentiment expressed on the seal—"I Love You"—would be returned to the giver with each letter received. This gift, however, also returns to the theme of absence; the seal is necessary because the friendship is sustained by correspondence, and the physical, speaking body is only imagined:

> And if thou coulds't behold it now,
> That face would all my feelings show;
> The deepening flush upon my cheek
> Would friendship's glad emotions speak.[27]

The symbolic value of the seal resides in its intermediary function. The words engraved upon its side—"T'amo"—stand in for those written on the human heart:

> For though thou'lt read upon this seal,
> Two words expressing what I feel,
> With depth beyond the graver's art,
> Thou'lt find them written on *my heart*,
> While *thine* as kind emotions move thee,
> Wilt echo 't'amo!' or, 'I love thee!' (21–26)

The seal prompts a reciprocal declaration of affection and affirmation of friendship. Together with the brooch and reticule that also spell and "speak" the love that exists between these friends, the seal epitomizes the function of the objects as reminders and expressions of affection during the physical separation of the women.

Two other birthday poems refer to gifts, though the evocative objects they accompany have less enduring value, being designed to be consumed in use rather than treasured over time, and thus their mediation of the relationship between Opie and Lemaistre is somewhat different. These gifts also share another characteristic: each was given at a time when the women apparently lived in some proximity, or when Opie at least believed there would be an opportunity for them to meet. Thus the gift need not stand in for a tangibly absent body but could rather offer a different kind of compliment. In "To Mrs. Lemaistre with an Almanack, on her Birthday—5th June—1817, Soon After her Return From Abroad," Opie comments once more on the importance of what has become an annual ritual marking their friendship:

> For many a year to hail this day
> Friendship, & I as is our duty
> Have brought a votive gift, & lay
> To thee, fair shrine of worth, & beauty.[28]

The dual figuring of the givers as "Friendship, & I" provides a curious image of the relationship itself as having agency. In exploring Anna Barbauld's assertion that "far dearer were the name of FRIEND," Laura Tallon comments that she "treat[s] 'friend' as a third but superior category to 'painter' or 'poet,' in the rivalry between the sister arts." Here, Opie offers a formation that further elevates the idea of female friendship.[29] She writes as if the idea of friendship itself has become a third party in the relationship, or that though each might be a separate "friend," the union of their sentiments constitutes a third entity, and that the relationship represents more than the sum of its individual parts.

The "votive gift" in this year is another item designed for personal daily use—a frequent reminder of the giver in the form of an almanac or daybook. Although these items were often elegantly designed, we get little sense of the physical qualities of the almanac from the poem and must speculate on them to some extent. It is perhaps the curious quirk of the gift enclosure poem that it need not describe in detail the object immediately before the recipient's eyes, even though it provides a gloss for interpreting the gift. The almanac is described as "a present . . . / That with the *useful* only classes" because it "shows how Time's swift pinion passes."[30] The almanac, unlike the brooch, the reticule, and the seal, is a consumable rather than a lasting object, kept close for a year but thereafter, if preserved at all, only consulted rarely. Indeed, Opie herself elegantly reduces its value because it is merely a pragmatic reminder for her friend, while she herself comments that though

> Such aid I highly rate
> That aid *this* year I proudly scorn
> Since now with smiling lip I date
> From the *glad hour* of thy return.[31]

This year's gift becomes the pretext for a pretty compliment, as the dates that will be marked by the calendar pale in significance to the date given precedence by affection, the "*glad hour*" of the friend's return. The almanac is not the same caliber of evocative object as the others, documenting as it does the passing of the year rather than standing in for the physical presence of someone separated by space. It offers instead the potential to inscribe the dates in which to anticipate the tangible presence of the female friend.

In 1819, Opie's gift was an object similarly short-term in its utility: "An Ivory Box Containing a Remedy for the Headach[e]—." Once again the friends were no longer widely separated, and Opie writes, "Hail happy change! No more I'm forc'd to send / My birthday offering to my distant friend."[32] Instead, the women can meet in person: "Now in her hand I can my tribute place, / And breathe my heart-felt wishes face to face, / Can friendship's prayer with friendship's kiss impart" (3–5). Opie exults in the possibility of being "face-to-face" to give "friendship's kiss" in person, and of placing the birthday tribute directly "in her hand." This year, the gift need not prompt memory nor bear a constant presence—it can instead serve a different function.

With longstanding friendship comes familiarity with the travails of time and mortality, and the "votive lay" of previous year, "To Mrs. Lemaistre at Malvern, on her Birthday—5th June 1818," accompanied no gift, but rather expressed concern for the ill health that appears to have been dogging Elizabeth's husband and Opie's friend, John Gustavus Lemaistre. The lyric expresses a different aspect of sociability, an empathetic sympathy with domestic trials and recognition that the good health of loved ones is the only gift that really matters:

> A wish *denied,* & life's best charms are o'er—
> A wish, if *granted,* thou can'st ask no more—
> 'Tis, that again upon thy husband's brow
> Health's faded brilliance may serenely glow;
> 'Tis, that once more from pain, & dimness free
> His eyes may gaze on all he loves *in thee*.[33]

With the birthday tribute of 1819, Opie found the right material gift, announced in the title: "An Ivory Box Containing a Remedy for the Headach[e]." Gloating that "Not empty verse alone thy sight shall meet," Opie proclaims: "My gift shall useful be as well as sweet. / For lo! this casket's ivory bounds contain, / A cure for languor, & a balm for pain."[34] The gift is designed not to cure Elizabeth Lemaistre's ills, but those of her husband: should his brow show signs of "nervous anguish," and his "clos'd eylids pain's inflictions mark," then she will be able to administer the "Remedy." What fascinates, however, is the proclamation of Opie's role in this process. She asserts that, "arm'd" by the giver, Lemaistre will "assert a power that's *new*" and cure her husband's "*headaches*," just as she had previously cured his "*heart-aches.*" Opie plays both physician (she loved to help her father, Dr. Alderson, and her letters are filled with reflections on diagnoses and possible prescriptions) and Cupid for her friend, strengthening spousal ties and the bonds of friendship in one stroke.

Amelia Opie's object poems remain poignantly moving, even at this distance of time. Peter Schwenger writes:

> For many the familiar presence of things is a comfort. Things are valued not only because of their rarity or cost or their historical aura, but because they

seem to partake in our lives; they are domesticated, part of our routine and so of us. Their long association with us seems to make them custodians of our memories; so that sometimes, as in Proust, things reveal us to ourselves in profound and unexpected ways. Yet all this does not mean that things reveal themselves, only our investments in them. And those investments carry with them a melancholy in the very heart of comfort.[35]

This sense of melancholy obtains in Opie's poems—the objects are charged with the burden of memory, of standing in for someone in absence, of resisting the fading from memory of those no longer present. This is perhaps most clearly expressed in the second of the Twiss portrait poems, but the vein is clear in the birthday gift poems as well. Consciously given to compensate for loss, they nevertheless continue to exist as daily paradoxical reminders not just of a friend but of her absence. The depth of this melancholy, however, expresses the intensity of the emotion of friendship. The tradition of the annual "votive lay" honoring both Elizabeth Lemaistre and her relationship with Opie testifies to forty years of conscious celebration of the steadfast love between two female friends. Only once in the extant sequence did Opie's mindfulness slip, and that event too was marked: the poem from 1844 carries the subtitle "(Alas! not *birthday verses,* as *usual,* but heartfelt apologies for not having written any! the first *omission* during 35 years!)," and concludes,

> Then Oh! forgive my tardy Muse
> And think thou still art dear as ever;
> Nor now this humble meed refuse
> But say, ''tis better *late* than *never*—"[36]

In spite of the rueful resort to proverbial wisdom in the line "better late than never," Opie's "tardy Muse" nonetheless confirms that the recipient of the verses is "still as dear as ever." The sequence of birthday poems written to Lemaistre suggests the importance of poetic composition as an integral and sustained aspect of social connections, and in particular of the celebration of female friendship.

Notes

1. The earliest of Opie's poetic "gift enclosures," these verses were addressed to Maria Riddell (1772–1808). They are found in a letter to Sir James Mackintosh, January 22, 1808 (BL Add. MS. 52451B):

Will you think me *very* vain, & conceited if I venture to give you ten lines of mine to Mrs. Riddell which I think *more* french still, tho' far behind their model.—Perhaps you know she is very covetous of paper, & I wasted so much of her note paper at her house, in fruitless endeavours to make a likeness of her, & Maria, that she scolded me unmercifully—So when I reached Town again I went to Bond Street, bought the most beautiful french note paper that could be procured, & sent it to her with the following lines.

>Accept these sheets with roses grac'd
>And borders form'd with grecian taste,
>Too classic far for thee to scorn 'em
>But truth Maria, bids me say
>Whatever charms they now display
>Thy hand with *greater* will adorn 'em—
>Nay, plainest of the plain might be
>The page that is thy thoughts' recorder,
>For who that boasts a note from thee
>Would *waste one* look upon its *border*. (1–10)

Collected Poems of Amelia Alderson Opie, eds. Shelley King and John B. Pierce (Oxford: Oxford University Press, 2009), 144, 515.

2. Opie's letters to her cousin Henry Perronet Briggs and his wife have frequent references to the pleasure his gift of a prism brought her: "Tell Henry Briggs his prism is the *delight of my* eyes! & of all beholders! If David's does as well, my end is fully answered" (Opie to Eliza Alderson, November 13, 1829, Huntington); see note to poem 272, *Collected Poems of Amelia Alderson Opie*, 570. Opie's biographer, Cecilia Lucy Brightwell, also notes, "Bright colours Mrs. Opie delighted in, and she had a sort of passion for prisms. She had several set in a frame, and mounted like a pole-screen, and this unique piece of furniture stood always in her window, and was a constant source of delight to her." *Memorials of the Life of Amelia Opie* (Norwich: Fletcher & Alexander, 1854), 334.

3. Opie, "To A Prism Sent from London to My Friend David," *Collected Poems of Amelia Alderson Opie*, 29–30.

4. Bill Brown, "Objects, Others, and Us (The Refabrication of Things)," *Critical Inquiry* 36, no. 2 (2010): 191.

5. Ibid., 191.

6. Sherry Turkle, "Introduction: The Things That Matter," in *Evocative Objects: Things We Think With*, ed. Sherry Turkle (Cambridge, MA: MIT Press, 2009), 5.

7. For a full discussion of this poem see Shelley King, "Representation, Memory and Mourning in Amelia Opie's 'On the Portraits of Deceased Friends and Relatives, which Hang Around Me,'" in *Performing the Everyday: The Culture of Genre in the Eighteenth Century*, ed. Alden Cavanaugh (Newark: University of Delaware Press, 2007), 120–29.

8. Christopher Kent Rovee, *Imagining the Gallery: The Social Body of British Romanticism* (Stanford, CA: Stanford University Press, 2006), 171.

9. The portrait is described as follows: "Seen to waist, in profile, ¾ face to left, in black dress to throat, short sleeves, shewing well-modelled arms; dark auburn hair in

short curls on forehead, black hair wound closely round the head; her right hand holds a netting needle; highly finished picture, shewing the influence of Sir. T. Lawrence." John Jope Rogers, *Opie and His Works* (London: Paul & Domenic Colnaghi & Co., 1878), 171.

10. Amelia Opie, "Memoir," in John Opie, *Lectures on Painting* (London: Longman, Hurst, Rees, & Orme, 1809), 26.

11. For a more detailed treatment of points made here regarding this companionate marriage and the development of mutual talents to enhance the careers of each, see my "Portrait of a Marriage: John and Amelia Opie and the Sister Arts," *Studies in Eighteenth-Century Culture* 40 (2011): 27–62.

12. Opie, "Lines Addressed to Mr Opie on his having painted for me a picture of Mrs. Twiss," *Collected Poems of Amelia Alderson Opie*, 1–4.

13. Although none of the birthday poems to Lemaistre based on gifts was published, Opie did place one of the other birthday poems (which might themselves be considered as gift objects) in the *European Magazine* (1822). Written in French and dated 1813 in the manuscript version, it is the earliest extant poem in the series, and its publication places the friendship between the two women in the public sphere.

14. Laura Tallon, "'Friendship, better than a Muse, inspires': Anna Letitia Barbauld Claims the Sister Arts for Female Friendship," in this volume.

15. Opie, "Portrait the Second" in "On the Portraits of Deceased Relatives and Friends, Which Hang Around Me," *Collected Poems of Amelia Alderson Opie*, 1–10.

16. Ibid., 24–32.

17. As a gift from her husband and an item of property furnishing a domestic space, the portrait falls into a specific category of object defined in legal terms as paraphernalia: "In the realm of married women's property, there is the old category, paraphernalia, describing a particular kind of thing, namely, the wife's clothes and personal ornaments. . . ." Susan Staves, *Married Women's Separate Property in England, 1660–1833* (Cambridge, MA: Harvard University Press, 1990), 148. Such things were considered appropriately transmitted from woman to woman.

18. Opie, "To _____ With Cowper's Poems," *Collected Poems of Amelia Alderson Opie*, 1–4.

19. Quoted in Brightwell, *Memorials*, 376.

20. The birthday poem for 1818, "To Mrs. Lemaistre at Malvern, On Her Birthday—5th of June—1818," offers "the votive lay to / Friendship due" (10), while that of 1822, "To Mrs. Lemaistre on Her Birthday—5th June—1822," asserts "Such is the heart that on thy natal day / To thee Eliza pours her votive lay, / For thee the Muse's wreath essays to twine, / And lays once more her offering on thy shrine" (9–12). In 1833, "Again, Eliza, Let me Hail That Day" opens "Again Eliza, let me hail that day / Which claims the tribute of a votive lay" (1–2) and Opie proclaims too the memorial value of the exercise to the poet: "Oh! Long may'st thou receive our annual lays / (To *me* memorials of sweet vanish'd days)" (7–8).

21. Opie, "To Mrs, Lemaistre—On her Birthday—5th of June 1815," *The Collected Poems of Amelia Alderson Opie*, 7–10

22. Opie, "To Mrs. Lemaistre at Paris on her Birthday—the 5th of June 1816 with a ridicule worked with the flower called 'Forget me not,'" *The Collected Poems of Amelia Alderson Opie*, 1–4.

23. Opie, "To Mrs. Lemaistre on her Birthday—5th of June—1822," *The Collected Poems of Amelia Alderson Opie*, 1–3.

24. Opie, "To Mrs. Lemaistre at Paris on her Birthday—the 5th of June 1816 with a ridicule worked with the flower called 'Forget me not,'" *The Collected Poems of Amelia Alderson Opie*, 9–14.

25. Ibid., 21–24.

26. Opie, "Go youth beloved," *The Collected Poems of Amelia Alderson Opie*, 13–16.

27. Opie, "A Three-sided Seal on Which is Engraved T'Amo," *The Collected Poems of Amelia Alderson Opie*, 7–10.

28. Opie, "To Mrs. Lemaistre with an Almanack, on her Birthday—5th June—1817, Soon After her Return From Abroad," *The Collected Poems of Amelia Alderson Opie*, 1–4.

29. Tallon, "Friendship, better than a Muse, inspires," in this volume.

30. Opie, "To Mrs. Lemaistre with an Almanack, on her Birthday—5th June—1817, Soon After her Return From Abroad," *The Collected Poems of Amelia Alderson Opie*, 9–10.

31. Ibid., 13–16.

32. Opie, "An Ivory Box Containing a Remedy for the Headach[e]—," *The Collected Poems of Amelia Alderson Opie*, 1–2.

33. Opie, "To Mrs. Lemaistre at Malvern, on her Birthday—5th June 1818," *The Collected Poems of Amelia Alderson Opie*, 17–22.

34. Opie, "An Ivory Box Containing a Remedy for the Headach[e]—," *The Collected Poems of Amelia Alderson Opie*, 9–12.

35. Peter Schwenger, *The Tears of Things: Melancholy and Physical Objects* (Minneapolis: University of Minnesota Press, 2006), 3.

36. Opie, "To Elizabeth Lemaistre (Alas! not *birthday verses*, as *usual*, but heartfelt apologies for not having written any! the first *omission* during 35 years!)," *The Collected Poems of Amelia Alderson Opie*, 21–24.

Afterword

*Researching, Writing, and Teaching
Women's Tributes to Women*

BETTY A. SCHELLENBERG

In their introduction to this volume, Jessica Cook and Laura Runge bring into focus a vital and complex tradition of women's commemorations of one another. It is a tradition that crosses boundaries between passionate and chaste literary modes, between divergent political and status allegiances, and between private exchange and public expression. Yet the commemorations discussed in this volume, like those received and created by Mary Delany, share a common commitment to the careful crafting of an object worthy of its intellectual, emotional, and social charge. From the early commemoration by Martha Fowke of Mary, Lady Chudleigh's enabling mentorship to the gift poems sent by Amelia Opie to Elizabeth Vassall Lemaistre, her friend of many years, a number of the writings analysed in the foregoing collection arise out of spaces of private correspondence and friendship. At the same time, it is clear that the tribute as it is explored here always has an agenda, one that reaches beyond that "woman-centered space" to achieve public rhetorical aims.[1] That publicity is as variable as the commemorative mode itself—while as literary historians we tend to focus on print publication, a number of the preceding essays demonstrate that circulation within extended scribal networks could serve as an equally powerful, or even more effective, mode of reaching target audiences and accomplishing a tribute's goal.

An important cumulative rhetorical effect of these carefully crafted tributes, as underscored by our editors, is women's claim to agency and guardianship of their own honor and capacity for friendship. They made that claim in the face of a persistent narrative of women's inferiority and contingency despite their own publicly recognized achievements. But their claims also reach beyond their own time in stubborn resistance to the simplifications of literary discourses that dichotomize and separate women writers from their female foremothers and contemporaries. The woman writers represented in this volume have done their part in providing us with the materials from which to construct a framework that will carry forward their celebration of achievement. To preserve their voices and actually enable them to speak and be heard, however—to disrupt the cycle of forgetting that many scholars have noted as the fate women writers in history are condemned to—we must connect the dots between three essential tasks, none of which can accomplish the goal alone: as researchers, we must strain to hear those muted voices in the archives; as writers, we must find ways to ventriloquize what we have heard; and as teachers, we must reconstruct a new and truer narrative together with our students. At best, these three enterprises will stimulate, enrich, and mirror one another. If they remain fragmented, or if the final piece of the picture is overlooked, the most well-intentioned efforts will be as soundless as the proverbial tree falling in an empty forest.

The foregoing essays showcase and offer a polemic for the ongoing value, as an indispensable starting point, of painstaking archival research into the individual and unique writing lives of eighteenth-century women. Tedious and frustrating as such work can sometimes be, it is the primary means to that sort of "thick contextualization" called for by Laura Mandell as cited in the editors' introduction.[2] Such contextualization, in turn, inevitably yields insights that challenge received notions of a particular woman or category of woman. I will illustrate with an example from my own experience. Catherine Talbot (1721–1770), the posthumous daughter of a well-connected clergyman and lifelong member of the household of the influential Bishop of Oxford and ultimately Archbishop of Canterbury Thomas Secker, is generally classified as a first-generation Bluestocking, thus as a socially conservative writer with a strongly moralistic strain to her work. Talbot's devotional writings received the tribute of posthumous publication as *Reflections on the Seven Days of the Week,* edited and published in 1770, the year of her death, by her longtime correspondent Elizabeth Carter. Carter prefaced this short devotional publication with the hope "that the good Sense, and exalted piety of these Reflections, may render them of some Use to the World in general" as well as offering "an Opportunity of profiting by her Thoughts" to those acquaintances who "are no longer permitted to enjoy the Blessing of her Example." This published celebration is deeply felt, sincere, and well deserved. It also accords with the manuscript correspondence of Elizabeth Montagu, the Bluestocking hostess and author, whose relationship with Talbot was for the most part mediated by their mutual friend Carter. Thus Montagu writes of Talbot to Carter, even before the former's death, that she "venerat'd" her as "the most pure, holy, & righteous" person she had ever known, as one who could already, even before her death, be called "without presumption . . . our Angel."[3]

But the corroboration between the high-flown praise of the printed Carter edition of Talbot's writings and the correspondence held in the Montagu collection of the Huntington Library needs to be triangulated with a manuscript volume entitled "Wrestiana," found in the Bedfordshire and Luton Archives and Records Office, as well as with correspondence between Talbot and an even more long-term friend, Jemima Yorke, second Marchioness Grey, and with Talbot's journals, distributed between Bedfordshire and the British Library. "Wrestiana" carefully preserves occasional and coterie pieces produced by members of the coterie centered at the country estate of Wrest around Lady Grey and her husband Philip Yorke, eventually the second Earl of Hardwicke. Through her childhood friendship with Grey, Talbot was a member of this coterie, which was particularly active in the early 1740s. So highly respected were her talents that the Yorke-Grey circle called her "Sappho," invited her contribution to the otherwise all-male collaborative publication *Athenian Letters* (1741–43), and wrote several mock-heroic pieces featuring her alternately as the Elizabethan "Ladie C-th-r-na T-lb-t, . . . Maide of Honour to the Queene," who elopes with her lover and "learn[s] Greeke in a fort-nighte," and as the heroine of the epic "Borlaciad," which concludes with a dream-vision of "a Long Line of her Posterity. . . . Generals, Wits, Deans of Ch:Ch: [Christchurch], Poetesses, Bishops, Royal Mistresses, Emperors, & Pope Joans."[4] The posthumous tribute printed by Talbot's admiring friend Carter and endorsed by Montagu in copies she distributed among young people of her acquaintance is markedly unlike these affectionate mock-heroic tributes conveyed to Talbot by Grey on behalf of the group of friends gathered at Wrest. In the writings of this coterie, Talbot features not as self-denying object of veneration, but as an intellectual, serious, yet sharp-witted member of a high-spirited and talented group of young peers. This is the Talbot who could note at the end of a day at Wrest that she had "Writ two Sonnettos (abusive) in five Minutes & produced as my Evenings Work. At the instigation of A. writ a third before Supper."[5]

It is important to note that many of Talbot's productions as a young wit were quite widely known in her time through apparently extensive circulation in scribal networks. At one point, she found herself identified by a fellow dinner guest as the "famous" author of "Verses of Mine forsooth that she had seen at Bath 14 Years ago." In another case, a witty letter of welcome written to a newborn cousin in 1742 was copied by Thomas Birch into one of his carefully compiled volumes of important literary artifacts (now held in the British Library), resurfaced as a "Ghost" enclosed in a letter to Talbot from a more recent acquaintance in 1761, and finally appeared in print in the

Gentleman's Magazine a month after Talbot's death.[6] Indeed, her experience serves as proof of Harold Love's assertion that publication through manuscript circulation, while it might "operat[e] at relatively lower volumes and under more restrictive conditions of availability than print publication, was still able to sustain the currency of popular texts for very long periods and bring them to the attention of considerable bodies of readers."[7] In order to accurately represent and understand Talbot's place as an author in the eighteenth-century literary landscape, we need to contextualize her writing not only in terms of print, but with regard to other media as well.

Thus, as Catherine Ingrassia's discussion of Mary Barber's and Laetitia Pilkington's posthumous praise of Constantia Grierson illustrates as well, even with respect to a single individual, one tribute may not tell the whole story. But to arrive at this multi-faceted "true narrative" of Catherine Talbot involves work in at least three substantial archival collections, on two continents, as well as access to rare eighteenth-century publications in print or digital facsimile form.[8] Small wonder that it has taken Claudia Kairoff and others many years to piece together the archival traces that suggest the identities behind the pen names "Laura" and "Valeria" in Anne Finch's "The Circuit of Appollo," and that Kathryn King is still searching for the Haywood admirer hiding behind "MA. A." Of course some of the evidence has been lost forever, likely the victim of chaotic households, difficult lives, and a lack of perceived value, as Katharine Kittredge explains of Mary Leadbeater's letters to Melesina Trench. Many of Talbot's letters that might have contributed to bridging some of the gaps in her story were either accidentally destroyed by Grey's descendants at Wrest or apparently discarded by Carter's nephew after the publication of his aunt's "edited" correspondence. But often materials are simply widely scattered and awaiting the patient sleuth who will gather references from correspondences, contemporary newspaper notices, and miscellany poems into a single narrative, as demonstrated by the new light Christine Gerrard's essay sheds on Martha Fowke's alignments and motivations. Materials may be preserved in such a fragmented state that no one has yet been able to contextualize them—will any of the twenty-five-odd missing birthday poems that Opie wrote to Lemaistre still turn up? The digitization of catalogues and even collections has furthered this work tremendously, but digitization of pre-existing catalogues alone cannot unearth the many bits of poetry or passing references that were simply not recognized, decades ago when the original catalogues were created, as of potential interest to a future researcher who might be working on a then-obscure or unknown woman writer. Many if not all of the authors contributing to this collection would affirm that the archival possibilities for their own objects of inquiry are far from exhausted.

As a result, one stumbles onto enough lucky finds to be left wondering how many other keys that might have unlocked great mysteries have been one file folder further into the cabinet. A particularly generative discovery for my recent study of eighteenth-century literary coteries began with passing references in studies by David Fairer and David Allan[9] to the Brotherton Collection of manuscript poetry collections at the University of Leeds. Intrigued, I carried out a remote catalogue search for poems by George Lyttelton, Elizabeth Carter, Thomas Edwards, Catherine Talbot, William Shenstone, Hester Mulso Chapone, and other scribal authors connected with the circles I was studying. To my surprise, I turned up, in a single mid-century collection, not only Lyttelton and Edwards, but also Thomas Birch, Isaac Hawkins Browne, and Charles Yorke—all names associated with the Yorke-Gray circle that had celebrated Catherine Talbot as "Sappho." The concentration was no coincidence; that collection turned out to have been compiled by Lady Mary Capell, a peripheral member of the coterie who appears with some regularity in the Talbot-Grey correspondence. Catalogue records of the volume's contents list attributions for most of its male-authored poems, including a cluster of verses addressed to the compiler by Charles Yorke, Philip Yorke's brother and the wit with whom Talbot exchanged the sparring sonnets noted above. Many of these attributions come from the volume itself, in the style of "Wrote by Mr. C___ Y___e," but the collection also preserves anonymous poetry, some of which has been identified subsequently to be the work of William Whitehead and Thomas Edwards, for example. The third-to-last poem in the volume, however, titled "Ode, Occasion'd by Reading Sonnets in the Style & Manner of Spenser, written by Tho. Edwards Esq," remains unattributed.

This poem is immediately recognizable to anyone familiar with the career of Hester Mulso Chapone as the launching point for her fame as a precocious young poet in the late 1740s and 1750s. A piece praising Edwards for his praise of Samuel Richardson's *Clarissa*, it cemented Mulso's membership in Richardson's most select literary coterie, and from thence led to the circulation of her manuscript poetry to the likes of Thomas Birch, also a member of the Yorke-Grey coterie, and, through Elizabeth Carter, to the Bluestocking coterie of Elizabeth Montagu and George Lyttelton. Meanwhile, the poetry book's entry in the Adam Matthews database of the collection notes that "letters by [Capell] to Dr Thomas Birch held in the British Library confirm her interest in literature and also her handwriting in this volume."[10] In fact, providing the kind of corroboration that makes the researcher's heart sing, this correspondence does much more: Birch's first preserved letter to Capell offers her "a very fine Ode, which I mention'd to your Ladyships, of Miss Mulsoe, address'd to Mr. Edwards on Occasion of some of his Sonnets in the Style & Manner of Spenser, particularly one to Mr. Richardson, prefix'd to the last Edition of his Clarissa. It was communicated to me under the Restriction, of not multiplying Copies: But I cannot deny it the Honour of a place in Lady Mary's Quarto, which consigns such pieces to Immortality." Capell replies that she has indeed copied the poem "into the *Sacred Book*."[11]

Hester Mulso's poetry, under her married name of Chapone, saw print publication in 1775 on the heels of her very successful *Letters on the Improvement of the Mind*, and her reputation as a first-generation Bluestocking would have made her poem relatively easy to identify for a late eighteenth-century reader who gained a glimpse of Capell's "Sacred Book." Yet, as feminist literary historians have not failed to note with dismay, Fame's trumpet fell silent within a couple of generations for the majority of women writers of the period, putting an end to the "Immortality" afforded by Capell's book. Thus, there is an ongoing urgency not only to enhance the usefulness of the archive through identifications and catalogue additions, but also to report our findings about the women whose writings are preserved in scattered repositories. But how to tell these stories in a manner that will resonate? We must speak to the current preoccupations of researchers—but we must do so, as our co-editors remind us, in a manner that will not simply cater to the presuppositions of predominant gender narratives and literary histories. This is seldom the work of a single article or even of an essay collection; it involves reiteration and patient but firm turning of the wheel before the rudder shifts and the ship changes course. It is instructive to note how many years it has been since the initial recovery work on Eliza Haywood by way of Pope's abuse in Book Two of *The Dunciad* before critics have had even minimally adequate biographical facts and enough firm attributions of Haywood's astonishingly extensive and varied output before them to be able to argue, as does Kathryn King, for Haywood's pursuit of fame as in the service of civic virtue rather than as the flaunting of a brazen sexual notoriety. Indeed, a significant portion of a literary historian's career can be invested in such a cause of recovery.

Fortunately, critical preoccupations often advance the goal of furthering insight into eighteenth-century women's writings. As theoretical perspectives shift, new windows open up to illuminate what might not have been visible through an earlier lens. Thus, in this volume, Shelley King profits from developments in object theory to take us beyond simplistic associations between the feminine and the material in her sophisticated analysis of Amelia Opie commemorating friends through gifts of "evocative objects." Similarly, renewed attention to the dynamics of local and transnational cultural transfer allows Laura Tallon and Natasha Duquette to argue for the ambition and seriousness of their respective subjects—Anna Laetitia Barbauld in her bold deployment of contemporary aesthetic theories of the sister arts to legitimize her own work, and Helen Maria Williams in her courageous and even risky insistence on the power of female friendship as a counterweight to political divisions. And in an insight that arguably challenges critical suppositions underpinning even this collection, Susan Lanser suggests that Anna Seward's "tribute" to the Ladies of Llangollen serves to give the "Circuit of Apollo" trope a "queer and ultimately fatal twist, evacuating the material underpinnings of literary encomium" in acquiescence to an early heteronormative literary discourse.

If challenges arise in researching and writing the complexly contextualized stories of women's commemorations of one another in a manner that recognizes at once both their uniqueness and the reader's moment in literary history, then the ultimate test comes in embodying this commitment and imparting it to new scholars and students of the period. We are all familiar with the pressures exerted in the classroom toward simplifying generalizations, binary frameworks, and narratives that connect the dots—and that connect somehow with narratives encountered elsewhere. When is generalization a tool and when is it a straitjacket? Nicolle Jordan's comparison of an Anne Finch tribute poem with a Jane Barker dedication, for example, leads us to see that a tribute poem might in fact fail where a prose dedication can succeed. In a similar paradox, the teachable truth that eighteenth-century women poets valued and developed the genre of the friendship poem is inadequate to the complicated dynamics of the Hill coterie that Gerrard describes. Yet those dynamics and the way they play out in the many feminocentric poems of Richard Savage's *Miscellaneous Poems and Translations by Several Hands* would not be beyond the comprehension of any student who has ever been member of a clique. Striking a balance between touchstones or guideposts and nuanced variations has always been the task of the teacher, however; the force of this collection is to argue that a number of the points of reference themselves need to be re-examined and reconstructed.

This volume further suggests that the most effective means of teaching women praising women and of contributing to the broad recognition of this widespread and richly varied strain in eighteenth-century poetry is to dedicate substantial segments of, or even entire, course syllabi to the topic of tributes—not as a unique subset of poetry by women, but as a substantial poetic tradition that might serve as a tool for examining the very concept of a tradition. Such an organizing concept is surely as viable as those of the literary prize or Oprah's Book Club, or the creation of a canon that has been used to structure many an advanced undergraduate course. I confess that I have sometimes been a step behind my own students in this regard. Teaching a course in eighteenth-century women poets some years ago, I gave my students a short essay writing assignment in which they had the option to make an argument for a particular poem's place in the canon—requiring, of course, that they consider the very notion of a canon and the criteria upon which it should be based. To my surprise, every one of the students who selected this topic wrote from the assumption that their chosen poem was canonical and defended that status, whereas I, knowing how recent modern attention to their chosen poem and poet in fact was, had expected arguments for prospective inclusion. Roger Lonsdale's 1989 anthology was our primary course text, and for these students, a modern anthology containing the poems they were studying was all they needed to lead them to conclude that their selection was of acknowledged value, and that their task was to locate that value in the poem. My students needed to hear the story of how recent the recovery of those poems was, how fragile their inclusion in a course curriculum. But I also needed to learn from them that it is possible, and it is my responsibility, to sustain the recovery of these poems and these poets on a regular basis, over and over, in the company of my students.

The past decade has seen the increased blurring of lines between the archive of rare books and manuscripts, the scholarly edition or critical study, and the classroom organized according to distinct role divisions of teaching and learning. Full-text facsimile archives such as *Eighteenth-Century Collections Online* and the *American Antiquarian Society Historical Periodicals Collection* allow students (at least at subscriber institutions) to carry out their own archival work, with the aid of the rich contexts provided by resources like *Orlando: Women's Writing in the British Isles*. Manuscript hands (not to mention idiosyncratic cataloguing systems) can be struggled over in the *British Literary Manuscripts* database or *Literary Manuscripts: 17th and 18th Century Poetry from the Brotherton Library*. As a result, learners can become researchers in the virtual archive, and in the process, become directly involved in bearing witness to eighteenth-century women writers. Indeed, the very models of the traditional classroom and the scholarly monograph as the sites of learning about the past are being productively challenged. The experiences afforded by online exhibitions such as *What Jane Saw*, created by Janine Barchas to contextualize Jane Austen through the Boydell Shakespeare Gallery and Joshua Reynolds's paintings, supplement the classroom experience and open up learning to those beyond the academy. In turn, the mainstream success of publications like *My Life in Middlemarch* by Rebecca Mead, and *The Paper Garden: An Artist Begins Her Life's Work at 72*, a combination of poetic memoir and an artist biography of Mary Delany by Molly Peacock, has demonstrated that engagement and commemoration across the span of centuries are not solely the purview of the hyper-specialized academic scholar and her readers. New links in the chain of commemoration continue to be forged; the Circuit of Apollo is not yet complete.

Notes

1. The description is Paula Backscheider's, in her discussion of the feminocentric tradition of the friendship poem as a "woman-centered space . . . tend[ing] to be occasional, vernacular, and unpretentious and about things the woman knows." *Eighteenth-Century Women Poets and Their Poetry: Inventing Agency, Inventing Genre* (Baltimore: Johns Hopkins University Press, 2005), 175–76.

2. Laura C. Mandell, "Gendering Digital Literary History: What Counts for Digital Humanities," in *A New Companion to Digital Humanities*, ed. Susan Schreibman, Ray Siemens, and John Unsworth (Chichester, UK: Wiley-Blackwell, 2015), 511–23.

3. Elizabeth Montagu to Carter, October 31 [1769] and [January 17, 1770], The Huntington Library, mo 3261 and mo 3272.

4. Lady Grey to Catherine Talbot, May 22, [1743] and July 14, 1743, Bedfordshire and Luton Archives and Records Service (BLARS) L30/21/3/10 and 12.

5. Talbot, Wrest Journal, BLARS L30/106/30. Here Talbot also records one of her "abusive" sonnets, a lighthearted, witty riposte to Charles Yorke for a teasing sonnet addressing her as "Miss" and for writing a letter to the critic William Warburton while in the company of herself and Grey:

> Master, who fir'd with sacred rage of Prose
> Dost waste thy hours in idle letters vain
> To absent Friends, unmindfull of the twain
> Fair present Dames, while the full period flows
> Restrain Thy Pen, & spend one thought on those
> Who elsewhere might the best poetick strain
> From Bards of Cam or Isis well obtain
> Unask'd unwish'd—O no let calm repose
> Soft in ye Cushion'd Chair Thy Eyelids seal
> Lest words unpleasing should perhaps offend
> The gentle Ear—Miss! Hatefull is the name
> O mayst Thou Miss the praise of learned Will,

And when Thy Steps from fair Vacuna bend,
Much mayst Thou Miss, each now neglected Dame! (BLARS L30/106/30)

6. Talbot, Wrest Journal, June 11, 1745, BLARS L 30/106, n.p.; Thomas Birch, British Library Add. MS 4291, ff. 271–72; Talbot to E. Berkeley, n.d. [after 1761], British Library Add. MS 39312, ff. 319–20; *Bluestocking Feminism: Writings of the Bluestocking Circle, 1738–1785, Vol. 3: Catherine Talbot & Hester Chapone*, ed. Rhoda Zuk (London: Pickering and Chatto, 1999), 167.

7. Harold Love, *Scribal Publication in Seventeenth-Century England* (Oxford: Clarendon, 1993), 38.

8. In addition to the Huntington Library's Montagu Collection and the BLARS holdings cited here, portions of Talbot's own journals and of her correspondence are held at the British Library among the Berkeley papers and the Birch Collection. Together, these add complexity to the rather one-sided portrayal of Talbot found in Montagu Pennington's 1809 edition of Carter-Talbot letters and fill in details suggested by Rhoda Zuk in her edition of Talbot's works cited above.

9. David Fairer, *English Poetry of the Eighteenth Century 1700–1789* (London: Pearson Education, 2003); David Allan, *Commonplace Books and Reading in Georgian England* (Cambridge: Cambridge University Press, 2010).

10. From the catalogue description of MS Lt 119, *Literary Manuscripts: 17th and 18th Century Poetry from the Brotherton Library, University of Leeds,* Adam Matthews Digital, 2006, http://www.literarymanuscriptsleeds.amdigital.co.uk.proxy.lib.sfu.ca/document.aspx?documentid=10495, accessed July 25, 2018.

11. Thomas Birch to Mary Capell, August 24, 1751 and Capell to Birch, August 31, 1751, British Library Add. MS 4302 ff. 43–44. For an account of a similar archival experience, see Katharine Kittredge's "'It Spoke Directly to the Heart': Discovering the Mourning Journal of Melesina Trench," *Tulsa Studies in Women's Literature* 25 (2006): 335–45.

Bibliography

Allan, David. *Commonplace Books and Reading in Georgian England*. Cambridge: Cambridge University Press, 2010.
Andreadis, Harriette. "Re-Configuring Early Modern Friendship: Katherine Philips and Homoerotic Desire." *Studies in English Literature, 1500–1900* 46, no. 3 (Summer 2006): 523–42.
Anonymous. "The Session of the Poets, to the Tune of Cook Lawrel." In *Poems on Affairs of State: from the Time of Oliver Cromwell, to the Abdication of K. James the Second*, 206–211. London, 1697.
Anonymous. *The Session of the Poets, Holden at the Foot of Parnassus Hill, July the 9th, 1696*. London, 1696.
Austen, Jane. *Northanger Abbey*. Edited by Susan Fraiman. New York: W. W. Norton & Company, 2004.
Backscheider, Paula R. and Catherine Ingrassia, eds. *British Women Poets of the Long Eighteenth Century: An Anthology*. Baltimore: Johns Hopkins University Press, 2009.
Backscheider, Paula R. *Eighteenth-Century Women Poets and their Poetry: Inventing Agency, Inventing Genre*. Baltimore: Johns Hopkins University Press, 2005.
———. *Elizabeth Singer Rowe and the Development of the English Novel*. Baltimore: Johns Hopkins, 2013.
———. "Inverting the Image of Swift's 'Triumfeminate.'" *Journal for Early Modern Cultural Studies* (2004): 37–71.
Backscheider, Paula R. and John J. Richetti, ed. *Popular Fiction by Women 1660–1730*. New York: Oxford University Press, 1996.
Ballaster, Ros. "Manley, Delarivier (c.1670–1724)." In *Oxford Dictionary of National Biography*, Oxford University Press, 2004; online edn, May 2009. http://www.oxforddnb.com.go.libproxy.wakehealth.edu/view/article/17939, accessed 28 July 2015.
———. *Seductive Forms: Women's Amatory Fiction, 1684–1740*. Oxford: Clarendon Press, 1992.
Bannet, Eve Tavor. "The Narrator as Invisible Spy: Eliza Haywood, Secret History and the Novel." *Journal for Early Modern Cultural Studies* 14, no. 4 (Fall 2014): 143–62.
Barbauld, Anna Letitia. "On Friendship." In *The Works of Anna Barbauld with a Memoir by Lucy Aikin, Vol. II*, edited by Lucy Aikin, 351–55. New York: G & C Carvill et al, 1826.
———. "To Miss E. Belsham, afterwards Mrs. Kenrick" (1771). In *The Works of Anna Lætitia Barbauld*, edited by Lucy Aikin. 2 vols. London: Longman, Hurst, Rees, Orme, Brown, and Green, Paternoster-Row, 1825.
———. *The Poems of Anna Letitia Barbauld*. Edited by William McCarthy and Elizabeth Kraft. Athens: The University of Georgia Press, 1994.
Barber, Mary. *Poems on several occasions*. London, 1734.

BIBLIOGRAPHY

Barker, Jane. *A Patch-Work Screen for the Ladies*. In *The Galesia Trilogy and Selected Manuscript Poems of Jane Barker*, edited by Carol Shiner Wilson. New York and Oxford: Oxford University Press, 1997.

———. *The Galesia Trilogy and Selected Manuscript Poems of Jane Barker*. Edited by Carol Shiner Wilson. New York: Oxford University Press, 1997.

Barnard, Teresa. *Anna Seward: A Constructed Life*. Aldershot, Hampshire, UK: Ashgate, 2009.

Behn, Aphra. "The Feign'd Curtizans, or, A Nights Intrigue." In Vol. 6 of *The Works of Aphra Behn*, edited by Janet Todd. 7 vols. Columbus: Ohio State University Press, 1996.

———. "The History of the Nun: or, the Fair Vow-Breaker." In Vol. 3 of *The Works of Aphra Behn*, edited by Janet Todd. 7 vols. Columbus: Ohio State University Press, 1996.

———. Preface to *The Luckey Chance; or, An Alderman's Bargain, A Comedy*. In *The Rover and Other Plays*, edited by Jane Spencer. Oxford: Oxford University Press, 1995.

———. *The Lucky Chance*. In Vol. 7 of *The Works of Aphra Behn*, edited by Janet Todd. 7 vols. Columbus: Ohio State University Press, 1996.

Bermingham, Ann. *Learning to Draw: Studies in the Cultural History of a Polite and Useful Art*. New Haven, CT: Yale University Press, 2000.

Birch, Thomas. Papers in the British Library.

Blakemore, Steven. *Crisis in Representation: Thomas Paine, Mary Wollstonecraft, Helen Maria Williams*. Madison: Fairleigh Dickinson Press, 1997.

Bowers, Toni. "Jacobite Difference and the Poetry of Jane Barker." *English Literary History* 64 (1997): 857–69.

Boyd, Elizabeth. *The Happy-Unfortunate; or, the Female-Page: A Novel*. London: T. Edlin, 1732.

———. *Variety: A Poem, In Two Cantos*. Westminster: Warner and Creake, 1727.

Boyle, John, fifth Earl of Cork and Orrery. *Remarks on the Life and Writings of Dr. Jonathan Swift*, ed. João Fróes. Newark: University of Delaware Press, 2000.

Budd, Adam. "'Merit in Distress: The Troubled Success of Mary Barber." *Review of English Studies* 53.210 (2002): 204–27.

Brewer, John. *The Pleasures of the Imagination: English Culture in the Eighteenth Century*. New York: Farrar Straus Giroux, 1997.

Brideoake, Fiona. "'Extraordinary Female Affection': The Ladies of Llangollen and the Endurance of Queer Community." *Romanticism on the Net* No. 36–37 (2004–5). http://id.erudit.org/iderudit/011141ar.

Brightwell, Cecilia Lucy. *Memorials of the Life of Amelia Opie*. Norwich: Fletcher & Alexander, 1854.

Brown, Bill. "Objects, Others, and Us (The Refabrication of Things)." *Critical Inquiry* 36, no. 2 (2010): 183–217.

———. *A Sense of Things: The Object Matter of American Literature*. Chicago: University of Chicago Press, 2003.

Brown, Susan, Patricia Clements, and Isobel Grundy, eds. *Orlando: Women's Writing in the British Isles from the Beginnings to the Present*. Cambridge: Cambridge University Press Online, 2006. http://orlando.cambridge.org/.

BIBLIOGRAPHY

Burke, Edmund. *A Philosophical Enquiry into Our Ideas of the Sublime and the Beautiful.* London: Routledge, 1958.

Cameron, William J. "Anne, Countess of Winchilsea: A Guide for the Future Biographer." PhD diss., Victoria College, Wellington, New Zealand, 1951.

Carroll, John J., ed. *Selected Letters of Samuel Richardson.* Oxford: Clarendon Press, 1964.

Carter, Elizabeth. *Poems on Several Occasions.* London: Rivington, 1762.

Chittister, Joan. *The Friendship of Women: A Spiritual Tradition.* Erie, PA: Benetvision, 2000.

Clarke, Norma. *The Rise and Fall of the Woman of Letters.* London: Pimlico, 2004.

Clayden, Peter. *The Early Life of Samuel Rogers.* London: Smith, Elder & Co., 1887.

Clayton, Thomas. "Suckling, Sir John (bap. 1609, d. 1641?)." *Oxford Dictionary of National Biography,* Oxford University Press, 2004; online edn, Jan 2008. http://www.oxforddnb.com.go.libproxy.wakehealth.edu/view/article/26757.

Clery, Emma J. *The Feminization Debate in Eighteenth-Century England: Literature, Commerce and Luxury.* Houndmills, Basingstoke, UK: Palgrave Macmillan, 2004.

Cokayne, G.E. *The Complete Peerage.* Edited by Geoffrey H. White. Vol. 12, Part 1. London: St. Catherine Press, 1953.

Cole, Rebecca Heinwitz. *Spanish America and British Romanticism.* Edinburgh: Edinburgh University Press, 2010.

Coleman, Deirdre. "Firebrands, letters and flowers: Mrs. Barbauld and the Priestleys." In *Romantic Sociability: Social Networks and Literary Culture in Britain, 1770–1840,* edited by Gillian Russell and Clara Tuite. New York: Cambridge University Press, 2002.

Cook, Jessica. "Mary Leapor and the Poem as Meeting Place." *Eighteenth-Century Theory and Interpretation* 57, no. 3 (2016): 365–83.

Curran, Stuart. "Anna Seward and the Dynamics of Female Friendship." In *Romantic Women Poets: Genre and Gender,* edited by Maria Crisafulli and Cecilia Pietropoli, 11–21. Amsterdam: Rodopi, 2007.

Davis, Karen E. "Martha Fowke: 'A Lady Once Too Well Known.'" *English Language Notes,* 23, no. 3 (1986): 32–36.

Delany, Mary. *Autobiography and Correspondence of Mary Granville, Mrs. Delany.* Edited by Augusta Hall (Lady Llanover). 6 vols. Bentley 1861, 1862. Cambridge: Cambridge University Press, 2011.

Delights for the Ingenious: Or, a Monthly Entertainment for the Curious of both Sexes. London, 1711.

DeLucia, JoEllen. *A Feminine Enlightenment: British Women Writers and the Philosophy of Progress 1759–1820.* Edinburgh: Edinburgh University Press, 2015.

Devine, Harriet. "Anna Seward." In *The Literary Encyclopedia, English Writing and Culture of the Romantic Period,* edited by Daniel Robinson. First published 27 November 2002. http://www.litencyc.com/php/speople.php?rec=true&UID=4027.

Donoghue, Emma. *Passions Between Women: British Lesbian Culture 1668–1801.* London: Scarlet Press, 1993.

Dryden, John. "To the Memory of Mr. Oldham" (1684). *Poems 1681–1684.* Edited by H. T. Swedenberg. Vol. 2 of *The Works of John Dryden.* Berkeley: University of California Press, 1972.

———. "To the Pious Memory of the Accomplished Young Lady Mrs Anne Killigrew, Excellent in the Two Sister Arts of Poesie and Painting. An Ode" (1686). *Poems, 1685–1692*. Edited by Earl Miner and Vinton A. Dearing. Vol. 3 of *The Works of John Dryden*. Berkeley: University of California Press, 1969.

———. "To Sir Godfrey Kneller" (1694). *Poems, 1693–1696*. Edited by A. B. Chambers, William Frost, and Vinton A. Dearing. Volume 4 of *The Works of John Dryden*. Berkeley: University of California Press, 1974.

Dubrow, Heather. *The Challenges of Orpheus: Lyric Poetry and Early Modern England*. Baltimore: Johns Hopkins University Press, 2008.

Duquette, Natasha. Introduction to *Julia, a novel interspersed with poetical pieces*, by Helen Maria Williams, xi–xxxi. London: Pickering and Chatto, 2009.

———. "Julie and Julia: Tracing Intertextuality in Helen Maria Williams's Novel." In *Editing Women's Writing*, edited by Amy Culley and Anna Fitzer. London: Routledge, 2016.

———. *Veiled Intent: Dissenting Women's Aesthetic Approach to Biblical Interpretation*. Eugene, OR: Pickwick, 2016.

Eberle, Roxanne, ed. *The Correspondence of Amelia Alderson Opie: An Online Archive of Networks and Letters*. https://ctlsites.uga.edu/eberle/ameliaopieletters/.

Eger, Elizabeth. "The Bluestocking Circle: Friendships, Patronage and Learning." In *Brilliant Women: 18th-Century Bluestockings*, edited by Elizabeth Eger and Lucy Peltz, 21–55. London: National Portrait Gallery, 2008.

———. "Paper Trails and Eloquent Objects: Bluestocking Friendship and Material Culture." *Parergon: Journal of the Australian and New Zealand Association for Medieval and Early Modern Studies* 26, no. 2 (2009): 109–38.

Eicke, Leigh A. "Jane Barker's Jacobite Writings." In *Women's Writing and the Circulation of Ideas: Manuscript Publication in England, 1550–1800*, edited by George L. Justice and Nathan Tinker, 137–57. New York: Cambridge University Press, 2002.

Elias, A.C. "Editing Minor Writers: The Case of Laetitia Pilkington and Mary Barber." In *1650–1850: Ideas, Aesthetics, and Inquires in the Early Modern Era*, edited by Kevin L. Cope, Volume 3, 129–47. New York: AMS Press, 1997.

———. "A Manuscript Book of Constantia Grierson's." *Swift Studies* 2 (1987): 33–56.

———ed. *Memoirs of Laetitia Pilkington*, 2 vols. Athens and London: University of George Press, 1997.

———. "Senatus Consultum: Revising Verse in Swift's Dublin Circle, 1729–1735." In *Reading Swift: Papers from the Third Münster Symposium on Jonathan Swift*, edited by Hermann J. Real and Helgard Stover-Leidig, 250–67. Munich: Wilhelm Fink Verlag, 1998.

Elizabeth Montagu and the Bluestocking Circle. http://www.elizabethmontaguletters.co.uk/the-project.

Ezell, Margaret, ed. *The Poems and Prose of Mary, Lady Chudleigh*. New York: Oxford University Press, 1993.

Fairer, David. *English Poetry of the Eighteenth Century 1700–1789*. Harlow and London: Pearson Education, 2003.

Feldman, Paula. "Note on the Texts of *Peru* and 'Peruvian Tales." In *Peru and Peruvian Tales* by Helen Maria Williams, 41–42. Guelph, Ontario: Broadview Press, 2014.

Fenves, Peter. "Politics of Friendship, Once Again." *Eighteenth-Century Studies* 32, no. 2 (Winter 1998–1999): 133–55.
Ferguson, Frances. *Solitude and the Sublime.* London: Routledge, 1993.
Ferguson, Moira. "'The Cause of My Sex': Mary Scott and the Female Literary Tradition." *Huntington Library Quarterly* 50, no. 4 (Autumn 1987): 359–77.
Finch, Anne. *The Cambridge Edition of the Works of Anne Finch, Countess of Winchilsea.* Edited by Jennifer Keith and Claudia Thomas Kairoff. 2 vols. Cambridge: Cambridge University Press, forthcoming.
———. *Miscellany Poems on Several Occasions.* London, 1713.
———. *Miscellany Poems with Two Plays By Ardelia.* Manuscript Fnb3, Folger Shakespeare Library, Washington, D.C.
———. *The Poems of Anne Countess of Winchilsea.* Edited by Myra Reynolds. Chicago: University of Chicago Press, 1903.
Frevert, Ute. *Men of Honour: A Social and Cultural History of the Duel.* Translated by Anthony Williams. 1991; repr., Cambridge: Polity Press, 1995.
Frye, Susan and Karen Robertson, eds. *Maids and Mistresses, Cousins and Queens: Women's Alliances in Early Modern England.* Oxford: Oxford University Press, 1999.
Gerrard, Christine. *Aaron Hill: The Muses' Projector, 1689–1750.* Oxford: Oxford University Press, 2003.
Gray, Thomas. *The Progress of Poesy. A Pindaric Ode. The Poems of Thomas Gray, William Collins, and Oliver Goldsmith.* Edited by Roger Lonsdale. New York: W. W. Norton, 1969.
Greer, Germaine "'Alme in Liberte Avvezze': Aphra Behn's Version of Tasso's Golden Age." In *Aphra Behn, 1640–1689: Identity, Alterity, Ambiguity,* edited by Mary Ann O'Donnell, Bernard Dhuicq, and Guyonne Leduc, 225–33. Paris: Harmattan, 2000.
Greer, Germaine, Susan Hastings, Jeslyn Medoff, and Melinda Sansone, eds. *Kissing the Rod: An Anthology of Seventeenth-Century Women's Verse.* New York: The Noonday Press, Farrar Straus Giroux, 1988.
Grundy, Isobel. "'Slip-Shod Measure' and 'Language of Gods': Barbauld's Stylistic Range." In *Anna Letitia Barbauld: New Perspectives,* edited by William McCarthy and Olivia Murphy, 23–36. Lewisburg, PA: Bucknell University Press, 2014.
Guest, Harriet. *Small Change: Women, Learning, Patriotism, 1750–1810.* Chicago: University of Chicago Press, 2000.
Guskin, Phyllis, ed., *Clio: The Autobiography of Martha Fowke Sansom (1689–1736).* Newark: University of Delaware Press, 1997.
———ed. "'Not originally intended for the Press'; Martha Fowke Sansom's Poems in the Barbados Gazette." *Eighteenth-Century Studies* 34, no. 1 (2000): 61–91.
Hagstrum, Jean. *The Sister Arts: The Tradition of Literary Pictorialism and English Poetry from Dryden to Gray.* Chicago: The University of Chicago Press, 1958.
Hallberg, Robert Von. *Lyric Powers.* Chicago and London: University of Chicago Press, 2008.
Hammond, Anthony, ed., *A New Miscellany of Original Poems, Translations and Imitations by the Most Eminent Hands.* London, 1720.
Handley, Stuart. "Colepeper, Thomas, third baronet, of Preston Hall (c. 1656–1723)." In *History of Parliament Online.* http://www.historyofparliamentonline.org/volume/1690-1715/member/colepeper-%28culpeper%29-sir-thomas-1656-1723.

———. "Wythens, Sir Francis (c.1635–1704)." In *Oxford Dictionary of National Biography*, Oxford University Press, 2004; online edn, Jan 2008. http://www.oxforddnb.com.go .libproxy.wakehealth.edu/view/article/30178.

Haywood, Eliza. *Epistles for the Ladies*. Edited by Christine Blouch and Alexander Pettit. In Set I, vol. 2 of *Selected Works of Eliza Haywood*, edited by Alexander Pettit. 6 vols. London: Pickering & Chatto, 2000–1.

———. *The Fair Captive: A Tragedy*. London: Jauncy and Cole, 1721.

———. *Female Spectator*. Edited by Kathryn R. King and Alexander Pettit. In Set II, vol. 2 of *Selected Works of Eliza Haywood*, edited by Alexander Pettit. 6 vols. London: Pickering & Chatto, 2000–2001.

———. *The Invisible Spy*. Edited by Carol Stewart. London: Pickering & Chatto, 2014.

———. *Memoirs of the Baron de Brosse*. London: Browne and Chapman, 1725.

———. *Poems on Several Occasions*. In *The Works of Mrs Eliza Haywood; Consisting of Novels, Letters, Poems, and Plays*. 4 vols. London: Browne and Chapman, 1724.

———. *A Wife to be Lett: A Comedy*. London: Browne and Chapman, 1724.

Heinwitz Cole, Rebecca. *Spanish American and British Romanticism: 1777–1826*. Edinburgh: Edinburgh University Press, 2010.

Hughes, Barbara. *Between Literature and History: The Diaries and Memoirs of Mary Leadbeater and Dorothea Herbert*. New York: Peter Lang, 2010.

Hurley, Ann and Kate Greenspan, eds. *So Rich a Tapestry: The Sister Arts and Cultural Studies*. Lewisburg, PA: Bucknell University Press, 1995.

Jonson, Ben. *The Poems of Ben Jonson*. Edited by George Burke Johnston. Cambridge: Harvard University Press, 1985.

Joy, Louise. "Emotions in Translation: Helen Maria Williams and the 'Beauties Peculiar to the English Language.'" *Studies in Romanticism* 50, no. 1 (2011): 145–77.

Kairoff, Claudia. *Anna Seward and the End of the Eighteenth Century*. Baltimore: The Johns Hopkins University Press, 2012.

Keane, Angela. "The Market, The Public, and the Female Author: Anna Laetitia Barbauld's Gift Economy." *Romanticism: The Journal of Romantic Culture and Criticism* 8, no. 2 (2002): 161–78.

———. *Women Writers and the English Nation in the 1790s*. Cambridge: Cambridge University Press, 2000.

Keith, Jennifer. *Poetry and the Feminine from Behn to Cowper*. Newark: University of Delaware Press, 2005.

Kelley, Theresa M. *Clandestine Marriage: Botany and Romantic Culture*. Baltimore: Johns Hopkins University Press, 2012.

Kelly, Gary. *Women, Writing, and Revolution, 1790–1827*. Oxford: Clarendon Press, 1993.

Kennedy, Deborah. *Helen Maria Williams and the Age of Revolution*. Lewisburg, PA: Bucknell University Press, 2002.

———. *Poetic Sisters: Early Eighteenth-Century Women Poets*. Lewisburg, PA: Bucknell University Press, 2013.

Kim, Jane E. "My Brother's Keeper: The Striving of Siblings in Joanna Baillie's *De Monfort*." *European Romantic Review* 23, no. 6 (December 2012): 707–26.

King, Kathryn R. "The Constructions of Femininity." In *A Companion to Eighteenth-Century Poetry*, edited by Christine Gerrard, 431–43. Chichester, UK: John Wiley and Sons, 2014.

———. "Eliza Haywood, Savage Love, and Biographical Uncertainty." *Review of English Studies* New Series 59, no. 242 (2008): 722–39.

———. *Jane Barker: Exile*. New York: Oxford University Press, 2000.

———. "New Contexts for Early Novels by Women: The Case of Eliza Haywood, Aaron Hill, and the Hillarians, 1719–1725." In *A Companion to the Eighteenth-Century Novel and Culture*, edited by Paula R. Backscheider and Catherine Ingrassia, 261–75. Malden, MA: Blackwell, 2005.

———. "The Pious Mrs. Haywood; or, Thoughts on *Epistles for the Ladies* (1748–1750)." *Journal for Early Modern Cultural Studies* 14, no. 4 (Fall 2014):187–208.

———. *A Political Biography of Eliza Haywood*. London: Pickering & Chatto, 2012.

King, Shelley. "Portrait of a Marriage: John and Amelia Opie and the Sister Arts." *Studies in Eighteenth-Century Culture* 40 (2011): 27–62.

———. "Representation, Memory and Mourning in Amelia Opie's 'On the Portraits of Deceased Friends and Relatives, which Hang Around Me.'" In *Performing the Everyday: The Culture of Genre in the Eighteenth Century*, edited by Alden Cavanaugh. Newark: University of Delaware Press, 2007.

Kittredge, Katharine. "'For the Benefit of Young Women Going into Service': Late Eighteenth-Century Proto-Young Adult Novels for Labouring Class Girls." *Women's Writing* 23, no. 1 (2016): 106–26.

———. "'It Spoke Directly to the Heart': Discovering the Mourning Journal of Melesina Trench," *Tulsa Studies in Women's Literature* 25 (2006): 335–45.

———. "Missing Immortality: The Case of Melesina Trench (A Neglected, Celebrated, Dismissed and Rediscovered Woman Poet of the Long Eighteenth Century)." *Aphra Behn Online: Interactive Journal for Women in the Arts 1640–1830* 1, no. 1 (Spring 2011).

———. "Wingless Women Living Backward on the Moon: Melesina Trench's *The Moonlanders*, 1816." *Science Fiction Studies* 101, no. 34 (March 2007): 19–41.

Labbe, Jacqueline. "Every Poet Her Own Drawing Master: Charlotte Smith, Anna Seward and *ut pictura poesis*." In *Early Romantics: Perspectives in British Poetry from Pope to Wordsworth*, edited by Thomas Woodman. New York: St. Martin's Press, 1998.

Laird, Mark. "Introduction," in *Mrs. Delany and Her Circle*, edited by Mark Laird and Alicia Weisberg-Roberts. New Haven, CT: Yale University Press, 2009.

Laird, Mark, and Alicia Weisberg-Roberts, eds. *Mrs. Delany and her Circle*. New Haven, CT and London: Yale University Press, 2009.

Lanser, Susan "Befriending the Body." *Eighteenth-Century Studies* 32, no. 2 (Winter 1998-1999): 179–98.

———. *The Sexuality of History: Modernity and the Sapphic, 1565–1830*, Chicago: University of Chicago Press, 2014.

Lanyer, Aemilia. *Salve Deus Rex Judaeorum*. London: Printed by Valentine Simmes for Richard Bonian, 1611.

BIBLIOGRAPHY

Leadbeater, Mary. *The Cottage Dialogues Among the Irish Peasantry.* Dublin: J. & J. Carick, 1811.

———. *Extracts and Original Anecdotes for the Improvement of Youth.* Dublin: R.M. Jackson, 1794.

———. *The Leadbeater Papers.* London: Bell and Daldy, 1862.

———. *Poems by Mary Leadbeater (Late Shackleton).* London: Longman, Hurst, et al.; Dublin: Martin Keene, 1808.

Leapor, Mary. *The Works of Mary Leapor.* Edited by Richard Greene and Ann Messenger. Oxford: Oxford University Press, 2003.

Levy, Michelle. "Barbauld's Poetic Career in Script and Print." In McCarthy and Murphy, eds., *Anna Letitia Barbauld: New Perspectives*, 37–58.

Lister, Anne. *I Know My Own Heart: The Diaries of Anne Lister 1791–1840.* Edited by Helena Whitbread. London: Virago, 1988.

Lonsdale, Roger, ed. *Eighteenth Century Women Poets: An Oxford Anthology.* Oxford and New York: Oxford University Press, 1989.

Love, Harold. *Scribal Publication in Seventeenth-Century England.* Oxford: Clarendon, 1993.

Lucas Papers. Bedfordshire and Luton Archives and Records Service.

Mandell, Laura C. "Gendering Digital Literary History: What Counts for Digital Humanities." In *A New Companion to Digital Humanities*, edited by Susan Schreibman, Ray Siemens, and John Unsworth. Chichester, UK: Wiley-Blackwell, 2015.

Manley, Delarivier. *Secret Memoirs and Manners of several Persons of Quality, of both Sexes. From the New Atalantis, an Island in the Mediterranean.* Edited by Rosalind Ballaster. 1709; rpt. London: Penguin, 1992.

Martinez, Michele. "Women Poets and the Sister Arts in Nineteenth-Century England." *Victorian Poetry* 41, no. 4 (Winter 2003): 621–28.

McCarthy, William. *Anna Letitia Barbauld: Voice of the Enlightenment.* Baltimore: The Johns Hopkins University Press, 2008.

———. "'We Hoped the *Woman* Was Going to Appear': Repression, Desire, and Gender in Anna Letitia Barbauld's Early Poems." In *Romantic Women Writers: Voices and Countervoices*, edited by Paula R. Feldman and Theresa M. Kelley. Hanover, NH: University Press of New England, 1995.

McGovern, Barbara. *Anne Finch and Her Poetry: A Critical Biography.* Athens: University of Georgia Press, 1992.

Medoff, Jeslyn. "The Daughters of Behn and the Problem of Reputation." In *Women, Writing, History 1640–1740*, edited by Isobel Grundy and Susan Wiseman. Athens: University of Georgia Press, 1992.

Mellor, Anne K., "'Anguish No Cessation Knows': Elegy and the British Woman Poet, 1660–1834." In *The Oxford Handbook of the Elegy*, edited by Karen Weisman, 442–62. Oxford: Oxford University Press, 2010.

Messenger, Ann. *Pastoral Tradition and the Female Talent: Studies in Augustan Poetry.* New York: AMS, 2001.

Miscellaneous Poems and Translations. By several hands. Publish'd by Richard Savage, Son of the late Earl Rivers. London, 1726.

Mitchell, Christopher. *The French Atlantic Triangle: Literature and the Culture of the Slave Trade.* Durham, NC: Duke University Press, 2008.

Montagu Collection. The Huntington Library, San Marino, California.
Moore, Lisa. *Dangerous Intimacies: Toward a Sapphic History of the British Novel.* Durham, NC: Duke University Press, 1997.
———. *Sister Arts: The Erotics of Lesbian Landscapes.* Minneapolis: University of Minnesota Press, 2011.
Moretti, Franco. *Atlas of the European Novel 1800–1900.* London: Verso, 1998.
Morris, Adelaide. "Woman Speaking to Women: Retracing the Feminine in Anna Laetitia Barbauld." *Women's Writing* 10, no. 1 (2003): 47–72.
Murphy, Olivia. "Riddling Sibyl, Uncanny Cassandra: Barbauld's Recent Critical Reception." In *Anna Letitia Barbauld: New Perspectives,* edited by William McCarthy and Olivia Murphy, 277–298. Lewisberg, PA: Bucknell University Press, 2013.
Neill, Anna. "The Sentimental Novel and the Republican Imaginary." *Diacritics* 23 (1993): 36–47.
'O Ciosáin, Niall. *Print and Popular Culture in Ireland 1750–1850.* NY: St. Martin's Press, 1997.
O'Donnell, Mary Ann. *Aphra Behn: An Annotated Bibliography of Primary and Secondary Sources,* 2nd ed. Burlington, VT: Ashgate, 2004.
Olive, Barbara. "The Fabric of Restoration Puritanism: Mary Chudleigh's *The Song of the Three Children Paraphras'd.*" In *Puritanism and its Discontents,* edited by Laura Runge Knoppers, Newark: University of Delaware Press, 2003.
———. "A Puritan Subject's Panegyrics to Queen Anne," *Studies in English Literature* 42, no. 3 (2002): 475–99.
Opie, Amelia Alderson. *The Collected Poems of Amelia Alderson Opie.* Edited by Shelley King and John B. Pierce. Oxford: Oxford University Press, 2009.
———. "Memoir." *Lectures on Painting.* By John Opie. London: Longman, Hurst, Rees, & Orme, 1809.
Overton, Bill, ed., *A Letter to My Love: Love Poems by Women First Published in the Barbados Gazette, 1731–7.* Newark: University of Delaware Press, 2001.
Peacock, Molly. *The Paper Garden: An Artist Begins Her Life's Work at 72.* New York: Bloomsbury, 2010.
Pearson, Jacqueline. *The Prostituted Muse: Images of Women and Women Dramatists 1642–1737.* London: Harvester Wheatsheaf, 1988.
Peltonen, Markku. *The Duel in Early Modern England: Civility, Politeness and Honour.* Cambridge: Cambridge University Press, 2003.
Philips, Katherine. *The Collected Works of Katherine Philips, The Matchless Orinda.* Edited by Patrick Thomas. Vol. 1, *The Poems.* Stump Cross, Essex, UK: Stump Cross Books, 1990.
Pilkington, Jack Carteret. *The real story of John Carteret Pilkington, Written by Himself.* London: 1760.
Pilkington, Laetitia. *Memoirs of Laetitia Pilkington.* Edited by A. C. Elias, Jr. Athens and London: The University of Georgia Press, 1997.
Pocock, J. G. A. *Virtue, Commerce, and History: Essay on Political Thought and History, Chiefly in the Eighteenth Century.* Cambridge: Cambridge University Press, 1985.
Poems by Eminent Ladies. London: R. Baldwin, 1755. *Eighteenth-Century Collections Online.*

Pope, Alexander. "Epistle to Mr. Jervas, With *Dryden's* Translation of *Fresnoy's* Art of Painting" (1716). *Minor Poems*. Edited by Norman Ault. Vol. 6 of *The Twickenham Edition of the Poems of Alexander Pope*, 11 vols., gen. ed. John Butt. New Haven, CT: Yale University Press, 1951–69.

———. *The Correspondence of Alexander Pope* Vol. III 1729–1735. Edited by George Sherburn. Oxford at the Clarendon Press, 1956.

Prescott, Sarah. *Women, Authorship, and Literary Culture, 1690–1740*. Houndsmill, Basingstoke, UK: Palgrave, 2003.

Radcliffe, Ann. *Romance of the Forest*. Edited by Chloe Chard. Oxford: Oxford University Press, 1986.

Ragussis, Michael. *Theatrical Nation: Jews and Other Outlandish Englishmen in Georgian Britain* Philadelphia: University of Pennsylvania Press, 2010.

Randolph, Grace Blome. *The Cookbook of Grace Blome* (1697), Manuscript V.b.301, Folger Shakespeare Library, Washington, D.C.

Ready, Kathryn. "Mind Versus Matter: Anna Barbauld and the 'Kindred Arts' of Painting and Poetry." *Eighteenth-Century Women: Studies in Their Lives, Work, and Culture* 6 (2011): 229–52.

Reynolds, Myra. *The Learned Lady in England 1650–1760*. Boston and New York: Houghton Mifflin Co, 1920.

———. *The Poems of Anne Countess of Winchilsea: From the Original Edition of 1713 and From Unpublished Manuscripts*. Chicago: Chicago University Press, 1903.

Robinson, Philip. "Traduction ou Trahison de *Paul et Virginie?* L'Exemple de Helen Maria Williams." *Revue d'histoire littéraire de la France* 89 (1989): 843–55.

Rogers, John Jope. *Opie and His Work*. London: Paul & Domenic Colnaghi & Co., 1878.

Rosenbaum, Susan. "'A Thing Unknown, without a Name': Anna Laetitia Barbauld and the Illegible Signature." *Studies in Romanticism* 40, no. 3 (Fall 2011): 369–99.

Rovee, Christopher Kent. *Imagining the Gallery: The Social Body of British Romanticism*. Stanford, CA: Stanford University Press, 2006.

Runge, Laura. "Dueling." In *The Encyclopedia of British Literature 1660–1789*, edited by Gary Day and Jack Lynch. Blackwell, 2015.

Sampson, Julie, ed. *Mary, Lady Chudleigh: Selected Poems*. Exeter, UK: Shearman Books, 2009.

Schellenberg, Betty A. "The Professional Female Writer," in *The Cambridge Companion to Women's Writing in Britain, 1660–1789*, edited by Catherine Ingrassia. Cambridge: Cambridge University Press, 2015.

Schimmelpenninck, Mary Anne. *Theory on the Classification of Beauty and Deformity*. London: John and Arthur Arch, 1815.

Schwenger, Peter. *The Tears of Things: Melancholy and Physical Objects*. Minneapolis: University of Minnesota Press, 2006.

Scott, Mary. *The Female Advocate*. London: Joseph Johnson, 1774. Brown University: *Women Writers Online*.

Scott, Sarah. *A description of Millennium Hall, and the country adjacent: together with the character of the inhabitants, and such historical anecdotes and reflections, as may excite in the reader proper sentiments of humanity, and lead the mind to the love of virtue*. London: J. Newbery, 1762.

Seward, Anna. *Llangollen Vale, with Other Poems.* London: G. Sael, 1796.

———. *Letters of Anna Seward: Written Between the Years 1784 and 1807. In Six Volumes.* Edinburgh: George Ramsay, 1811.

———. *Monody on Major André by Miss Seward (author of the Elegy on Capt. Cook.) To which are added letters addressed to her by Major André in the year 1769.* London: J. Jackson, 1781.

———. *The Poetical Works of Anna Seward; with Extracts from her Literary Correspondence, edited by Walter Scott, Esq.,* 3 vols. Edinburgh: James Ballantyne, 1810.

Sigler, David. "'The Ocean of Futurity which has no Boundaries': The Deconstructive Politics of Helen Maria Williams's Translation of *Paul and Virginia.*" *European Romantic Review* 23, no. 5 October 2012: 575–92.

Smith, Orianne. *Romantic Women Writers, Revolution, and Prophecy: Rebellious Daughters, 1786–1826.* Cambridge: Cambridge University Press, 2013.

Spedding, Patrick. *A Bibliography of Eliza Haywood.* London: Pickering and Chatto, 2004.

Spencer, Jane. *Aphra Behn's Afterlife.* Oxford: Oxford University Press, 2000.

Staves, Susan. *A Literary History of Women's Writing in Britain, 1660–1789.* Cambridge: Cambridge University Press, 2006.

———. *Married Women's Separate Property in England, 1660–1833.* Cambridge, MA: Harvard University Press, 1990.

Stone, Lawrence. *The Family, Sex and Marriage in England, 1500–1800.* New York: Harper & Row, 1977.

Suckling, Sir John. *Fragmenta Aurea. A Collection of All the Incomparable Peeces, Written by Sir John Suckling. And Published by a Friend to Perpetuate His Memory.* London, 1646.

———. *The Works of Sir John Suckling.* Edited by Thomas Clayton. Vol. 1, *The Non-Dramatic Works.* Oxford: Clarendon, 1971.

Swift, Jonathan. *The Correspondence of Jonathan Swift, Volume III 1724–1731.* Edited by Harold Williams. Oxford: Clarendon Press, 1963.

Talbot, Catherine. Papers in the British Library.

Tasso, Torquato. *Jerusalem delivered; an heroic poem: translated from the Italian of Torquato Tasso, by John Hoole.* Vol. 2. 2nd ed. London: printed for R. and J. Dodsley, P. Valliant [sic], T. Davies, J. Newbery and Z. Stuart, 1764. Eighteenth Century Collections Online.

Taylor, Elizabeth. "Song" ("Ye Virgin Pow'rs defend my heart"); "To Mertill who desir'd her to speak to Clorinda of his Love"; "Song" ("Strephon has Fashion, Wit, and Youth"). In *Miscellany, Being a Collection of Poems by Several Hands,* edited by Aphra Behn, 69–73. London, 1685.

Thaddeus, Janice Farrar. "Mary Delany, Model to the Age." In *History, Gender & Eighteenth-Century Literature,* edited by Beth Fowkes Tobin. Athens: University of Georgia Press, 1994.

Todd, Janet. *The Sign of Angelica: Women, Writing, Fiction 1660–1800.* New York: Columbia University Press, 1989.

Trench, Melesina. *Aubrey: In Five Cantos.* Southampton: T. Baker, 1818.

———. *Compaspe and Other Poems.* Southampton: T. Baker, 1817.

BIBLIOGRAPHY

———. *Laura's Dream, or, The Moonlanders*. London, 1816.
———. Letters to Mary Leadbeater. Beinecke Library. OSB MSS 50.
———. *Mary Queen of Scots, an Historical Ballad: with Other Poems*. London: John Stockdale, 1800.
———. "The Recollections of Melesina Trench, with Extracts from her Diary and Correspondence." Autograph draft. Hampshire Record Office, ref. 23M93/2/1, n.d.
———. *The Remains of the late Mrs. Richard Trench*. Ed. Richard Chenevix Trench. London: Parker, Son and Bourn, 1862.
———. *Thoughts of a Parent on Education*. London: John W. Parker, 1837.
Turkle, Sherry. "Introduction: The Things That Matter" to *Evocative Objects: Things We Think With*. Cambridge, MA: MIT Press, 2009.
Van Lennep, William, Emmett L. Avery, Arthur H. Scouten, George W. Stone, Jr., and Charles B. Hogan, eds. *The London Stage 1660–1800: A Calendar of Plays, Entertainments and Afterpieces, Together with Casts, Box-Receipts and Contemporary Comment Compiled from the Playbills, Newspapers and Theatrical Diaries of the Period*. Vol. 1, 1660–1700. Carbondale: Southern Illinois University Press, 1960–68.
Vickery, Amanda. *The Gentleman's Daughter: Women's Lives in Georgian England*. New Haven, CT: Yale University Press, 1998.
Vieth, David M. *Attribution in Restoration Poetry: A Study of Rochester's Poems of 1680*. New Haven, CT: Yale University Press, 1963.
Wahl, Elizabeth Susan. *Invisible Relations: Representations of Female Intimacy in the Age of Enlightenment*. Stanford, CA: Standford University Press, 1999.
Watkins, Daniel P. *Anna Letitia Barbauld and Eighteenth-Century Visionary Poetics*. Baltimore: John Hopkins University Press, 2012.
Weisberg-Roberts, Alicia. "Introduction (1): Mrs. Delany from Source to Subject." In *Mrs. Delany and her Circle*, edited by Mark Laird and Alicia Weisberg-Roberts. New Haven, CT and London: Yale University Press, 2009.
Wendorf, Richard, ed. *Articulate Images: The Sister Arts from Hogarth to Tennyson*. Minneapolis: University of Minnesota Press, 1983.
Whitehall Evening Post. (London) April 27, 1799.
Wikborg, Eleanor. "The Expression of the Forbidden in Romance Form: Genre as Possibility in Jane Barker's *Exilius*." *Genre* 22 (1989): 3–19.
Wilcher, Robert. *The Discontented Cavalier: The Work of Sir John Suckling in Its Social, Religious, Political, and Literary Contexts*. Newark: University of Delaware Press, 2007.
Williams, Carolyn and Angela Escott and Louise Duckling, eds. *Woman to Woman: Female Negotiations During the Long Eighteenth Century*. Newark: University of Delaware Press, 2010.
Williams, Helen Maria. "Introductory Remarks on the Present State of Science and Literature in France" to *Poems on Various Subjects*, ix–xliii. London: Whittaker 1823.
———. *Julia, a novel interspersed with poetical pieces*. Edited by Natasha Duquette. London: Pickering and Chatto, 2009.
———. *Letters Written in France in the Summer of 1790 to a Friend in England*. Oxford: Woodstock Books, 1989.
———. *Memoirs of the Reign of Robespierre*. London: John Hamilton Ltd., 1929.
———. "To Mrs. Montagu" in *Peru, a Poem in Six Cantos*, iii-vi, London: T. Cadell, 1784.

———. *An Ode on the Peace.* London: T. Cadell, 1783.
———. *Paul and Virginia by Bernardin Saint-Pierre.* Oxford: Woodstock, 1989.
———. "Preface" to *Paul and Virginia by Bernardin Saint-Pierre,* iii-ix. Oxford: Woodstock, 1989.
Wilmot, John, Earl of Rochester. *Poems on Several Occasions, by the Right Honourable, the E. of R———.* Antwerp [London], 1680.
———. *Poems, &c. on Several Occasions: with Valentinian, A Tragedy.* London, 1691.
——— *The Poems and Lucina's Rape.* Edited by Keith Walker and Nicholas Fisher. Chichester, UK: Wiley-Blackwell, 2013.
Wilputte, Earla. *Passion and Language in Eighteenth-Century Literature: The Aesthetic Sublime in the Work of Eliza Haywood, Aaron Hill, and Martha Fowke.* Basingstoke, UK: Palgrave Macmillan, 2014.
Winn, James A. *"When Beauty Fires the Blood": Love and the Arts in the Age of Dryden.* Ann Arbor: The University of Michigan Press, 1992.
Wollstonecraft, Mary. *Collected Letters of Mary Wollstonecraft.* Edited by Janet Todd. New York: Columbia University Press, 2003.
———. "Chapter 4: Observations on The State of Degradation to Which Woman is Reduced by Various Causes." *A Vindication of the Rights of Woman.* Edited by Sylvana Tomaselli. New York: Cambridge University Press, 1995.
Woolf, Virginia. *A Room of One's Own.* San Diego: Harcourt, 1981.
Wordsworth, William. *The Complete Poetical Works of Wordsworth: Cambridge Edition.* Boston and New York: Houghton Mifflin, 1904.
Wright, Angela. *Britain, France, and the Gothic, 1764–1829: The Import of Terror.* Cambridge: Cambridge University Press, 2013.
Wyett, Jodi. "'No Place Where Women Are of Such Importance': Female Friendship, Empire, and Utopia." *The History of Emily Montague, Eighteenth-Century Fiction* vol. 16, no. 1 (2003): 33–57.
Zuk, Rhoda, ed. *Vol. 3: Catherine Talbot & Hester Chapone. Bluestocking Feminism: Writings of the Bluestocking Circle, 1738–1785,* 6 vols. Edited by Gary Kelly. London: Pickering and Chatto, 1999.

Contributors

JESSICA COOK is a Continuing Instructor and M.A. Advisor at the University of South Florida. Her scholarly work focuses on women poets of the long eighteenth century and place studies. She has published articles on Mary Leapor and Clara Reeve, and also writes on the eighteenth century and contemporary popular culture for the website *ABO Public*, a public scholarship forum for the open access scholarly journal *ABO: Interactive Journal for Women in the Arts, 1640–1830*.

NATASHA DUQUETTE is Associate Dean and Professor of English at Tyndale University College in Toronto, Ontario. She is the author of *Veiled Intent: Dissenting Women's Aesthetic Approach to Biblical Interpretation* (Pickwick, 2016) and has edited two essay collections: *Sublimer Aspects: Interfaces between Literature, Aesthetics, and Theology* (Cambridge Scholars, 2007); and *Jane Austen and the Arts: Elegance, Propriety, and Harmony* (Lehigh University Press, 2013). For the Chawton House Library Series, she produced a scholarly edition of Helen Maria Williams's *Julia, a novel interspersed with poetical pieces* (Pickering & Chatto, 2009).

CHRISTINE GERRARD is Professor of English Literature in the English Faculty at the University of Oxford, and Barbara Scott Fellow and Tutor in English at Lady Margaret Hall Oxford. She has recently been a Mellon Foundation Teaching Fellow at the Ashmolean Museum, Oxford, working on a project designed to engage students with classical influences on eighteenth century literature and culture. She is currently completing an edition of Jonathan Swift's *A History of the Four Last Years* as part of the Cambridge edition of the *Complete Works of Jonathan Swift*. She is also editing the eighteenth-century volume for the *Oxford History of Poetry in English*. Her main interests are in political writing of the period 1660–1760, and eighteenth-century poetry, particularly women's poetry.

CATHERINE INGRASSIA is Professor of English at Virginia Commonwealth University in Richmond, Virginia. Her publications include *Authorship, Commerce, and Gender in Early Eighteenth-Century England* (Cambridge,

1998); *"More Solid Learning": New Perspectives on Pope's* Dunciad (co-edited with Claudia Kairoff, Bucknell, 2000), and *Companion to the Eighteenth-Century Novel and Culture* (co-edited with Paula Backscheider, Blackwell, 2005). A past editor of *Studies in Eighteenth-Century Culture*, she has edited Eliza Haywood's *Anti-Pamela* (Broadview, 2004), co-edited *British Women Poets of the Long Eighteenth Century* (Johns Hopkins, 2009), and published essays on the literature and culture of eighteenth-century England. Most recently she edited the *Cambridge Companion to Women's Writing in Britain, 1660–1789* (2015). She is currently working on a book-length project titled "Cultures of Captivity in the Long Eighteenth Century."

NICOLLE JORDAN is an Associate Professor of British literature at the University of Southern Mississippi. Intersecting with feminism and ecocriticism, her scholarship focuses on the relationship between landscape and women's property ownership. She has published articles on Jane Barker, Anne Finch, William Godwin, Elizabeth Montagu, Lady Mary Wortley Montagu, and Sarah Scott.

CLAUDIA THOMAS KAIROFF is a professor of English at Wake Forest University, where she teaches Restoration and Eighteenth-Century British Literature. She has published *Alexander Pope and His Eighteenth-Century Women Readers* (Southern Illinois University Press, 1994), *Anna Seward and the End of the Eighteenth Century* (Johns Hopkins, 2012), and numerous articles on Pope and on women poets. With Catherine Ingrassia, she co-edited *"More Solid Learning": New Perspectives on Alexander Pope's* Dunciad (Bucknell University Press, 2000). She has co-edited with Jennifer Keith *The Works of Anne Finch, Countess of Winchilsea*, a two-volume critical edition forthcoming from Cambridge University Press, and is working on a monograph about gender, religion, and politics in the writings of Anne Finch.

KATHRYN R. KING is Professor Emerita of Literature at the University of Montevallo and former Director of Faculty Development. Her research focuses on the lives, texts, and professional careers of women writers in the long eighteenth century. Her books include *A Political Biography of Eliza Haywood* (Pickering & Chatto, 2012) and *Jane Barker, Exile: A Literary Career 1675–1725* (Oxford, 2000). She is co-editor (with Alexander Pettit) of Haywood's *Female Spectator* (Pickering & Chatto, 2001), and has published articles in *RES, ELH, JEMCS, The Eighteenth-Century, Studies in the Novel*, and many other journals. She has held ACLS, NEH, and other fellowships, is former editor of the eighteenth century section of *Literature Compass*, and is currently working on periodical culture at mid-century.

SHELLEY KING is Professor and Head of the Department of English Language and Literature at Queen's University, in Kingston, Ontario. She and John B. Pierce have co-edited a number of Amelia Opie's works: *The Collected Poems of Amelia Alderson Opie* (Oxford, 2009); *Adeline Mowbray* (Oxford World's Classics, 1999); and *The Father and Daughter with Dangers of Coquetry* (Broadview, 2003). She is also co-editor with Yael Schlick of *Refiguring the Coquette: Essays on Culture and Coquetry* (Bucknell University Press, 2008). She has published articles on Opie's poetry and fiction in journals including *Eighteenth-Century Studies, Studies in Eighteenth-Century Culture,* and *Romanticism on the Net.*

KATHARINE KITTREDGE is Professor of English at Ithaca College where she teaches courses in the Women's and Gender Studies program, as well as courses in children's literature and science fiction. She is the editor of *Lewd and Notorious: Female Transgression in the Eighteenth Century* (University of Michigan Press, 2003), and has published numerous articles on Anglo-Irish author and diarist Melesina Trench.

SUSAN S. LANSER is Professor Emerita of English, as well as Women's, Gender and Sexuality Studies, and Comparative Literature at Brandeis University. She has published widely on gender, narrative, and eighteenth-century subjects. Her books include *The Sexuality of History: Modernity and the Sapphic 1565–1830* (University of Chicago Press, 2014), which won the American Historical Association's Joan Kelly Award and honorable mention for the Louis D. Gottschalk Prize. She is past president of the International Society for the Study of Narrative and was 2017–2018 president of the American Society for Eighteenth-Century Studies.

LAURA L. RUNGE is Professor and Chair of English at the University of South Florida, where she has taught eighteenth-century British literature, women's literature, and digital humanities. Author of *Gender and Language in British Literary Criticism, 1660–1790* (Cambridge, 1997) and co-editor with Pat Rogers of *Producing the Eighteenth-Century Book: Writers and Publishers in England, 1650–1800* (University of Delaware Press, 2009), she has published widely on women authors from Aphra Behn to Mary Robinson. She is a founding editor of the online journal *ABO: Interactive Journal for Women in the Arts, 1640–1820.*

CONTRIBUTORS

BETTY A. SCHELLENBERG is a Professor of English at Simon Fraser University. Her interests in women's writing, scribal circulation, and intermediation inform her recent book *Literary Coteries and the Making of Modern Print Culture* (Cambridge, 2016). Other publications include *Samuel Richardson in Context* (co-edited with Peter Sabor, Cambridge, 2017); an edited volume of Samuel Richardson's 1750–1754 correspondence (Cambridge, 2015); *The Professionalization of Women Writers in Eighteenth-Century Britain* (Cambridge, 2005); and *Reconsidering the Bluestockings* (co-edited with Nicole Pohl, Huntington Library Press, 2003).

LAURA TALLON is a high school English teacher at Fontbonne Academy in Massachusetts, where she teaches courses on British literature and women's writing. She has published on Anne Finch in *Eighteenth-Century Life*, and is currently working on a book project on gender and the sister arts.

Index

abolition, 134–35
actresses, 26, 27, 61, 76, 179
Africa, 132, 133, 135
Aikin, John, 106
Allan, David, 198
ambition, 9, 10, 13, 14, 15, 39, 68, 70, 90, 115, 172, 179, 200
American Antiquarian Society Historical Periodicals Collection, 201
American Revolution, 123, 125–26
Andover, Lady, 2, 13
André, John, 125–26, 137
Andreadis, Harriette, 120n22
Anglicanism, 35n18, 56, 127
Anne (queen of England), 54
anonymous, 23, 24, 33, 46, 47, 60, 69, 77, 179, 183, 198
Apollo, 3, 4, 9, 11, 22–23, 25, 27, 29–33, 40, 62, 65, 96, 99, 114, 143, 146, 150, 200, 202
Arendt, Hannah, 177, 178
aristocratic, 71, 75, 131, 163, 164
Aristotle, 7
Astell, Mary, 7
Aston, 55, 64
Athenian Letters, 196
Austen, Jane, 1, 7, 202

Backscheider, Paula R., 4, 8, 9, 16, 53n19, 67n20, 89, 94, 100n3, 102n57, 124, 143, 202n1
Baillie, Joanna, 128, 137, 138n9, 139n24
Ballaster, Ros, 17n6, 34n11
Ballitore, 155, 156, 157, 159, 164, 166, 167, 168, 169
Ballybarney, 164, 165, 167, 168–69, 174n73
Bannet, Eve Tavor, 77
Barbados, 60
Barbados Gazette, 60, 63
Barbauld, Anna Letitia Aikin, 9, 14, 15, 39, 104–18, 137, 180, 187, 200; "On Friendship," 137; "On Mrs. P[riestley]'s Leaving Warrington," 106; *The Poems of Anna Letitia Barbauld*, 16n1, 120n15; "A Summer Evening's Meditation," 116; "To a Lady with some Painted Flowers," 111, 112–13; "To Miss E. Belsham, afterwards Mrs. Kenrick," 108; "To Mrs. P[riestly] with some Drawings of Birds and Insects," 9, 15, 106–18
Barber, Mary (pseud. Sapphira), 10, 14, 59, 87–102, 197; *Poems on several occasions*, 87, 89, 90, 91–94, 95, 96, 99
Barker, Jane, 11, 13, 36, 43–52, 70, 71, 200; *The Amours of Bosvil and Galesia*, 36, 43, 44, 46, 48, 49; *The Galesia Trilogy and Selected Manuscript Poems*, 16n1, 48; *A Patch-Work Screen for the Ladies*, 49, 50–52, 53n24, 84n14
Barnard, Teresa, 16n1, 126
Bath, 111, 162, 173n30, 183, 196
Beattie, James, 127
beauty, 38, 59, 73, 87, 98, 110, 111, 112, 124, 128, 158, 161, 176, 180, 181, 187
Bedfordshire and Luton Archives and Records Office, 196
Behn, Aphra (pseud. Astrea), 2–4, 5, 6, 9, 23, 26, 27–28, 29, 31, 52n6, 70, 72; "The Feign'd Curtizans," 17n7; "The Golden Age," 27–28; "The History of the Nun: or, the Fair Vow-Breaker," 17n7; preface to *The Luckey Chance*, 6, 18n25, 70
Beinecke Library, 156, 167
Belfast Magazine, 161, 162
Bermingham, Ann, 111, 112
Bernardin de Saint-Pierre, Jacques-Henri, 124, 130, 149; *Paul et Virginie*, 124, 130, 131, 132, 135, 149
Birch, Thomas, 196, 198–99
Bishop, Henry Rowley, 186

223

INDEX

Blakemore, Steven, 130
Blome, Grace (pseud. Laura), 3, 29, 31–32, 33, 197
Bluestockings, 2, 4, 10, 12, 69, 123, 127, 128, 129, 137, 195, 198, 199
Bodleian Library, 29
Bond, William, 59
bookseller, 25, 55, 82, 88, 99, 160, 161, 163
botany, 111–13, 134–35
Botticelli, Sandro, *La Primavera*, 116
Bowers, Toni, 53n21
Boyd, Elizabeth, 72; *The Happy-Unfortunate*, 72; *Snail*, 72; *Variety*, 72–73
Boyle, John, fifth Earl of Cork and Orrery, 100n3
Brackley, 11
Brereton, Jane, 72
Brewer, John, 145, 146
Brideoake, Fiona, 143, 145, 153n18
Bridgeman, Diana, 61
Brightwell, Cecilia Lucy, 191n2; *Memorials of the Life of Amelia Opie*, 182, 191n2
Britain, 88, 113, 126, 144, 145, 146, 153n15
British Library, 196, 198, 203n8
British Literary Manuscripts database, 201
Brown, Bill, 177
Browne, Isaac Hawkins, 198
Brownlow, Elizabeth. *See* Cecil, Elizabeth Brownlow, Countess of Exeter
Budd, Adam, 90, 99
Bulstrode, 2, 13
Burghley House, 43, 44–46, 51, 45
Burke, Edmund, 111, 124, 133, 136, 145, 152n9; *Philosophical Enquiry into the Origin of our Ideas of the Sublime and the Beautiful*, 124; *Reflections on the Revolution in France*, 145
Butler, Lady Eleanor, 5, 15, 43, 129, 142–54

calabash, 133, 135
Cameron, William J., 30
Capell, Lady Mary, 198–99
Carew, Thomas, 22
Caribbeana, 60
Carter, Elizabeth, 4–5, 70, 80, 127, 195–96, 197, 198
Carteret, Lord John, 93, 94
Cary, Henry, 143

Catholicism, 35n18, 147, 154n25, 174n73
cavalier, 22, 58
Cavendish, Anne (wife of John Cecil, fifth Earl of Exeter), 45
Cavendish, Margaret Bentick, Duchess of Portland, 2, 12
Cavendish, Margaret, Duchess of Newcastle, 23
Cecil, Elizabeth Brownlow, Countess of Exeter, 11, 36, 43–46, 48–49, 53n24, 47
Cecil, William, first Lord Burghley, 44
Centlivre, Susannah, 72
Chandler, Mary (Martha Fowke's mother), 57
Chapone, Hester Mulso, 198–99; *Letters on the Improvement of the Mind*, 199
character, 13, 170–71
Charles I (king of England), 22
Charles II (king of England), 28, 57
chastity, 2, 5–6, 28, 150, 194
Cheltenham, 183
Chenevix, Richard, 165
childbirth, 15, 167, 170
childhood, 28, 41, 160, 196
children, 10, 32, 35n18, 54, 89, 91, 132–33, 145, 156, 157, 159, 161, 163, 164, 167, 168, 169, 172
Chittister, Joan, 123
Chudleigh, Mary, Lady, 5, 13–14, 54–66, 194; *Essays Upon Several Subjects in Prose and Verse*, 58; *The Ladies Defence*, 54, 58, 60; *Poems on Several Occasions*, 54, 58
Cibber, Colley, 10, 91, 182
civic virtue, 14, 68, 82, 199
civility, 81
Clarissa (Richardson), 18n21, 78, 198, 199
Clarke, Norma, 70, 82
class difference, 10, 15, 95, 139n28, 155–72
classical, 68, 81, 82, 114
classics, knowledge of, 88–89, 95, 96; allusions to, 32
Clayden, Peter, 139n24
Clayton, Thomas, 33n2
Clery, Emma J., 81
Clifden, Viscount, 160
Clifford, Margaret, Countess of Cumberland, 41
Cockburn, Catherine Trotter, 9

INDEX

Cokayne, George Edward, 25, 35n18
Cole, Rebecca Heinwitz, 124
Coleman, Deirdre, 119n9
Colepeper, Thomas, third Baronet, 29
Collins, William, 104, 119n2
Colman, George, 93, 95; *Poems by Eminent Ladies,* 93, 113
commemoration, 3, 4, 5, 11, 12, 72, 73, 81–82, 123, 179, 182, 194, 200, 202
competition, 1, 9, 14, 21, 22, 26, 27, 61, 88, 90, 92, 93, 96, 99, 104, 115, 180
Condorcet, Nicolas de, 134
Cook, Jessica, 19n46, 194, 219
Cornwallis, Elizabeth (pseud. Clarissa), 145
correspondence, vii, 1, 2, 7, 11, 15, 59, 142, 149, 155, 156, 159, 162, 166, 169, 172, 183, 187, 194, 195, 196, 197, 198, 199, 203n8. *See also* letters
coterie, 9, 11, 13, 31, 48, 53n24, 62, 63, 69, 71, 78, 79, 84n17, 196, 198, 200. *See also* writing circle
Covent Garden, 68, 77
Coventry, 55
Cowley, Abraham, 30, 31, 38, 39, 40, 77
Cowper, William, 181
Curran, Stuart, 151, 154n26

Darwin, Erasmus, 144, 145
daughter, 10, 15, 25–26, 28, 35n18, 41, 45, 48, 52n14, 54, 56, 89, 101n31, 116, 121n38, 145, 155, 156–57, 159, 169, 170, 179, 181, 195
Davenant, William, 22, 23
David, Pierre Jean, 176, 191n2
Davis, Karen E., 67n25
death, 3–5, 27, 28, 29, 30, 54, 55, 56, 61, 64, 65, 70, 77, 78, 79, 80, 87, 88, 111, 126, 137, 138n11, 142, 148, 149, 151, 155, 170, 179, 181–82, 183, 186, 195, 197; of children, 54, 56, 157; of mother, 54, 58, 156; of parents, 55
dedication, 2, 4, 11, 13, 19n46, 36, 43–53, 73–74, 88, 93, 94, 128, 146, 200
Delany, Mary (pseud. Aspasia), 2, 7, 12–13, 111–12, 194, 202
Delany, Patrick, 89, 90, 98
de Las Casas, Bartolomé, 125
De la Warr, Anne, Lady, 61

Delights for the Ingenious, 55, 64, 66n5
DeLucia, JoEllen, 143
Denham, John, 23, 38, 39, 40
Deva (river), 146–47, 150
Devine, Harriet, 125
Devonshire, 55, 56, 57, 64
Dinbren, 142
dissenter, 106, 103, 127
Dixon, Sarah (pseud. Valeria?), 31–32, 33, 35n16, 197
Donne, John, 59
Donnellan, Anne, 12
Donoghue, Emma, 7
Drury Lane, 76
Dryden, John, 23, 26, 56, 70, 104–5, 106, 107, 108, 109, 111, 113, 114; "MacFlecknoe," 114; "To Sir Godfrey Kneller," 104, 107; "To the Memory of Mr. Oldham" (1684), 111; "To the Pious Memory of the Accomplished Young Lady Mrs Anne Killigrew," 113
Du Fossé, Thomas and Monique, 129, 139n28
Dublin, 14, 87, 88, 89, 91, 97, 157, 160, 170
Dubrow, Heather, 85n33
Duck, Stephen, 89
duels, 5, 17n21
Duquette, Natasha, 9, 14, 21, 26, 46, 111, 123–41, 200, 219
Dyer, John, 60, 62, 83n13

Eastwell, 31, 37
Eberle, Roxanne, 16n1
Edgeworth, Maria, 140n48, 161, 171–72
Edgeworth, Richard Lovell, 145, 161
education, 10, 42, 63, 89, 95, 96, 155, 164, 169
Edwards, Thomas, 198–99
Eger, Elizabeth, 2, 129
Eicke, Leigh A., 53n21
Eighteenth-Century Collections Online, 201
elegy, 15, 33, 54–56, 63, 66n6, 113, 137, 143–44
Elias, A. C., 67n22, 88, 89, 90, 91, 92, 93, 95, 98, 99, 102n60
Elizabeth I (queen of England), 44
Elizabeth Montagu and the Bluestocking Circle (website), 16n1

225

INDEX

Enlightenment, 5, 6, 14, 61, 81
epistle, 24, 29, 32, 39, 59, 70, 78–80, 91, 97, 105, 107, 157. *See also* correspondence; verse epistle
epistolary fiction, 78
epitaph, 13, 55–58, 60, 63, 64–65, 151
epyllion, 123, 127
erotic, 3, 21, 39, 62, 151, 180
estate, 11, 13, 25, 36–53, 89, 147, 155, 196
Etherege, George, 23
eulogy, 93, 130, 144, 148
Exeter, Countess of. *See* Cecil, Elizabeth Brownlow, Countess of Exeter
Ezell, Margaret, 16n1, 66n1, 66n14

Fairer, David, 198
fame, 2, 3–4, 6, 9, 12, 14, 26, 40, 41, 56, 63, 68–86, 96, 105, 106, 108–9, 118, 128, 142, 179, 198, 199. *See also* reputation
Farmer's Journal, 162
father, 38–41, 45, 49, 58, 89, 90, 96, 106, 133, 139n28, 145, 183, 189
Feldman, Paula, 139n23
Female Politician, The (MA. A.), 75
femininity, 42–43, 81, 113, 124, 147, 172
feminism, 2, 14, 42, 51, 59, 63, 64, 69, 81–82, 132, 199
Fenves, Peter, 17n20
Ferguson, Frances, 141n66
Ferguson, Moira, 118
Fielding, Henry, 77
Finch, Anne, Countess of Winchilsea (pseud. Ardelia), 1, 3–4, 8, 9, 11, 13, 15, 21–53, 59, 70, 81, 105, 114, 116, 147, 197, 200; "Ardelia's Answer to Ephelia," 29; "The Circuit of Appollo," 1, 3–4, 8, 9, 11, 13, 21–31, 81, 197; "An Epistle to Mrs. Catherine Flemin," 24; *Miscellany Poems, With Two Plays*, 26; "Nocturnal Reverie," 116; "Petition for Absolute Retreat," 147; "To the Honourable Lady Worsley at Long-leat," 36–43
Finch, Heneage, Earl of Winchilsea, 28, 30, 37
Fisher, Lydia Jane, 156, 157; "A Memoir of Mary Leadbeater," 159
Fleming, Catherine, 24
Folger Shakespeare Library, 25, 26, 29, 30, 35n15

Fordyce, Dr., 108
Fowke, Martha (pseud. Clio), 5, 13–14, 54–67, 70, 81, 194, 197; *Clio; or a Secret History*, 60; *The Epistles of Clio and Strephon*, 59; "The Innocent Inconstant," 59
Fowke, Thomas, 108
Fox, George, 166
France, 11, 22, 35n18, 37, 123, 129–30, 132, 134–35, 137, 139n28, 145, 185. *See also* Paris
freedom, 59, 115, 117, 119n11, 130, 132, 141n62
Freemantle, Bridget, 10
French Revolution, 129, 145
Fresnoy, 104–5; *Art of Painting*, 104–5
Frevert, Ute, 6
friendship, 1, 2, 4, 5–6, 7, 8, 9, 10, 12–13, 14, 15, 16, 22, 31, 32, 34n8, 39, 42, 50, 58, 59, 61, 62, 63, 64, 65, 71, 72, 73, 75, 77, 79, 82, 87, 89, 90, 92–97, 99, 100, 104–22, 123–41, 142, 143, 145, 146–48, 150, 151, 152n9, 153n18, 155–75, 176–93, 194, 195, 196, 200, 202; female, 7, 9, 8, 13, 39, 60, 104–22, 123–41, 146–48, 176–93, 200; friendship poems, 7, 8–9, 102n57, 124, 200, 202n1; male, 6–7
Frye, Susan, 11
Fulham, 62

Garrick, David, 144
gender, 1, 2, 3, 5, 6, 10, 13, 14, 15, 21, 26, 36, 41, 52, 70, 76, 105, 106, 108, 110, 111, 113, 114, 115, 132, 136, 163, 180, 199
Genesis, 125, 138n9
genius, 4, 40, 42, 62–63, 65, 68, 85n47, 89, 93, 126, 127–28, 147, 158, 172, 177
gentleman, 5
Gentleman's Magazine, 4, 80, 102n46, 143, 197
geography, 89
George III (king of England), 2, 155, 182
Gerrard, Christine, 5, 13–14, 21, 25, 54–67, 197, 200, 219
gift, 2, 6, 13, 31, 73, 96, 97, 106, 107, 111, 118, 119n11, 158, 178–81, 191n2, 192n13, 192n17, 194; objects, 7, 107, 176, 181–90, 200
Girondist, 129–31

INDEX

Gloucester, Duke of, 54
Glyndŵr, Owain, 146
Godmersham, 37, 39, 52n4
Gothic, 144
Granville, Ann, 7, 8, 101n16
graveyard poetry, 56
Gray, Thomas, 104, 114, 119n2
Greer, Germaine, 28
Grey, second Marchioness. *See* Yorke, Jemima, second Marchioness Grey
Grierson, Constantia, 10, 14, 87–103, 197; "To Mrs. Mary Barber," 87, 93–95
Grub Street, 10, 69
Grundy, Isobel, 114
Guest, Harriet, 81, 86n66, 126
Guskin, Phyllis, 16n1, 59, 67n23
Gwynedd, Hywel ab Owain, 146
Gwynn, Nell, 2

Hagstrum, Jean, 118n1, 119n7
Hall, Augusta, 2
Hallberg, Robert Von, 81
Hammond, Anthony, 58; *A New Miscellany of Original Poems*, 58
Hampshire, 155
Hampshire Chronicle, 162
Hampshire Record Office, 156
Hampstead, 128, 137
Handel, 116; *Rindaldo*, 116, 122n49
Handley, Stuart, 34n10
Hayley, William, 145
Haymarket, 77
Haywood, Eliza (pseud. Ardella), 3, 6, 14, 46, 56, 59, 60, 61, 63, 68–86, 197, 199; *Epistles for the Ladies*, 78–80; *The Fair Captive: A Tragedy*, 71; *Female Spectator*, 68; *The Invisible Spy*, 77; *Love in Excess*, 71–72; *Memoirs of the Baron de Brosse*, 83n4; *Poems on Several Occasions*, 84n17; *The Rash Resolve*, 61, 74; "To Mr. Walter Bowman," 84n18; "The Vision," 71, 77; *A Wife to be Lett: A Comedy*, 76
Hebrew, 81, 97, 125, 133
Henrietta Marie (wife of Charles I), 7
Henry IV (king of England), 146
Henry VIII (king of England), 146
heterosexuality, 7, 74, 105

Hill, Aaron (pseud. Hillarius), 56, 60–63, 71, 77, 78–79, 200; "The Vision," 77, 78–79
Hill, Margaret Morris (pseud. Miranda), 62, 81–82
honor, 1, 5–6, 28, 194
Hope, Nicholas, 60
Horatian, 62
Huber, Therese, 149; *Die Ehelosen*, 149
Hughes, Barbara, 159, 164

Ingrassia, Catherine, 5, 10, 14, 21, 87–103, 197, 219
Ireland, 2, 11, 90, 93, 94, 113, 142, 145, 153n15, 166, 169. *See also* Ballitore; Dublin
Irish Rebellion (1798), 157
irony, 6, 7, 23, 24, 38, 54, 81, 183

Jacobite, 48, 51, 79
Jacobite Rebellion of 1715, 58
James II (king of England), 30, 35n18, 41
jealousy, 62–63, 96, 104, 185
Jennens, Susanna, 10
Johnson, Samuel, 76, 114, 144; "The Vanity of Human Wishes," 114
Jones, Mary, 59
Jonson, Ben, 22, 41, 147
Jordan, Nicolle, 11, 13, 21, 22, 36–53, 73, 84n28, 200, 220
Joy, Louise, 132
justice, 87, 94, 125, 129, 139n29, 140n39, 151, 171

Kairoff, Claudia, 8, 13, 16n1, 21–53, 143, 152n9, 153n14, 197, 220
Keane, Angela, 119n11, 124
Keith, Jennifer, 16n1, 35n15, 52n6, 108
Kelley, Theresa, 111, 112
Kelly, Gary, 140n48
Kemble, Charles, 179
Kennedy, Deborah, 31, 35n16, 139n28
Kent, 3, 9, 11, 21, 24, 25–33, 35n18
Killigrew, Anne, 105, 113
Kim, Jane E., 138n9
King, Kathryn R., 6, 14, 25, 46, 48–49, 51, 67n20, 68–86, 197, 199, 220
King, Shelley, 7, 15, 26, 107, 119n7, 120n13, 176–193, 199, 221

INDEX

Kittredge, Katharine, 11, 15, 32, 155–75, 197, 203n11, 221
Kraft, Elizabeth, 16n1

Labbe, Jacqueline, 119n7
laboring class, 10
Ladies Diary, 55
LaFanu, William P., 162
Laird, Mark, 121n28
lampoon, 24, 57
Lancashire, 11
landlord, 165
landowner, 134, 157, 166
landscape, 2, 38, 44–45, 49–51, 143, 145, 150–51, 197
Lanser, Susan, 5, 7, 9, 14–15, 21, 43, 129, 142–54, 200, 221
Lanyer, Aemilia, 41, 147; "The Description of Cooke-ham," 41, 51, 147
Latin, 88, 95–96, 97, 106. See also classics
LaTouch, Elizabeth, 166
Leadbeater, Mary, 11, 15, 32, 155–75, 197; *The Annals of Ballitore*, 159, 164, 168; "Ballitore," 158; *The Cottage Dialogues*, 161, 162, 168; *Extracts and Original Anecdotes for the Improvement of Youth*, 159; *The Leadbeater Papers*, 156; *Poems by Mary Leadbeater*, 160–61
Leapor, Mary (pseud. Mira), 10–11, 52n6, 59
Lee, Mary Sydenham, 54, 56, 58
Lee, Richard, 56
legacy, 1, 4, 5, 6, 8, 77, 78, 88, 92, 113, 118, 170
Lemaistre, Elizabeth Vassall, 7, 15, 107, 178, 180, 182–93, 194, 197
Lemaistre, John Gustavus, 183–84, 185, 189
lesbian, 2, 5, 15, 74, 150
letters, 2, 4, 6–8, 16n1, 34n6, 37, 38, 51, 59, 76, 123, 129, 139n30, 140n32, 144, 149, 155–75, 186, 189, 191n2, 196, 197, 198, 199, 202, 203n8. See also correspondence
Levy, Michelle, 122n47
libertine, 2, 59, 62
Lichfield, 142, 145
Lincolnshire, 43, 44
Lister, Anne, 142
literary circle, 55, 57, 63. See also coterie; writing circle

Literary Manuscripts: 17th and 18th Century Poetry from the Brotherton Library, 201
Llangollen, 14, 43, 142–54, 200
Locke, John, 110, 177
Logan, Charles, 58
London, 1, 8, 10–11, 24, 25, 33, 37, 50, 55–56, 57, 58, 69, 74, 82, 101n30, 116, 123, 125, 127, 129, 139n28, 144, 155, 160, 165, 171, 176, 180, 183
Longinian sublime, 71. See also sublime
Longleat, 37, 39–40, 42
Longman & Company, 183
Lonsdale, Roger, 17n16, 84n22, 121n41, 201
Love, Harold, 197
Lucretian, 58
lyric, 2, 15, 29, 74, 80, 85n33, 107, 114, 126, 176–93
Lyttelton, George, 198

Mackenzie, Henry, 128, 139n24
Madagascar, 133
Maidstone, 28, 29, 31
Mallet, David, 60
Mancini, Hortense, Duchess of Mazarin, 2
Mandell, Laura C., 12, 195
Manley, Mary Delarivier, 3, 9, 24, 26, 28, 34n6, 72
manuscript, 6, 10, 13, 21–35, 60, 70, 74, 78, 84n17, 95, 99, 100n3, 101n30, 120n25, 161, 164, 182, 192n13, 195, 196, 197, 198, 201
marriage, 2, 7, 12, 25, 28, 29, 30, 33, 89, 97, 110, 112, 139n28, 144, 179, 192n11; same-sex, 144–45
Martinez, Michele, 109, 122n47
Marvell, Andrew, 57
Mary Beatrice (wife of James II), 27–28
Mary Magdalene, 79–80
masculinity, 6, 9, 13, 14, 23, 39, 40, 42, 56, 62, 63, 77, 82, 105, 109, 111, 113, 116, 120n22, 124, 128, 134, 180
Massachusetts, 183
Mauritius, 131–35
Mazarin, Duchess of. See Mancini, Hortense, Duchess of Mazarin
McCarthy, William, 16n1, 106, 121n31
Mead, Rebecca, *My Life in Middlemarch*, 202

INDEX

Meath, Bishop of, 161
Medoff, Jeslyn, 17n6
Mellor, Anne K., 54
memoir, 16n1, 60, 87, 89–103, 152n9, 159, 179, 183, 202
memory, 5, 14, 15, 56, 62, 82, 88, 107, 113, 126, 128, 137, 138, 149, 151, 176, 185, 186, 189, 190
mentor, 11, 14, 21, 57, 60, 61, 62, 71, 123, 127, 128, 129, 137, 145, 171, 194
Merian, Maria Sibylla, 112, 121n31
Messenger, Ann, 31, 32, 35n18
military, 125
misogyny, 13, 15, 16, 22, 24, 64, 80
Mitchell, Christopher, 135
Montagu, Elizabeth, 9, 12, 14, 46, 111, 123–29, 132, 137, 195–96, 198; *Essay on the Writings and Genius of Shakespear*, 127, 128
Montagu, Mary Wortley, Lady, 61
Montagu Collection, 196, 203n8
Montaigne, Michel de, 7
More, Hannah, 10, 127, 173n26
Morris, Adelaide, 122n44
Moser, Mary, 112
mother, 7, 10, 37, 54, 57, 58, 64, 74, 96, 121n38, 124, 130, 131, 132, 140n39, 156, 158, 159, 160, 168, 181, 194
mourning, 4
Murphy, Olivia, 121n37
muse, 3, 9, 14, 21, 22, 25, 27, 38, 39, 41, 50, 62, 64, 65, 68, 72, 87, 91, 95, 96, 97, 99, 100, 104–10, 117, 144, 180, 184, 190, 192n20

names, 21, 25, 28, 32, 46, 55, 139n28, 171, 197, 198; difficulty tracing women's, 25–27
National Library of Scotland, 182
Neill, Anna, 132
neoclassical, 39, 69, 77
neoplatonic, 57, 58, 59
New York Public Library, 182
Newnham, 31, 35n18
Norris, Richard, 58
Northamptonshire, 10–11
Northanger Abbey, 1, 7
Norwich, 179, 180, 183
novelist, 9, 56, 73, 74, 80, 122n44, 128

'O Ciosáin, Niall, 155
O'Donnell, Mary Ann, 16n1
Oldfield, Anne, 61
Olive, Barbara, 66n7
Opie, Amelia Alderson, 7, 15, 26, 107, 176–93, 194, 197, 200; *Dangers of Coquetry*, 179; "Go Youth Beloved," 186; "Lines Addressed to Mr. Opie," 178, 179–80; "Memoir," 192n10; "On the Portraits of Deceased Relatives and Friends," 178, 180–81; "To A Prism," 176; "To Mrs. Lemaistre, at Malvern," 189; "To Mrs. Lemaistre, at Paris," 184–85; "To Mrs. Lemaistre, with an Almanack," 187
Opie, John, 178, 179–80
Orlando: Women's Writing in the British Isles, 95, 102n51, 201
Orpheus, 74–75
Orrery, Lord, 99, 100n3
Ovid, 70, 75, 96
Oxenden, Elizabeth, Lady, 29, 33

painting, 7, 14, 104–5, 109–13, 116, 118, 123, 127, 130, 158, 178, 180–81, 202. *See also* sister arts
panegyric, 76, 142, 143, 148, 158
Paris, 123–24, 125, 129–31, 137, 184, 185
Parnell, Thomas, 31, 59; "A Night Piece on Death," 56
patriarchy, 5, 7, 15, 43, 46, 122n44, 132, 143
peace, 22, 113, 123, 125–27, 132, 136, 150, 153n14, 185
Peacock, Molly, 16n2, 202
Pearson, Jacqueline, 17n6
peasant, 155, 161, 165, 169, 171, 172
Peltonen, Markku, 5
pen names, 21, 25–27, 28, 29, 32, 34n8, 70, 197. *See also* pseudonyms
personification, 108, 125–27, 130, 132
Peru, 123–28
Pettit, Alexander, 16n1
Pforzheimer Collection, 182
Philips, Katherine (pseud. Orinda), 2–3, 7, 8, 9, 26–27, 29–30, 31, 34n8, 70, 77, 105, 108–10, 111, 114, 120n22
Phoebus, 40, 96. *See also* Apollo
Pilkington, Jack Carteret, 101n19

INDEX

Pilkington, Laetitia van Lewen, 10, 14, 59, 67n22, 80, 87–103, 197; *Memoirs*, 87, 91, 94, 96, 98–99, 101–3
Pilkington, Matthew, 90, 91, 97, 98, 102
Piozzi, Hester Thrale, 141n68, 142, 159
Pix, Mary, 3, 24, 34n6
Plas Newydd, 142–43, 146–49
Plutarch, *Lives*, 32
Pocock, J. G. A., 17n19
poems: commendatory, 29, 72; country house, 13, 36–51, 147, 153n19; friendship, 7, 8–9, 102n57, 124, 200, 202n1; gift, 15, 106, 177–78, 181–90, 194; occasional, 15, 37, 58, 176–93; pastoral, 28, 29, 32; sessions, 8, 13, 21–33; tribute, 1, 6, 8, 21, 63, 87, 88, 93–96, 99, 158, 164, 171, 200. *See also* elegy; epitaph; epyllion; lyric; sonnet; verse epistle
Poems by Eminent Ladies, 93, 113
Poems by the Most Eminent Ladies of Great-Britain and Ireland, 113
poetic convention, 4, 5, 54, 74, 76, 77, 106; of country house poetry, 36, 38, 39, 41, 42, 147; of elegy, 54; of sister arts, 106–18
Ponsonby, Sarah, 5, 15, 43, 129, 142–54
Pope, Alexander, 26, 31, 56, 59, 62, 66, 69, 82, 83, 88, 90, 104–9, 111, 114, 199; "Dunciad," 34n8, 69, 82, 199; "Epistle to Mr. Jervas," 104–9; *Windsor-Forest*, 114
Portland, Duchess of. *See* Cavendish, Margaret Bentick, Duchess of Portland
portrait, 13, 15, 16, 42, 44, 47, 58, 59, 62, 75, 89, 94, 107, 127, 130, 143, 170–71, 178–93
Post, Elizabeth, *Het Land*, 149
Prescott, Sarah, 11, 73
Preston Hall, 29, 58
Priestley, Mary (pseud. Amanda), 14, 15, 39, 104–22
Priestley, Joseph, 106, 107
print, 12, 23, 25, 26, 30, 33, 48, 53n24, 55, 60, 61, 67n16, 77, 88–89, 91, 99, 101n30, 127, 131, 144, 160, 163, 164, 194, 196, 197, 199
printer, 83, 87, 88, 93, 164
property (land), 13, 36–53, 157
Protestant, 37, 147, 168, 170

provinces, 11, 13, 32, 144
Prude, The (MA. A.), 73–75
pseudonyms, 13, 58, 61–62. *See also* pen names
publishers, 75, 77, 139n24, 164, 172, 183
Puritans, 56, 64, 66n7

Quakers, 155, 157, 160, 166, 169, 176

Radcliffe, Ann, 138n11
Ragussis, Michael, 153n15
Randolph, Grace Blome. *See* Blome, Grace
Ready, Kathryn, 110
Reeve, Clara, 69, 73, 80; *Progress of Romance*, 69
Reign of Terror, 124, 129, 130, 137
Renaissance, 74, 82, 118
reputation, 2–4, 5, 6, 10, 14, 45, 54, 56, 58–60, 63, 64, 68, 69, 75, 80, 87, 89, 91, 97–98, 105, 179, 199. *See also* fame
Restoration, 23, 57, 62
Reynolds, John, 55
Reynolds, Joshua, 127, 202
Reynolds, Myra, 17n11, 90
rivalry, 9, 62, 88, 90, 102n57, 109, 188
Robertson, Karen, 11
Robespierre, Maximilien, 129, 130–31, 137
Robinson, Philip, 131–32, 140n48
Rochester, Earl of. *See* Wilmot, John, Earl of Rochester
Rogers, John Jope, 192n9
Roland, Marie-Jeanne, 9, 14, 111, 124, 129–41, 152n9
romanticism, 62, 63, 144, 145, 153n13, 177–78
Romney, George, 119n2, 127
Rosenbaum, Susan, 107
Rousseau, Jean-Jacques, 112
Rovee, Christopher Kent, 178
Royal Academy, 112, 179, 180
Runge, Laura, 1–20, 194, 221

same-sex couples, 15, 21, 143–54
same-sex desire, 43, 120n22
same-sex friendships, 104, 109–11, 120n22, 180
Sampson, Julie, 66n7
Sappho, 55, 74–75, 196, 198. *See also* Talbot, Catherine

230

INDEX

satire, 22–24, 32, 68, 91
Savage, Richard, 56, 59, 60–63, 68, 69, 75, 83, 85n47; *Miscellaneous Poems and Translations*, 56, 60–63, 85n54, 200
Saville, John, 145
scandal, 14, 28–29, 59, 60, 63–64, 65, 73, 75, 155
Schellenberg, Betty, 69, 83n6, 194–203, 222
Schimmelpenninck, Mary Anne, 138n11
Schwenger, Peter, 189–90
Scott, Mary, *The Female Advocate*, 118
Scott, Sarah, *Millenium Hall*, 12–13
Scott, Walter, 142, 149, 151
Secker, Thomas, 195
Senatus Consultum, 98–99
sensibility, 74, 122n44, 123, 124, 168
Settle, Elkanah, 23
Sevenoaks, 29, 31
Seward, Anna, 5, 9, 14–15, 43, 104, 111, 123–41, 142–54, 159, 200; dubbed "Swan of Lichfield," 144; "A Farewell," 151–52, 154n26; "Llangonllen Vale," 43, 142–54; "Monody on Major André," 125–26
sexuality, 2, 5–6, 7, 23–24, 44, 59, 60, 62–63, 69, 74, 82, 83n2, 105–6, 108, 112, 116, 199
Shackleton, Richard, 160, 163
Shadwell, Thomas, 23
Shakespeare, Judith, 15
Shakespeare, William, 107, 127, 161, 202
Shelley, Percy, "Rosalind and Helen," 149
Shenstone, William, 198
Siddons, Sarah, 178, 179
Sidney, Sir Robert, 41
Sigler, David, 132, 141n62
Sir Charles Grandison (Richardson), 78
sister arts, 14, 104–22, 180, 188, 200
sisterhood, 2, 7–8, 12, 13, 32, 37, 100, 124, 130, 140n39, 145, 150, 178, 179
sister poets, 21–22
slavery, 133–36, 160, 162
Smith, Charlotte, 111
Smith, Orianne, 139n29
Sneyd, Honora, 145–46, 148
sociability, 15, 104, 111–12, 124, 129, 137, 176–93
Society for the Promotion of Christian Knowledge, 164

Society of Friends, 166, 183. *See also* Quakers
sonnets, 111, 123, 130–32, 135–38, 141n62, 142, 143, 149, 150, 196, 198–99, 202n5
Spedding, Patrick, 71, 74
Spencer, Jane, 3–4
Staves, Susan, 2, 80, 86, 153, 173n26, 192n17
stewardship, 36, 43–51
Stone, Lawrence, 17n19
Stuart line, 22, 23, 27, 37
sublime, 42, 71, 78, 80, 94, 97, 111, 124–25, 129–36, 139n30, 145, 151, 185. *See also* Longinian sublime
Suckling, Sir John, 22–24, 26, 31
Swift, Jonathan, 2, 59, 69, 88–91, 98, 100n3

Talbot, Catherine (pseud. Sappho), 195–98; *Reflections on the Seven Days of the Week*, 195, "Wrestiana," 196
Tallon, Laura, 9, 14, 21, 39, 104–22, 137, 180, 188, 200, 222
Tasso, Torquato, 27–28, 116; *Aminta*, 27; *Jerusalem Delivered*, 116
Taylor, Elizabeth. *See* Wythens, Elizabeth Taylor
tenants, 142, 157, 164–70, 174n73
Terence, 88
Thaddeus, Janice Farrar, 8
theatre, 25, 139n30
Thomas, Elizabeth, 3, 55, 60–61; *Miscellany of Poems*, 55, 60; "Ode on the Death of Lady Chudleigh," 61
Thomson, James, 60
Thornton, Bonnell, 68, 76, 93, 95; *Poems by Eminent Ladies*, 93, 95; *Spring Garden Journal*, 68
Thynne, Frances, Viscountess of Weymouth (mother of Lady Worsley), 37
Thynne, Thomas, first Viscount Weymouth, 33, 37–38, 39, 40–43
Tipper, John, 55
Todd, Janet, 16n1, 26
Tory, 31, 144
tradition, 15, 22, 37, 39–40, 43, 44, 46, 56, 58, 59, 81, 104, 105–18, 147, 165, 180, 184, 190, 194, 201
Treaty of Paris, 125

231

INDEX

Trench, Melesina, 11, 15, 32, 155–75, 197; *Compaspe and Other Poems*, 163; *Ellen: A Ballad*, 162, 163; *Laura's Dream, or, The Moonlanders*, 163; *Mary Queen of Scots*, 158; *Thoughts of a Parent on Education*, 155, 164
Trench, Richard Chenevix, 156, 170; *The Remains of the Late Mrs. Richard Trench*, 156
Tunstall, William, 58
Turkle, Sherry, 177
Twiss, Frances Kemble, 15, 107, 178–93

van Lewen, John, 89, 97
verse epistle, 10, 104, 108, 111. *See also* epistle
Vickery, Amanda, 7
Victor, Benjamin, 60, 62
Vieth, David M., 23
Virgil, 96, 99, 112; *The Aeneid*, 160; *Eclogue*, 112

Wahl, Elizabeth Susan, 18n30
Wales, 8, 11, 142, 146. *See also* Llangollen
Waller, Edmund, 23, 58
war, 22, 123, 125–27, 145, 146, 148, 153n14. *See also* American Revolution; French Revolution; Welsh War of Independence
Warrington Academy, 106, 113
Warwickshire, 24
Washington, George, 125
Waterford, Bishop of. *See* Chenevix, Richard
Watkins, Daniel P., 114
Weekly Intelligencer, 162
Weisberg-Roberts, Alicia, 19n57
Welsh, 79, 143, 144, 146, 150, 152n8, 153n15
Welsh War of Independence, Last, 146
Wendorf, Richard, 119n7
West Indies, 134
Westminster Abbey, 3
What Jane Saw (website), 202
Whig, 144–45
Whitehall Evening Post, 179
Whitehead, William, 198
widow, 94, 132, 155, 167, 169, 183
wife, 10, 23, 29, 45, 57, 62, 64, 76, 77, 81, 88, 89, 106, 145, 159, 160, 168, 178, 180, 191n2, 192n17

Wikborg, Eleanor, 52n10
Wilcher, Robert, 33n2
Williams, Helen Maria, 9, 14, 26, 46, 111, 123–141, 200; "Introductory Remarks on the Present State of Science and Literature in France," 139n31; *Julia, a novel*, 124, 127, 128–29; *Letters Written in France*, 123, 129; *Memoirs of the Reign of Robespierre*, 140n39; *An Ode on the Peace*, 123, 125–27, 136; *Paul and Virginia by Bernardin Saint-Pierre*, 124, 130–37; *Peru*, 123, 124–25, 127–28; "Sonnet: To the Calbassia Tree," 130, 132, 135–37; "To Mrs. Montagu," 127–28
Wilmot, John, Earl of Rochester, 6, 23, 26, 33n5, 57, 59
Wilputte, Earla, 66n14, 71, 79, 84n17
Wilson, Carol Shiner, 16n1, 52n9
Wilsthorpe, 44
Winchilsea, Countess of. *See* Finch, Anne, Countess of Winchilsea
Winn, James A., 104, 105
Wollstonecraft, Mary, 112, 129, 137, 140n32; *Vindication of the Rights of Women*, 112, 129
women: artists, 1, 3, 5–6, 12, 14, 16, 106, 108, 111–13, 144, 158, 202; intellectuals, 1, 4, 6, 21, 61, 118, 123, 125, 127, 144; patrons, 1, 6, 10, 13, 26, 41, 43–53, 61, 90, 167; writers, 3, 6, 11, 12, 21, 23, 26, 30, 31, 36, 39, 61, 69, 72, 73, 78, 79, 80, 122n44, 125, 127, 128, 137, 182, 194, 195, 199, 201
women's creativity, 1, 6, 9, 13, 14, 24, 42, 63, 89, 105, 116, 131–32, 180
Woolf, Virginia, 3, 15, 81
Wordsworth, William, 142, 153–54n25; "To the Lady E.B. and Hon. Miss P.," 149–50
Worsley, Frances, Lady, 11, 33, 36–43, 51
Wrest, 196–97
Wright, Angela, 130–31
writing circle: Aaron Hill's, 56, 60–63, 71, 77–78, 200; at Dublin, 14, 87–103; in Kent, 3, 9, 25–33; at Wrest, 196–97
Wycherley, William, 23
Wyett, Jodi, 18n30
Wythens, Elizabeth Taylor (pseud. Alinda or Olinda), 28–29, 31, 33, 34n10, 34n11;

"Song" ("Strephon has Fashion, Wit and Youth"), 29; "Song" ("Ye Virgin Pow'rs defend my heart"), 29; "To Mertill who desir'd her to speak to Clorinda of his Love," 29
Wythens, Sir Francis, 28

Yearsley, Ann, 10; *Poems Upon Several Occasions,* 10

York, 160
Yorke, Charles, 198, 202n5
Yorke, Jemima, second Marchioness Grey, 196, 197, 198
Yorke, Philip, second Earl of Hardwicke, 196, 198
Young, Edward, 60

Zuk, Rhoda, 203n6

www.ingramcontent.com/pod-product-compliance
Lightning Source LLC
Chambersburg PA
CBHW030439300426
44112CB00009B/1079

OLD SCHOOLS

Sara Guyer and Brian McGrath, series editors

Lit Z embraces models of criticism uncontained by conventional notions of history, periodicity, and culture and committed to the work of reading. Books in the series may seem untimely, anachronistic, or out of touch with contemporary trends because they have arrived too early or too late. Lit Z creates a space for books that exceed and challenge the tendencies of our field and in doing so reflect on the concerns of literary studies here and abroad.

At least since Friedrich Schlegel, thinking that affirms literature's own untimeliness has been named "Romanticism." Recalling this history, Lit Z exemplifies the survival of Romanticism as a mode of contemporary criticism as well as forms of contemporary criticism that demonstrate the unfulfilled possibilities of Romanticism. Whether or not they focus on the Romantic period, books in this series epitomize Romanticism as a way of thinking that compels another relation to the present. Lit Z is the first book series to take seriously this capacious sense of Romanticism.

In 1977, Paul de Man and Geoffrey Hartman, two scholars of Romanticism, team-taught a course called "Literature Z" that aimed to make an intervention into the fundamentals of literary study. Hartman and de Man invited students to read a series of increasingly difficult texts and through attention to language and rhetoric compelled them to encounter "the bewildering variety of ways such texts could be read." The series' conceptual resonances with that class register the importance of recollection, reinvention, and reading to contemporary criticism. Its books explore the creative potential of reading's untimeliness and history's enigmatic force.

OLD SCHOOLS

Modernism, Education, and the Critique of Progress

Ramsey McGlazer

Fordham University Press
New York 2020

Copyright © 2020 Fordham University Press

All rights reserved. No part of this publication may be reproduced, stored in a retrieval system, or transmitted in any form or by any means—electronic, mechanical, photocopy, recording, or any other—except for brief quotations in printed reviews, without the prior permission of the publisher.

Fordham University Press has no responsibility for the persistence or accuracy of URLs for external or third-party Internet websites referred to in this publication and does not guarantee that any content on such websites is, or will remain, accurate or appropriate.

Fordham University Press also publishes its books in a variety of electronic formats. Some content that appears in print may not be available in electronic books.

Visit us online at www.fordhampress.com.

Library of Congress Cataloging-in-Publication Data available online at https://catalog.loc.gov.

Printed in the United States of America

22 21 20   5 4 3 2 1

First edition

for Bob Glazer, Martricia McLaughlin,
and Ryan and Mariele McGlazer